The Seven Democratic Virtues

THE SEVEN DEMOCRATIC VIRTUES

WHAT YOU CAN DO TO OVERCOME TRIBALISM AND SAVE OUR DEMOCRACY

CHRISTOPHER BEEM

THE PENNSYLVANIA STATE UNIVERSITY PRESS
UNIVERSITY PARK, PENNSYLVANIA

Library of Congress Cataloging-in-Publication Data

Names: Beem, Christopher, author.
Title: The seven democratic virtues : what you can do to overcome tribalism and save our democracy / Christopher Beem.
Description: University Park, Pennsylvania : The Pennsylvania State University Press, [2022] | Includes bibliographical references and index.
Summary: "Outlines specific steps that average American citizens can take to reduce political polarization and safeguard democratic institutions"—Provided by publisher.
Identifiers: LCCN 2022019104 | ISBN 9780271093949 (cloth)
Subjects: LCSH: Democracy—United States. | Virtues. | Identity politics—United States.
Classification: LCC JK1726 .B444 2022
LC record available at https://lccn.loc.gov/2022019104

Printed in the United States of America
Published by The Pennsylvania State University Press,
University Park, PA 16802–1003

The Pennsylvania State University Press is a member of the Association of University Presses.

It is the policy of The Pennsylvania State University Press to use acid-free paper. Publications on uncoated stock satisfy the minimum requirements of American National Standard for Information Sciences—Permanence of Paper for Printed Library Material, ANSI Z39.48–1992.

TO MY TEACHERS

Walter Nicgorski

James L. Wiser

Franklin I. Gamwell

Jean Bethke Elshtain

Contents

Acknowledgments ix

Introduction 1

PART 1: THE DEMOCRATIC VICE 15

1. Tribalism 17
2. Tribal Alignment 34
3. Tribalism and Madison's Precautions 52

PART 2: DEMOCRATIC THINKING 65

4. Humility 67
5. Honesty 80
6. Consistency 97

PART 3: DEMOCRATIC ACTING 111

7. Courage 113
8. Temperance 127

PART 4: DEMOCRATIC BELIEF 145

9. Charity 147
10. Faith (and Hope) 163

Conclusion: Democratic Excellence 177

Notes 183

Bibliography 197

Index 216

Acknowledgments

Thanks to my McCourtney Institute for Democracy colleagues Michael Berkman, Jenny Harchak, and especially Jenna Spinelle. Jenna's talents as a thinker, writer, and editor are always enormously helpful but have been especially so throughout this project.

Pattie Beem, as usual, listened supportively to my developing thoughts and read drafts. Writing is a lonely endeavor, especially during a pandemic, and she made it ok. I am grateful. (Klode demanding to sit in the same chair as I wrote helped too, even if it did make it harder to type.) Connor Beem, our son, also offered thoughtful comments on a chapter draft. Tom Ellis once again pushed me to be more concrete and accessible. Sarah Cypher offered her editing expertise on a very early draft.

Thanks to Alan Abramowitz and Kelly Garrett for helping me think through the implications of their work.

Thanks to Penn State colleagues John Christman, Ben Jones, Amy Linch, Eduardo Mendieta, and especially John Gastil, who graciously read several proposal drafts and offered sound advice.

Thanks to the Penn State University Press. Professionalism has ebbed in the world of academic publishing. But Ryan Peterson was exemplary: responsive, timely, forthcoming, and encouraging. Laura Reed-Morrisson was an outstanding editor. Her work improved the book immensely. Thanks also to readers Michael Neblo and Peter Levine, whose work on democracy I admire and learn from.

Some ideas presented here first appeared in "The Burden of Truth: Hannah Arendt, Democracy, and Donald Trump's Lies," *The Critique* (January–February 2017). I first addressed the idea of democratic charity in the piece "In Appealing to 'Give Each Other a Chance,' Biden Recalls the Democratic Charity of Abraham Lincoln," *The Conversation*, November 10, 2020. I gave an earlier version of the chapter on honesty at a Rock Ethics Symposium at Penn State in 2020. Thanks to all for the opportunity.

INTRODUCTION

The riot finally at an end, Officer Harry Dunn looked around the Capitol Rotunda and surveyed the damage. Smoky residue from fire extinguishers hung in the air. Broken glass, empty canisters of pepper spray, and Trump and MAGA signage were all strewn about the floor. That hallowed space, now sullied and slandered. Dunn had just endured what he thought war must be like, with a crowd that was prepared for—itching for—a fight. He recalled the racist taunts he had endured, a Black man surrounded by a very white and very angry crowd. He shuddered at the loss of life, at the comrades who had been gravely injured. He thought about how close it had come to being much, much worse. How close he had come to taking a life. Or to losing his own.[1]

All this violence, this defilement of democracy, carried out by a frenzied mob unwilling to accept that a free and fair election had not gone their way, driven by a president promoting the childish delusion that the election had been stolen.

Dunn turned to his friend and colleague, one of dozens who had struggled vainly to stop the mob of thousands. "Is this America?" he asked.

The answer could only be yes. This *is* America. Reagan's shining city on a hill, Lincoln's last, best hope: with this act, America belied these beliefs and demeaned itself before history and the world.

But is this the America that we are stuck with, that we must acquiesce to? Is America now a place where our opponents are our bitter enemies, where the truth is just someone else's lie, and where winning justifies everything?

As Dunn proudly proclaimed, the terrorists didn't win that day. The vote securing the election went ahead that very same evening. Democracy endured. There had been no peaceful transfer of power—hardly—but there had been a transfer.

Yet the questions still linger: Is this America? Were the events of January 6, 2021, a shameful aberration that we have already started to put behind us, or is this just the way things are now? Is democracy something that has been tested and endured, or is it something that we can no longer sustain? Is it something that we even *want* to sustain? Those questions have not yet been answered. Like that smoke in the Rotunda, they still hang in the air.

Democracy Means Conflict

Democracy begins with this inescapable fact: people disagree. We all have different experiences, interests, objectives, and beliefs, and all this difference leads to disagreement. These disagreements are deep and abiding; we disagree about matters that are extremely important to us. Though a tyrant can try to subdue their expression, they cannot be overcome. And while some disagreements slowly disappear as societies grow and change, many are simply never going away.

Because disagreement is inevitable, so is conflict. We are not just going to disagree—we are going to fight about those disagreements. Unless we are able to manage that conflict, society will eventually descend into violence and civil war. Democracy is the alternative: to tyranny on the one hand, and civil war on the other. Democracy affirms the freedom that makes conflict unavoidable, but it seeks to channel and constrain that conflict so that in spite of it, society can remain at peace.

This midpoint between civil war and tyranny is one very good reason why a person might prefer to live in a democracy. But there are many more. It is well established that democracies are more likely to be freer, more creative and productive, with citizens experiencing less violence and less government corruption. People living in democracies have higher standards of living, higher levels of health, and higher levels of happiness than those in nondemocracies. There are good reasons why refugees, forced to leave everything behind, strive to come to democracies.

The argument for democracy, though, is not merely practical. It is also, and even primarily, moral. For among the many possible ways of organizing human society, democracy manifests a distinctively high respect for humanity. Simply because we are human beings, we all have the right to rule ourselves, to think and believe what we want, and to make decisions about how we live our lives. Democracy likewise affirms that we all have the capacity to do so. Education makes democracy work better, to be sure, and for this reason democrats have always been deeply interested in education. But simple common sense is sufficient for each of us to find our own way, to evaluate politicians and their platforms, and to decide which one conforms most to our interests and ideals. Whatever capacities we do or do not have, democracy insists that no one is a better position to determine my own interests than I am.

In his poem "Democracy," Langston Hughes writes that democracy is more than just another way of organizing society. Democracy means that I can "stand / On my two feet / And own the land." Democracy affords me the freedom, dignity, and accountability that my humanity demands. But that birthright is not merely for me or those like me. Every other citizen—Hughes refers to "the other fellow"—has that very same standing. To acknowledge the rights of others even as I demand my own: all of that is distinctively democratic. To speak of either freedom or equality without the other is to misapprehend democracy.

To be sure, there are those who are unpersuaded by Hughes's simple yet lofty words. Nor do they share his high opinion of democracy. They see the status quo as evidence not of something that can and must be corrected but of an endemic inadequacy that must be transcended.

Some on the far left argue that democracy as we experience it is not the opposite of authoritarianism; rather, it is just a more discreet form of it. Equality is not an ideal we strive for but a lie that serves to sustain power even as it masks it. And freedom? That is nothing more than what late-stage capitalism allows it to be. Whatever comes after what we have now is not entirely clear, but it will be more genuinely egalitarian, and it may well have to emerge from the ashes.

For many more on the right, democracy is not a lie but a threat. It is the means by which groups with different backgrounds, values, and objectives can exercise their rights and gain power. They fear that such a possibility endangers their status at the top of the cultural, economic, and political food chain. At minimum, these Americans are eager to manipulate the mechanisms of democracy so that it preserves the past and manifests something less than equality and majority rule. For these Americans, any democracy that demands a larger, and for that matter more authentic, measure of equality is not worthy of respect, let alone defense; it is something to be cordoned off.

Neither side is likely to find anything relevant or useful in what follows.[2] I can live with that. For there are many more Americans who feel no such disrespect. On the contrary, they take great pride in American democracy, and they earnestly want to see it endure. These Americans survey the current condition of that democracy and react with grave concern, even dread. Many times over the last few years I have been asked by people who feel this way—students, friends, and people who have found out what I do for a living—"What can I do? What can I do to help our democracy?"

This is the right way to frame the question. Of course it is impossible to ignore the slow-moving train wreck that is all around us. And it is equally difficult to ignore the actions of those whose pursuit of power, money, or status only furthers us along that path. Many argue that the correct response is political reform: changing our political institutions and procedures and electing representatives whose commitment to democracy overrides their rank self-interest. I don't disagree. But structures and procedures can only operate within a primary agreement about what behaviors we can rightfully expect from each other. Likewise, politicians respond to incentives, and right now the incentives line up to preserve and even exacerbate an appalling status quo. In what follows, I argue that the prerequisite to reforming our politics is the reform of our own actions and behaviors.

The late conservative firebrand Andrew Breitbart insisted that "politics is downstream from culture."[3] In other words, if you want to change the former, you first have to attend to the latter. For Breitbart, this meant that Republicans should have been more worried about making movies and writing songs than they were about voter registration in some congressional district. My assessment of what is unsatisfactory about our culture, let alone how we should work to restore it, diverges significantly from what Breitbart would and did say. But regarding this one very general point, at least, I agree: politics *is* downstream from culture. The sorry condition of the former therefore reflects and stems from the sorry condition of the latter. What's more, I agree that restoring that culture is not a job merely or even primarily for politicians. It is a responsibility that falls on all of us as citizens. For all of us, therefore, the appropriate question is the one that comes before questions of political reform: What can I do?

If you have that same question—if you are concerned about the condition of our democracy right now, you want that democracy to endure for yourself and for your children, and you want to know what you can do to help sustain it—then this is my effort to respond. To paraphrase the philosopher Philippa Foot, in the army of democratic virtue, we are all volunteers.[4] If you want to be one of those volunteers, keep reading.

Again, democracy allows human society to accommodate the inescapable fact of disagreement. It provides the means for channeling and constraining conflict, thereby avoiding the Scylla and Charybdis of tyranny and civil war. Sometimes, despite our best efforts, conflict will overwhelm our constraints. That ever-looming possibility is why democracies are fragile. This has always been so, but now we all know it to be true.

Tribalism is one basic, inescapable feature of human existence that crystallizes these difficulties. All human beings are driven to form groups, to cooperate within them, and to distrust and disparage outsiders. Now to say "all," "basic," and "inescapable" means that tribalism is not a category that defines some subset of human beings. It does not refer specifically or even primarily to a group of people in New Guinea or the Amazon. Nor does it refer to members of the nearly six hundred federally recognized tribes in the United States who use that word to describe themselves. For my purposes, it is a neurological term, reflecting the basic wiring of all human brains. Tribalism is part of our evolutionary blueprint; it manifests itself irrespective of the time, place, or culture in which humans find themselves. No matter who we are or where we live, we are all tribal.

From the very beginning, democracy's critics have argued that tribalism makes democracy unsustainable. And even its most ardent defenders have acknowledged that a democratic society is especially vulnerable to this vice and must find ways to moderate it. But the events of January 6, 2021, are simply the most inescapable illustration of this inescapable fact: tribalism is moderated no longer. It has swamped the banks of our democratic life and turned us into two ever more hostile camps. In this moment, the "other side" is no longer an opponent but an existential threat; norms of behaviors are for suckers; politics has become a zero-sum game. As more partisans—politicians and citizens alike—reflect this attitude, the rhetoric ratchets up, leading to ever more distrust, antagonism, and even enmity. Under such conditions, the future of our democratic society is something we can no longer assume. Tribalism means that fixing our politics is not primarily a political problem. It is a matter of reforming our political culture. If we are to stop the decline and preserve our democracy, we citizens have to recommit to behaviors that work against the most antidemocratic aspects of our humanity. And that means we must all turn (perhaps more accurately, return) to a set of specifically democratic virtues.

For many, the very idea sounds unappealing. Virtues have a "schoolmarm" kind of vibe. Prim and priggish. And it is true that virtues push against our natural inclinations. We are all inclined to eat too much, want what is not ours, lie when it suits our purposes, and so forth. As a result, in every society, virtuous behaviors are never easy. But virtues are also agreements—agreements made within groups, families, and societies. Developed over time, these agreements lay out basic understandings of how we should all behave toward ourselves and each other. By agreeing about their value and desirability, we give these virtues a standing that guides our interactions with each other. This agreement thus makes it possible for us to live together. And, ideally, to thrive.[5]

No matter how humans choose to live together, we always remain human beings. That is why many virtues are universal. All societies value hard work, fairness, and filial loyalty, for example. But societies are also distinctive. They all make different choices about how to organize themselves, and those choices reflect their answers to the most fundamental questions of human existence: How we should live together? What is important and valuable? What is it that makes us, us? These answers are not always articulated, but they are always there. In fact, they are inevitably implied in whatever ways we choose to organize our shared lives. Paraphrasing Isaiah Berlin, the political philosopher John Rawls wrote, "There is no social world without loss."[6] Every society favors some ways of life and undermines others, and it cannot be otherwise. A Tibetan monastery, a samurai village, and a modern democracy are all forms of human society, but they answer these questions very differently. The way they understand human virtues, the virtues they highlight, and the way their culture seeks to celebrate and cultivate them will all vary as well.

Virtues for a Democracy

So what virtues are most relevant for a democratic society? What virtues help us live together and even thrive in a democracy? To get at that question, we have to ask a prior one: What are the answers that democratic society gives to those most fundamental questions?

Democracy is a messy and contentious concept (just like its practice), so no set of answers is going to be without controversy. But we have to start somewhere. Any list of virtues implies some set of answers, and so too does the one to follow. It is only fair, then, that I start with mine. So, with no claim of completeness, here it is:

- There is a world out there, a reality, that is the same for all of us, even though we all perceive it differently, and that world exists regardless of whether we understand it or agree about it.[7]
- As citizens, all of us have equal standing, and within wide limits, an equal right to live life the way we want, to believe what we want, and to express those beliefs freely.
- People can disagree deeply, even passionately, about those beliefs and still live together peaceably.
- Our all-too-human commitment to our group identity or self-interest does not wholly overwhelm our commitment to reason, fairness, and the goals of liberty and justice for all.
- Despite the difficulties, it is nevertheless possible to genuinely hear arguments with which we disagree, to debate those arguments productively, and (sometimes) to even find ourselves persuaded.

Of course, there will be those who argue with this list. Is it sufficient? What is missing? And what is the standing of these claims? On what are they grounded? Those are surely arguments worth having.[8] But it is sufficient for my purposes. Moreover, I would argue that without them, or something very much like them, we are left with a conception of democracy that is deeply diminished. In fact, without them, it is hard for me to imagine what living in a democracy even means. Most importantly, it is difficult to sustain the idea that there is any point to framing *any* list of democratic virtues, let alone the account that is to follow.

The same questions about sufficiency or completeness arise with the virtues I list below. There are surely virtues that are important to a democratic society I will not consider. My aim is not to be comprehensive but to lay out the virtues we need right now—virtues that work against our all-too-human inclination toward tribalism, virtues that give us all the opportunity to step away from the abyss and that give us the tools to develop a more perfect union. In what follows, I seek to describe those virtues and show how they can help us—all of us—achieve this daunting but indispensable task.

What Follows

In chapter 1, referencing experimental work by Henri Tajfel and others, I show that the drive to form groups, to cooperate within them, and to treat our fellow members preferentially is buried deep in our brains and in our genes. This universal and inescapable feature of the human condition is called *tribalism*. We all belong to an astonishing variety of tribes, from those based on gender, race, ethnicity, and faith to those arising from the bands we listen to, the teams we follow, and the products we buy. For most of us, most of the time, these tribes push and pull us in different directions. They connect us with different people, cause us to value different things, and even bring us to speak and act in different ways, even if all of them genuinely reflect a part of ourselves. But tribalism always has a dark side. It inevitably causes us to favor *us* and denigrate *them*.

Chapter 2 reviews recent work by Lilliana Mason that shows that when our tribes align, when all our tribal identities separate into two distinct and antithetical groups, tribalism becomes vicious. It exacerbates our inclinations to view the other with distrust and even animosity. We come to see them as less worthy, less legitimate, less human versions of ourselves. Alan Abramowitz's analysis of the 2016 election shows that our current division into *us* and *them* turns predominantly on whether one regards dramatic changes in the United States since the 1960s as generally good or generally bad.

Democracy's critics and advocates have always known that tribalism is dangerous to democracies. In chapter 3, I review the writings of one very important American advocate, James Madison. Madison called tribes "factions," and he well understood the danger they represented. His solution was, in part, to expand the republic. The larger the republic, the greater number of tribes—and the smaller chance that they would come into alignment. But Madison, and for that matter just about all the Founders, also insisted that a democratic society required virtuous citizens. The last few years have demonstrated that we cannot rely on procedures to save us from our tribalistic selves. We need to recover a shared commitment to democratic virtue.

I break the democratic virtues down into three categories. Philosophers would call these categories intellectual virtues, moral virtues, and theological virtues. I call them democratic thinking, democratic acting, and democratic belief.

Aristotle split the virtues into two types: moral and intellectual.[9] The intellectual virtues help us understand and articulate the good and the just. Moral virtues identify ways for us to act so that we are more likely to achieve those goals. I am using a similar distinction. Intellectual virtues improve the thinking that being a democratic citizen requires and counter the vice of tribalism. But to call them intellectual virtues makes it sound as though they are reserved for philosophers. In the democratic context, that is exactly the wrong way to understand them. Call them instead the "democratic thinking" virtues.

In chapters 4, 5 and 6, I lay out the democratic thinking virtues of humility, honesty, and consistency.

Humility is often presented as merely a religious virtue. The English philosopher David Hume, in fact, called it a "monkish virtue" and argued that it was actually better seen as a vice. But democracy depends on assessing the world and then arguing about it. Tribalism leads to biases that make us see things as we want to see them, rather than how they genuinely are. I use the writings of St. Bernard of Clairvaux (a monk, as it happens) to argue that Hume was wrong. Humility starts with recognizing the truth about ourselves and our inescapable limitations. Recent research shows that those with high humility are best able to profess their own views while being open to the views of others. Humble people make the best democrats.

Tribalistic bias leads us unconsciously, albeit honestly, to believe things that are not true. When we lie, on the other hand, we consciously, deliberately, undermine the truth. Reviewing the actions of politicians from Franklin Roosevelt to Mitch McConnell, I show that while lying in politics is inevitable and sometimes even necessary, it is also sometimes pernicious. Contemporary Russian propaganda from media outlet RT and the falsehoods of Donald Trump show how democracy depends on a commitment to reflect facts honestly. Following the work of political theorist Hannah Arendt, I argue that committing to *honesty*, to the ideal of the truth, means we strive to limit ourselves to those falsehoods we genuinely believe.

Finally, we need to develop ways to mitigate the effects of our biases. We need to affirm that what is true when it affects me is also true when it affects you. Looking at work by Ralph Waldo Emerson and Winston Churchill, I argue that the virtue of *consistency* helps us affirm the classical ideal of justice: treating like things alike and different things differently. And since we are all better at seeing the bias in others than we are at seeing it in ourselves, taking on the perspective of our opponent is one essential means by which we can develop this virtue.

If honesty, humility, and consistency are virtues that improve our democratic thinking, helping us make the right decisions, we can think of moral virtues as helping us improve our actions. Call them "democratic acting" virtues. These action virtues come after the thinking virtues just as action should follow thoughtful consideration. Democratic acting virtues make us more likely to achieve the good. In classical Western philosophy, these virtues are called the *cardinal virtues*—temperance, courage, justice, and prudence. This list thus has a standing in Western ethics that, to say the least, merits our attention. Two of these four virtues are particularly important for understanding how a democrat ought to behave and, especially, how a democrat ought to address the vice of tribalism.[10] Democratic acting requires a distinctively democratic understanding of courage and temperance.

To engage politically at all means that we are expressing our opinions to those whose opinions we do not know and to those who we know do not agree with us. I call this everyday democratic courage. As partisan animosity rises, so too does the courage needed for even these little acts. In chapter 7, I argue that democratic courage demands that we scrutinize our own presuppositions, challenging both ourselves and those in our tribe.

Chapter 8 argues for a democratic notion of temperance. Unlike many ancient philosophers, Aristotle thought that anger could be properly directed and controlled. And when it was, its expression could be wholly legitimate, even virtuous. On the other hand, Aristotle thought hatred was not merely a more extreme version of the former. Hatred is permanent. It consumes us and becomes part of our very identity. Research on those leaving hate groups show the accuracy of Aristotle's description. Democratic temperance falls in the middle. It requires both that we accept anger toward our opponents as inevitable and that we also stop that anger from morphing into hatred. Some of the most basic features of democratic politics, including compromise and collaboration, are impossible without it. I close by showing how we can increase our prospects for temperance.

The theological virtues come from Thomas Aquinas. Writing in the thirteenth century, Thomas agreed with the ancients that the four cardinal virtues were a necessary means for achieving human happiness. They were seen as supreme virtues within the bounds of human reason. Theological virtues—faith, hope, and charity—"surpass" that reason. They make it possible for us to achieve a dimension of both happiness and excellence that we cannot achieve otherwise. I am arguing that a nontheological version of these faithful virtues is fundamental in restoring our democracy.

Chapter 9 presents a democratic understanding of charity. For Thomas, charity means the love and care we give to others, a love that begins with, and rests upon, our love for God. For democrats, charity simply means giving all our fellow citizens, even those in the other tribe, the benefit of the doubt. Abraham Lincoln affirmed this idea in his second inaugural address, and Joseph Biden reaffirmed it in his first. But just as it did for Thomas, democratic charity begins elsewhere: in this case, our commitment to others begins with our commitment to democracy. We give others the benefit of the doubt because we are committed to democracy, and we know that democracy works better when we do so. In the current climate, such charity is extremely difficult. The most pragmatic approach is to adopt a version of the "generous tit for tat" strategy developed in game theory.

Chapter 10 focuses on democratic faith. Thomas defined faith as believing or assenting to truths that are not evident in themselves. Democratic society likewise depends on an affirmation of principles that, to say the least, are less than demonstrable. In fact, work by Christopher Achen and Larry Bartels shows that those principles strain against the facts. Our votes are not the product of our careful consideration of the candidates and our self-interest. Rather, they are simply another manifestation of our tribal identity. But democratic society works better when we continue to affirm these principles despite insufficient evidence. The Freedom Riders did that. More recently, so did Greta Thunberg, Alexander Vindman, and Bryan Stevenson. These democrats show that tribalism is not the whole story. Sometimes, at least, people actively listen to and are even persuaded by protest. And sometimes so many join that history is changed, and society ends up more democratic. These acts, and countless others, affirm the ideal of democratic politics as a matter of faith.

Every democratic act depends on and manifests these virtues. They make democracy go. In the conclusion, I argue that by striving to practice them ourselves—and honoring their practice in others—we help keep our tribalism in check and thereby make our democracy better. Committing ourselves to democratic virtues is one political act, one pro-democracy act, that all of us can undertake. Just as importantly, this practice also makes us better human beings. In Aristotelian terms, committing ourselves to democratic virtue is how we achieve democratic excellence.

An Opportunity, at Least

I write on January 20, 2021, the first full day of the new Biden administration. As I reflect on his inauguration address, much that he had to say continues to echo in my head; his words resonate with so much in the pages that follow.[11] President Biden did not dispute the depth of our division. In fact, he referred to it as our "uncivil war." Moreover, he acknowledged that prospects for changing this reality might strike some as "a foolish fantasy." But he called on all Americans to move past the tribalism that divides us and to seek, together, a more perfect union. He said that we, all of us, at this moment, owe it to those who have preserved democracy to work just as hard to preserve it for those who will come after us. For Biden, that work centers on committing ourselves to many of the democratic virtues, including humility, temperance, courage, and faith.

The investiture of a new president is always an opportunity for that work to begin again. And particularly so now. In Biden's words, "And so today, at this time and in this place, let us start afresh. All of us." There are no guarantees. The hateful insurrection that took place days earlier, on the very steps where Biden took his oath of office, showed us just how low our democracy has sunk. It manifested the indifference—even aversion—that so many of our fellow citizens have for it. In the words of Amanda Gorman, who also spoke at the inauguration, there are many Americans who "would shatter our nation rather than share it, / Would destroy our country if it meant delaying democracy."[12] Biden's words might fall on deaf ears or be overwhelmed by events that we cannot begin to predict. The task is daunting, the prospects by no means assured. We can't know how long this opportunity will remain, nor even how genuine is the possibility of meaningful change. But we have not lost yet. We have this moment. Volunteers in the army of democratic virtue would do well to try to make the most of it.

PART I
The Democratic Vice

I

TRIBALISM

Where all think alike, no one
thinks very much.
—WALTER LIPPMANN

Virtues are hard. We know they are worth the effort, but they push us to act in ways that are contrary to our inclinations. Vices, on the other hand, are all too easy. They are choices toward which all of us have some inclination. That's why just about every human society has a very similar and familiar set of vices.

For all this universality, just as with virtues, societies are distinctive in the ways they understand and position vices. Martial cultures—the Spartans or the Vikings, say—felt particular animus toward cowardice. This vice was especially relevant because it was especially dangerous. If cowardice were to become widespread and extreme, the cultural core of these societies, and perhaps their very existence, would be threatened. Similarly, there are some vices that are especially relevant to, and especially dangerous for, a democracy. Tribalism is one such vice. I will show why that is so and why it is such a danger right now, but first I want to lay out just what I mean by the term.

Tribalism on the Brain

Tribalism starts as an inclination, too. The drive to form groups, to cooperate within them, to trust members, to treat them preferentially and with greater sympathy: all of this is instinctual. There are good reasons why this is so. In fact, it is part of the reason why you are reading these words. Tribes, and the trust and cooperation that they engendered, gave early hominids a competitive advantage against much larger and more powerful prey and predators—and against other hominids. Those who did not form these tribes, who did not learn trust and cooperation, did not have that advantage and therefore did not survive to pass on their genes. Those of us who are here now thus reflect the impact of that natural selection: "From the earliest cave evidence of our species, human evolutionary development occurred in the context of families and tribes. Already in the human remains found at Terra Amata, France, our ancestors 400,000 years ago were living in groups, with collections of families seeking the survival and protection that the tribe alone could provide. These several hundred thousand years of existence in small tribes means that our genetics are built around survival within this powerful social arrangement."[1] Just like our ancestors, we are all driven to find little sources of identity, the comfort and security of belonging, the feeling of being part of an *us*. Just so, we divide all other people into whether they are or are not in our tribe. To repeat, all of us possess this deep, and deeply human, instinct.

In contemporary society, tribalism manifests itself through the feeling of identity and belonging that connects us to an incalculable number of groups and social identities. Of course, for my purposes the most relevant are the two US political parties, Democrats and Republicans, but we'll get to that shortly. For now, start with "incalculable." We all can name dozens of our tribes: religious faiths, professions, people who share the same ethnic identity or heritage. Less obvious but still operative: sports fans, sports enthusiasts, hobbyists; dog people, cat people, ferret people; devoted owners of Harley-Davidson motorcycles, or Fender guitars, or Apple products;[2] fans of popular artists, Deadheads, Parrot Heads, Phish Heads (and all the other band fans whose names I am too old to know). At any moment, there are thousands of tribes, big and little, that make up American life. And all of us belong to many such tribes simultaneously.

As we grow up, we learn which groups we are effectively born into (race, ethnicity, sexual orientation, family history). Others we choose to belong to as a way of defining who we are to ourselves and others. Many of these "born into" tribes are effectively permanent, but many of the ones we choose are not; our interests and allegiances can wax and wane and even disappear completely. Finally, we learn whether and how these groups stand in relation to one another.

Nor do all our tribes serve the same purpose in our lives. My wife has a group of friends from college. Over the decades, they have been through it all with each other. That is one kind of tribe: intimate, caring, and mutually supportive. Some of these women are attorneys; as women in that profession, they belong to a different tribe, one that brings identity, status, and camaraderie but a much diminished sense of belonging.

Some of these distinctions are simply about size. A Bible-study group can be intimate; a parish, maybe; Catholicism can't be. But our tribes also differ according to the importance we give them. Consider popular bumper stickers. "I am the NRA," the Christian symbol of a fish, "I brake for unicorns": all these proclaim the driver's tribes, but they do not all necessarily evince the same level of passion and commitment. Finally, importance can depend on circumstance. We are more aware of our identity both when we are with tribe members who are all focused on the same thing—a PTA meeting, say—and, conversely, when we find ourselves surrounded by people who are different from us.[3]

Tribalism is grounded in this instinctual need to determine who is like us and who is different, and in our equally instinctual desire to be with those who are like ourselves. The term is *homophily*. After about nine months, all babies prefer (focus longer on) faces that are like their own.[4] And everyone who has gone to an integrated high school has noticed that the lunch tables in that same high school are often anything but.[5] But this inclination is not limited to race or ethnicity. Veterans who return from overseas combat frequently note that they feel more comfortable with veterans whom they have never met than with civilian acquaintances.[6] And in that same integrated high school, members of the football team or the theater kids might sit together irrespective of race. Of course, some of this separation is exacerbated, even mandated, by bigotry and discrimination. Some students sit together because that is effectively the only choice they have. But the point is that some of this separation takes place even when there are no such constraints. What drives us to separate is our preference for familiarity. Here, too, there are good reasons why this behavior was selected. In the groups we identify with, we know the social cues, the typical patterns of interaction, what is distinctively valued or denigrated. In tribes where we don't know these rules, we must expend more mental energy to pick up those idiosyncrasies, and we are more likely to make some mistake that only draws attention to our outsider status. The familiar is simply easier.

Another reason why tribalism is so operative in our lives is our innate need to categorize. When my middle son was little, upon being introduced to a character in any book, movie, or TV show, his first and inevitable question was: "Is he a good guy or a bad guy?" He was trying to make sense of this new story by placing characters in categories he already understood. This innate feature of the human brain was, as well, a survival strategy: predator, prey; safe to eat or not; good place to hunt; bad place to cross the river. These categories helped us survive in an infinitely complex world. Just about every animal that lives in groups manifests this same behavior, and for the same reason.[7]

Not only do we humans categorize, but we can't help but do so. In fact, we can't think without categories. Every time we see something or someone, we place that thing or that person into a category (or more than one). In cognitive scientist Stevan Harnad's words, "To cognize is to categorize."[8] The specificity of these categories depends on the depth of our investment. If you are not a beer geek, distinctions between a dry hopped or West Coast IPA will be lost on you and almost certainly a matter of indifference. "Beer" is quite sufficient as a category. But for those who do care, categories as specific as these are matters of serious discussion and debate: they are how members of the beer geek tribe identify themselves. Just so with coders, gardeners, model train enthusiasts, and so on. (As it happens, those who prefer craft beers over the traditional American pilsner are predominantly Democrats. As we shall see in the next chapter, this fanaticism about beer is just one of those little tribalistic markers that reinforce partisan identity.)

The categories we apply to people function the same way. They help make it possible for us to negotiate the complicated dynamics of interacting with a stranger. These categories obviously include racial and ethnic identities, but just about every human stereotype is likewise a category. If I see someone wearing a hunting cap, I will make assumptions. So too if I see someone with earlobe gauges. (What's more, people will often adopt these indicators as a signal to others that those assumptions are warranted.) Without conscious thought, we immediately size people up, determining what groups they fit into and what expectations we can have about who they are, what they want, and how we might relate to them. Of course, those determinations can be completely wrong. Comedy makes regular use of that kind of mistake. And being wrong enough times, or being wrong once but with significant enough effects, can cause us to modify our categories. But whether our expectations are reinforced or not, the process of categorization goes on. Indeed, it is genuinely unstoppable.

All these innate features of human behavior combine to create a very formidable predisposition. All of us seek out those with whom we are comfortable, those who are like us and with whom we share some aspect of our identity. We all instinctively categorize ourselves and the people we interact with into groups, into *us* and *them*.

Part of the legacy of tribalism is that we want fellow members (and by extension, ourselves) to succeed and to prevail over those tribes to which we do not belong. This desire is why people follow and enjoy sports. We want our team/tribe to win, and the deeper our investment, the greater our desire. Isabel Duarte and her colleagues showed Portuguese football fans videos of their team's successes and defeats while their brains were being scanned by an fMRI machine, which identifies parts of the brain that are activated during different tasks. Those parts of the brain showing increased activity suggest (but of course do not prove) that our tribal attachments are reinforced by chemicals in the brain: "Tribal love . . . represents a strong motivational state."[9] In other words, it's not simply that we want our tribe to win. It's that when our tribe does win, we receive feel-good chemicals, and when we lose, the brain releases chemicals that make us feel bad.

Fanaticism for a sports team might well represent an undue investment of time, energy, money, and (especially) emotion. (I would certainly admit as much for me.) But except for rare instances, like riots after a championship or soccer hooliganism, manifestations of our tribal instincts are basically harmless. The same holds true for those claiming a long-standing ethnic heritage or for fans of an entertainer or product. We take pleasure in the connection, in the feeling of belonging, but we also recognize that it doesn't matter much. Walking out of Lambeau Field (home of the Green Bay

Packers) decked out in my Chicago Bears regalia, I had to endure chants of "The Bears still suck." I didn't like it—not least because it was not wrong—but I never worried about my safety. In fact, in good Cheesehead fashion, when people did strike up a conversation, they welcomed me to Green Bay. So yes, Packer fans and Bears fans make up competing tribes, but as with most cases, tribal "warfare" goes no further than a snarky chant.

Yet even at its most benign, there is more to tribalism. Tribalism means favoritism, and favoritism implies unfairness. That unfairness is all the more perilous because it is unconscious.

Favoritism Is Innate

Developmental psychologist Rebecca Bigler randomly assigned elementary school children to "yellow" and "blue" groups and gave them T-shirts that corresponded to their groups. During the six-week summer session, the teachers were instructed not to show any preference for one group over the other but simply to distinguish between the two—for example, by instructing the yellow group to sit on one side of the room, with blue on the other side. After the session concluded, these children were shown photos of other children and then asked to divide resources among them. The children in the experiment did not know the children in the photos. They knew nothing about them except the color of their shirts: yellow or blue. Nevertheless, they consistently showed a strong unconscious preference for children wearing the shirt color that matched their own, giving those children a greater share of the resources they were asked to allocate.[10]

Another example. Henri Tajfel was a Jew who served as a French soldier during World War II. Captured by the Germans, he spent much of the war as a prisoner. Tajfel hid his Jewish identity from his captors, and that is why he survived. With this backstory, it is no surprise that he devoted his professional life to studying human dynamics relating to identity.

In 1970, Tajfel and his colleagues showed a small group of preadolescent boys a series of unidentified abstract paintings, some by Wassily Kandinsky and some by Paul Klee.[11] They asked the boys which paintings they liked. While they claimed that they separated the boys based on which painter they preferred, the actual separation was random. The boys were then individually asked to award points to every other boy, identified only by a code number and by the group to which he belonged. Even though their group identity was meaningless—and virtually instantaneous, to boot—the boys consistently gave more resources to the members of their own group. Then, just to reinforce the point, Tajfel repeated the experiment, only this time he *told* the boys that their groups were not based on their artistic choices but were random. Even so, they continued to show in-group favoritism.

In each of these experiments, the tribal attachment was not something the children were born with or some shared identity that they chose. Here, the tribes in question were created quickly, by others, and they rested on categories that were arbitrary, even meaningless. (Indeed, in one instance, the experimenters explicitly acknowledged that to be the case.) But none of that mattered. Without a moment's reflection, the children's tribal instinct kicked in and accepted and affirmed the terms of this instant *us* and *them*.[12] More to the point, this acceptance caused them to look upon the *us* more favorably. That is, they wanted *us* to win.

We simply *do* think of ourselves as belonging to tribes, and we simply *do* prefer our fellow tribe members to those who do not belong. And because we receive feel-good chemicals when our tribe wins, we are unlikely to be objective about any decision in which that outcome is at stake. Thus, to belong to a tribe is to be unable to view the world with impartiality. The very possibility of objectivity and fairness is compromised. As anybody who has been to a game knows, sports fans are hardly disinterested observers when it comes to fouls and close calls. In fact, as I note in chapter 6, fans are also far more inclined to look the other way when it is a member of their team who is accused of some bad behavior, on or off the court. But these inevitable features of sports fandom apply to all our tribes. All of us look more favorably on those who share our identity. This favoritism for those in the tribe, and distrust of those outside, thus leads, inevitably, to in-group bias.

What Is a Bias?

Since it is so relevant to what follows, let me take a minute to talk about what biases are and why we have them. A bias is an endemic inclination, one to which all of us are subject. People differ on how many discrete biases we are subject to, but in the words of Ben Yagoda, leaving aside the trivial ones and the duplicates, "a solid group of 100 or so biases have been repeatedly shown to exist."[13] A complete list would take us too far afield, but here are a few that have been well established through research:

- The *anchoring bias* means we tend to give undue influence to the first piece of information we hear.
- *Hindsight bias* means that once events are in the past, we tend to see them as much more explainable and predictable—even inevitable—than they ever really were.
- The *halo effect* means we tend to find people who are physically attractive more knowledgeable than those who are not.

Again, there are lots more. And as I will show, several biases are directly implicated in, and exacerbated by, our tribal identity. But the point is that all of these biases are part of our wiring. They are largely unconscious and effectively ubiquitous. And all of them cause us to think less effectively and accurately, leading us to reach conclusions that are less reliable than those we might otherwise be capable of. What is more, you cannot turn off these biases or outsmart them. All you can do is strive to diminish their effect.

It is fair to ask why that is the case. Why is it that the human brain, the most complex, exquisite single thing in the known universe, has all these built-in bugs? Because they are not bugs; they're . . . well, you know, features. The preeminent objective for any organism is staying alive and passing on its genes. To stay alive in the face of some danger, we usually need to react immediately. And our biases help us to do that. Our biases are part of our arsenal of what researchers term "Type 1" thinking, which helps us make sense of the world and respond to it with little time and effort.[14] If, for example, we give more weight to the first piece of information we encounter, we are less likely to get bogged down in determining which information is really accurate. These mental shortcuts are called *heuristics*. They may not be perfectly accurate, but they can get us to decisions that are pretty good most of the time. That makes them an effective survival strategy for responding immediately to some danger. And because we are all here, we can assume that the trade-off between speed and accuracy was a good one. So our biases are the legacy of surviving on the savanna, just like our need to identify with a tribe. And in both regards, these features of our humanity were selected because they were better at keeping us alive.

But human beings can also solve complex mathematical problems. We can assess our enemy's intent from their actions and devise a strategy based on that assessment. We can uncover a piece of rock, understand that it is in fact a fossil, and extrapolate hypotheses about when the animal lived, what it looked like, what it ate, and so forth. With these kinds of problems, we aim to consider the evidence or situation as accurately and objectively as possible so that we can make the best assessment, the best decision. This is called "Type 2" thinking. It is deliberate and deliberative. It takes longer. It requires focus and much more energy. (Because Type 1 and Type 2 thinking require such different amounts of time and focus, Daniel Kahneman calls them "thinking fast and slow.") For Type 2 problems, our biases are useless at best and more often lead us to the wrong conclusion. And again, the more we desire a certain outcome, the more likely those biases will come into play, and the more likely that negative outcome will result.

In-Group Bias

So how does bias operate with respect to groups? Whenever our tribe is involved in a dispute, our notion of what's fair is unconsciously modified. Just as in those close calls in sports, in-group bias causes us to process information differently. We more readily recall and give more weight to information that supports our side, and we find reasons to discount and even "forget" information that supports the other side.[15] And we do all this unconsciously and all in ways that favor *us* over *them*.

We all know examples of this bias, especially as it becomes more extreme. We have seen that bias can extend into overt prejudice: a racist, for example, is very explicit about her favoritism. Alternatively, we might know people who have experienced so much racism from the dominant social group that they have grown distrustful of any member of that group. (As we shall see, tribalism grows through the perception of and reaction to threat. Sometimes that threat is real and sometimes it isn't, but it is the perception that matters.) But the hard fact is that the difference between all of us and the racist is one of degree. The racist constructs her very identity around her inability to perceive the world accurately, but none of us are immune. Bias is operative in all of us, even if we insist that it is not. Like all biases, the in-group bias is not conscious. And that means that we don't always know that we are acting in a biased way, and we are always incapable of fully appreciating bias's effects.

Just as every *us* creates a *them*, favoritism toward some necessitates prejudice against others. For all of us, defining anyone as *them* affords that individual a different and diminished status. In short, the drive to form groups, the inclination to favor members over nonmembers, is of a piece with the fact that we have less connection to them, less inclination to trust them, and less investment in their winning. In fact, we are actually invested in their losing, even when we don't win. In that Klee and Kandinsky group experiment, a statistical analysis of the boys' decisions showed that their choices didn't lead to the maximum payoff for their side. Instead, the boys sought the maximum possible *difference* between their side and the other. In other words, the boys on Team Kandinsky were more interested in being as far ahead of Klee folk as possible than they were in making more money for themselves. The authors of study concluded, "It is the winning that seems more important to them."[16]

This flip side is likewise manifested neurologically. Mina Cikara examined brain activity of Red Sox and Yankees fans while showing them an animated baseball game.[17] These subjects were selected based on their knowledge of their team as well as their level of passion both for their team and against the other one. (That is, it was not enough that they loved their team; they also had to hate the opposing one.) Participants showed signs of pleasure when their team succeeded and pain when they failed. No surprise there. But the same patterns were elicited when their hated rival did badly or well. In fact, this pleasure obtained even when the failure took place against some other team: even when the Red Sox lost a game against the Orioles, for example, Yankees fans felt pleasure. In short, from a neurological point of view, the pleasure associated with my tribe's winning and your tribe's losing is quite similar. Schadenfreude is not a feeling that we are proud to have. It is a genuinely guilty pleasure—but it is real.

Worse, because we attach less significance to *them*, because we feel pleasure when they lose, we also are less interested in distinctions within that group. Just as types of beers are irrelevant to someone who drinks iced tea, all of *us* are less invested in *them*. Therefore, there is a neurological foundation for the bigot's almost inevitable claim: "They're all alike." But here again, the same inclination that leads a bigot to say vile things is present in all of us. We all possess the tribal instinct, and that instinct simply makes it easier for us to diminish individual differences among those outside our group. Ultimately, tribalism leads to dehumanization of the other. In languages all over the world, the word for our group, for *us*, corresponds to the word for *human*. (For example, the English word *barbarian* comes from an ancient Greek word for people who did not speak Greek.) And people attribute human descriptors (person, people, citizen) to members of their tribe, while they are more likely to use animal words (e.g., wild, creature, breed) to outsiders.[18] If you are not part of *us*, you are literally less of a human being.

This trail from dehumanization to discrimination reveals a natural human inclination. We might not be aware of it. But it is the rare human being who does not manifest this legacy of our tribal beginnings. Again, the danger of bias only begins with bigotry and unfairness. When this impulse to dehumanize is unchecked, *us* and *them* grows from unconscious favoritism to animus, enmity, and ultimately violence. Few patterns are more frequently represented in human history.

How Tribalism Becomes Vicious

As obvious as this point is, it is equally true and important to note that this does not always or even frequently take place. Bears fans don't go to war with Packers fans. So what is it that makes tribalism go too far? How can humans go from wearing our team's gear and cheering wildly to dehumanizing, devaluing, and even harming those who are not in our tribe?

As I have said, vices start as natural human inclinations. We might cut out from work some afternoon for something that is decidedly not work related. That action isn't something that qualifies us for employee of the year, but it doesn't make us degenerates, either. The difference here, as in most of human behavior, is a matter of degree. When our inclination overwhelms our self-control, our commitments, our better instincts, and our sense of perspective, then it becomes a vice. And the more overwhelmed, the more vicious we have become.

Belonging to a tribe is likewise a natural, even inescapable, disposition. It helps us feel connected to other people and lets us proclaim some little part of who we are to the world. Spending a Sunday afternoon watching our team, or LARPing, or hanging out online with fellow Star Wars nerds is probably not the best use of our time. We could be exercising, or reading Proust, or whatever. But it is hardly vicious. It is when our tribe comes to so dominate our lives that we shirk our responsibilities or lose touch with reality—or, most relevantly, when favoritism toward *us* bleeds into animus toward *them*—that that disposition becomes a vice. There are a number of ways that change can happen. Two are especially pertinent in our present circumstances.

Tribal Threats

Again, bonding with other family units into a tribal group was a very successful survival strategy. But this meant that the fate of the tribe was indistinguishable from that of every individual in it. If the tribe was safe, so was the individual; if the tribe fell apart or was defeated by another, the individual was in big trouble, too. So when the tribe was threatened, everyone in the tribe would respond in the way that humans respond to any threat, especially those that concern people and things we deeply value: they would defend those people and things with their lives. This response, "defend and aggress," is another genetic adaption that extends back far into our evolutionary history.

Thus, one way to enhance the destructive dimensions of tribalism is to make those in the tribe feel threatened. *Feel* is the correct word, for as I noted above, the threat may or not be real, and it may or may not be serious enough to warrant an aggressive response. But the brain does not wait around to make that kind of determination. Again, for good reasons, defend/aggress is a reaction; it is immediate and not subject to consideration or forethought. In his book *Tribalism: The Evolutionary Origins of Fear Politics*, Stevan Hobfoll speaks directly to this link between tribalism and defend/aggress: "We need this for survival, as thoughtfulness and careful consideration take time and also potentially threaten the solidarity of the tribe. At some point, even if the tribe is wrong, its members must fight without question for its survival or the tribe will perish. Although this linkage of loss-defend-aggress was imprinted when we were living in bands of 150 people, faced with harsh environmental challenges to survival from both nature and other warring tribes, they are nevertheless deeply ingrained in how our brains process information and how we react cognitively, emotionally, and in action."[19] And the more extreme the perceived threat—the more it is understood to involve the tribe's very survival—the more aggressive will be the response.

The Threats Americans Feel

As we all know too well, many Americans consider themselves and their tribe to be under threat right now in precisely this way.

- White Americans feel ever less comfortable and familiar in their own country. An influx of immigrants has changed their society in ways that they do not understand or approve. If those trends continue, their way of life—that is, the way things used to be—appears to be gone forever. For their part, those same immigrants feel unwelcome and even unsafe in the country they were so desperate to get to and to which they are so committed.
- Working people, and especially older men, feel threatened by the loss of a working wage. They remain prepared to give an honest day's work for an honest day's pay, but people have been replaced by robots and, some believe, by immigrants. The jobs are gone, and with them feelings of self-worth. Younger people see an economy controlled by that older generation that has left them saddled with insurmountable college debt and a planet that is on fire. And while baby boomers are only too happy to have the younger generation make the lattes, they stubbornly and smugly hold on to privileges that make it harder for young people to make their way in the world.
- Rural Americans feel threatened by an economy that is leaving them behind. Their towns' tax base slowly evaporates; opioid addiction brings crime, squalor, and death; the next generation cannot

find jobs and has to leave. Similarly, people of color believe that the latest case of police violence demonstrates that their second-class status in this society has never really changed, and the only difference is that now there is video.

- Evangelicals feel threatened by a culture that they believe denigrates them and their beliefs. Religious convictions against homosexual conduct, let alone trans people, are dismissed as benighted bigotry. Cultural acceptance, even indifference, regarding sinful behavior thus manifests a culture that has turned its back on God, one in which they no longer have a place. For their part, LGBTQ citizens feel that their hard-won social acceptance and even their right to be who they are are under attack by a powerful and bigoted subset of American society.
- Humiliation and victimhood characterize women's feelings as well. The rise of the Me Too movement has only exposed the raw sexism that pervades the country at the highest levels of government, business, sports, and entertainment. It treats women unfairly and leaves them unsafe. For men, the threat is that women now demand the end of due process: a single accusation of rape can destroy a man without any genuine recourse.
- Gun owners feel that the federal government wants to take their guns away and turn patriotic Americans into criminals for asserting their constitutional and God-given rights to defend themselves and their families. But as schoolchildren must endure yet another lockdown drill, their parents grow ever more fearful that the next mass shooting will take place in their own town, all because spineless politicians cower before the inordinate and irresponsible power of the National Rifle Association and its minions.

I have tried to present these feelings as accurately as possible. I don't know that all will recognize themselves in these descriptions, but I am confident that just about all Americans will find these expressions of threat familiar. Of course, it is almost certainly the case that one side of these oppositions is more accurate, more commensurate with reality, than the other. But again, the feeling of threat is what matters. If the feeling is real, that is sufficient; the ingrained responses of defend and aggress are almost inevitable.

I have paired these reactions to demonstrate how feelings of threat exacerbate each other. Just as the victim of a racist culture finds it hard to trust any member of the dominant group, any perceived threat leads to a reaction of defense and aggression. But perception is operative here as well. Reaction is itself a matter of interpretation: what we take as defense, they see as aggression, which in turn requires defense. Once this cycle begins, it is very difficult to stop. Lee Drutman describes this cycle of reaction and counterreaction, this descent of tribalism into animosity and violence, as a "doom loop."[20] There is solid evidence that that is exactly what is happening and exactly where we are heading.

Our Tribal Doom Loop

You may have heard of several studies that document the steeply increasing number of parents who would be unhappy if their child married a partisan from the other side. But did you know that among both Republicans and Democrats, the percentage of such objectors is now higher for partisanship than it is for religion or race?[21] Moreover, the more strongly partisan an individual is, the more likely they are to express this kind of animus. A recent Pew study found that "partisans who follow government and politics most closely are more likely than less attentive partisans to give a cold rating to the other party—and a warm rating to their own."[22] Strong partisans are not just cold to the other side; they have a visceral distrust and dislike of them. A study by Patrick Miller and Pamela Conover shows that "Democrats and Republicans with strong identities perceive the opposing party as rivals who are fundamentally immoral and cannot be trusted; likewise, they are enraged at each other for 'destroying American democracy.'"[23]

Strong partisans also identify closely with the wins and losses of their tribe. They are very happy when their side wins, and when they lose, they feel terrible. In fact, partisans were twice as sad that their tribe lost the 2012 US presidential election as American parents were to the shootings in Newtown, Connecticut, that same year and respondents living in Boston were to the Boston Marathon bombing in 2013.[24] I am only one parent, but based on my own reaction to the Newtown shooting, I can only say that that is very sad, indeed.

Finally, strong partisans display the same tribalistic inclination to dehumanize those on the other side. A study by Vanderbilt

University's Center for the Study of Democratic Institutions asked participants to rate their political opponents. Respondents who considered themselves strong partisans—from either partisan tribe—were equally likely to dehumanize opposing partisans. Research showed that "seventy-seven percent of our respondents rated their political opponents as less evolved than members of their own party."[25] This tendency held true for Republicans and Democrats equally. However, the stronger the partisan, the more likely they were to dehumanize their partisan opponents.

If all this is true, is it hard to figure out where this doom loop ends up? In 2018, political scientists Nathan Kalmoe and Lilliana Mason asked a group of Americans whether they agreed or disagreed with a set of statements about American politics. They found that 42 percent of partisans agreed with the statement that members of the other party "are not just worse for politics—they are downright evil." Almost one in five agreed that those in the other party "lack the traits to be considered fully human—they behave like animals." Finally, they asked this question: "What if the opposing party wins the 2020 presidential election. How much do you feel violence would be justified then?" As Thomas Edsall describes the results, "18.3 percent of Democrats and 13.8 percent of Republicans said violence would be justified on a scale ranging from 'a little' to 'a lot.'"[26] Of course, these numbers reflect a minority of partisans. The vast majority of Americans from both parties continue to reject violence as a legitimate response to any political event. But after the events of January 6, the idea of partisan violence can no longer shock us. The thousands involved in that insurrection may represent the feelings of many, many more. More than 159 million people voted in the 2020 election. It is quite likely, therefore, that the percentages documented by Kalmoe and Mason can be extrapolated to tens of millions of Americans—tens of millions who may see the other side as such a threat that their defeat justifies an extreme and destructive response. How much higher does that number have to go before our democracy becomes unsustainable? That is the question before us.

Let me sum up. Deep in our genetic birthright is our desire to connect, to become part of an *us*, to become part of a tribe. We all manifest that commitment in ways that are mostly, but not merely, benign. For at the core of tribalism is bias: favoritism and, as a result, unfairness. And that unfairness is pernicious because it operates beneath our conscious awareness. When our tribe is very important to us, and we think it is threatened, we defend it. That, too, is part of our genetic endowment. That response is both immediate and aggressive. Because it is, when one tribe reacts in this way, it is virtually inevitable that the other tribe will respond in kind. And once that cycle begins, it is very difficult to stop. This "doom loop" describes where we are now. There is one more reason why tribalism has become so dangerous for our democracy right now: tribal alignment. That is the subject of the next chapter.

2

TRIBAL ALIGNMENT

They came three thousand miles, and died,
To keep the Past upon its throne.
—JAMES RUSSELL LOWELL, AT THE GRAVE OF BRITISH SOLDIERS BURIED AT THE OLD NORTH BRIDGE

The story goes that there was a journalist who was writing a story about politics in Northern Ireland during "the Troubles." His research naturally took him to a pub, and as he was scribbling the day's notes, he struck up a conversation with a local patron. After a time, the man leaned in and asked, "So what are you, a Catholic or a Protestant?" "Neither," replied the journalist. "I'm an atheist." The Irishman leaned in still further, eyed the journalist, and asked, "Ah, but are you a Catholic atheist or a Protestant atheist?"

We all belong to many, many tribes. We are complex creatures, with many aspects to our lives and our personalities. Some of our tribes are very important to us, inseparable from our most essential sense of who we are. Some we belong to just for fun; we take them up and put them down as we move through life. But in Northern Ireland, in the midst of a long and bloody civil war, there was only one question, one operative *us* and *them*, and it had nothing to do with the theological status of Jesus's mother. All those other tribes that everyone belonged to, all the small and large social identities, all the ways in which people categorized each other, all of these were subsumed into the relentless and overwhelming struggle between the only two tribes that mattered. Any civil war you can name, almost by definition, is similarly constituted. This is the other way for tribalism to become vicious. It happens when one tribe, one form of identity, envelops all others. All the myriad tribes a person belongs to all line up behind this one tribe, until there is only one *us* and one *them*.

I expect you know where this is going. In the United States right now, politics has become for us what religion was for those in Northern Ireland—an *us* and *them* split that has aligned a vast array of otherwise distinct tribes into two overriding identities. And our current political culture manifests the results.

Us and *Them* in American Politics

With few exceptions, political campaigns in the United States have—for more than 170 years—constituted a simple binary choice. As a result, some polarization is neither unique nor surprising. In fact, it's inevitable. Parties win by uniting various coalitions, interest groups, tribes, call them what you will. And to build that coalition, to bring people together and create an *us*, you also inevitably create a *them*—people who are not part of our tribe. Again, as I showed in the last chapter, we human beings will always be inclined to stereotype and treat unfairly anyone who is a *them*. What is more, any campaign's effort to create that *us* and to move members to volunteer, give money, and vote frequently exploits that innate disposition toward division and animosity. Frequent hard-edged competition between these two parties is therefore entirely predictable. In the nation's history, eras of good feelings are few and far between.

It is also true that there have always been social categories that have both lined up and connected a person to one party or the other. If we were living in the 1950s, and I was an Irish Catholic union worker from Chicago, you could make some pretty good assumptions about my politics. Same if I were a Presbyterian bank president who belonged to a country club on the north shore of Lake Michigan. Just to say, partisan tribal alignment is not a new phenomenon. And, again, given that in American politics the prevailing choice is always between one party or the other, some of this is inevitable. Democracy depends on tribalism, and tribes can combine to move us to one side or the other.

Given all this, there is always something dangerous about democratic politics. In fact, political scientists have long noted that in order to contain this danger and maintain a stable democracy, it is important that our tribal identities be "cross-cutting"— that our identities do not all line up in the same partisan direction, and that many of our identities have no connection to politics at all.[1] But today, cross-cutting identities are uncommon, even rare. To a degree unseen since the Civil War, our current partisan split, this particular expression of *us* versus *them*, has overwhelmed and subsumed all others. And it has done so for many more Americans. Our tribal identity is no longer myriad and idiosyncratic but lined up and stark.

Now before I go any further, let me address an immediate response to this argument. It is true that a sizable number of Americans identify as independent, neither Republican nor Democrat. In fact, a Gallup poll early in 2021 set a record for the highest percentage of self-identified independents Gallup had ever recorded. There were as many self-identified independents (50 percent) as there were Democrats or Republicans (25 percent for each).[2] Since then, that percentage has retreated. But even at more customary levels, percentages for independents always outnumber those for both Republicans and Democrats. Regardless of the exact number, somewhere between one third to one half of Americans don't explicitly belong to either political party. That would appear to undermine the idea that these two partisan tribes dominate American culture.

Not exactly. A small number of Americans (7 percent) genuinely choose not to identify with or support either party, but these individuals are distinctive for their lack of interest in, and knowledge of, politics. They are independent because they just don't care that much. But most Americans who have chosen not to self-identify as Republican or Democrat are not really independent at all. According to a Pew Center report, 81 percent of self-described independents "lean" toward one party or the other. Among those leaners, their voting choices, policy preferences, and, most relevantly, their attitudes toward their tribe and the other are sometimes less ardent than those of avowed Democrats and Republicans, but they always manifest in the same direction: "Independents who lean toward one of the two parties have a strong partisan imprint. Majorities of Republican and Democratic leaners have a favorable opinion of their own party, and they are almost as likely as Republican and Democratic identifiers to have an unfavorable opinion of the opposing party."[3]

So if these independents aren't really all that independent, then why do they call themselves that? Samara Klar and Yanna Krupnikov argue that the rise in independents reflects a growing distaste for the condition of American politics and especially with political partisanship. These independents find it all exhausting and even embarrassing. Therefore, while their beliefs, attitudes, and voting behaviors are very similar to those who profess partisan identities, they are less inclined to profess them.[4] In sum, these independents belong to one tribe or the other; they are just quieter about it.

Whether they call themselves independents or are ardent supporters of one party or the other, partisanship has become, in the words of Lilliana Mason and Julie Wronski, "a tribe that binds all other identities together."[5] Each of the many tribes that we belong to now is more likely to reflect the overriding frame of partisan identity, reinforcing our sense of separateness, division, and animosity. And as these two tribes have emerged as the one operative definer of *us* and *them*, our common identity as Americans has accordingly declined, and our ability to sustain democratic politics has become far more difficult.

The Slow Decline of the Postwar Establishment

The reasons for this split are longstanding. We did not come to this condition overnight. It is best seen as the product of significant changes that have been developing since the end of World War II. At that moment, with its manufacturing infrastructure uniquely intact and facing a world eager to consume again, the American economy dominated the globe. Wages rose precipitously, and a middle-class income could be achieved by a single family breadwinner. That person was usually the father: overall employment rates for men were almost double those for women. And with precious few exceptions, leaders in politics and business were likewise almost universally men. What's more, those men were also almost exclusively white. The South was far more explicit and direct about it, but in the North as well, segregation of, and discrimination toward, African Americans and other racial and ethnic minorities was an established fact of social life. Finally, the vast majority of Americans were both Christian and regular churchgoers. In the 1950s, more than 95 percent of Americans identified as Christian.[6] This is the society that most baby boomers (myself included) grew up in: one in which American economic power was unquestioned and in which the white, male, Christian (WMC) cultural establishment was also unquestioned. But even then, powerful forces had begun to chip away at this social structure.

The End of Economic Dominance

As the rest of the world slowly rebuilt, the US manufacturing advantage began to decline, as did its economic preeminence. Competition heated up, and many jobs went offshore as companies sought cheaper labor in developing nations. Finally, automation (including robots) and computers eventually eliminated the need for so many assembly lines—and so many laborers: "Manufacturing and agriculture employed one in three workers just after World War II. Today, those sectors employ only one in eight."[7] The effects of these changes—good and bad—have not been distributed equitably. All over America, towns that depended on that one industry or that one factory reeled from the shift, and some have never fully recovered. Of course, economic growth has continued, but it has been driven by the comparative growth of service sector jobs, which offer lower wages and often no union support, and of highly skilled, professional jobs in the so-called knowledge economy. The latter are frequently in major metropolitan areas, and employees in these industries have become more transient and less attached to "place" than those in generations past. These changes, along with a dramatic lowering of the tax burden on those earning the most,[8] have led to historically high inequality levels and a hollowing out of the middle class.

Immigration

After hitting unprecedented highs in 1910, immigration to the United States slowly declined, reaching a modern low in 1970. Thereafter, immigration began a steady rise, to the point where in the 2000s, numbers of immigrants have once again approached 1910 levels. Two factors account for the change. First, Congress passed the Immigration and Nationality Act of 1965. This law eliminated national quota systems that many regarded as racist and created a new immigration system that favored skilled immigrants and family reunification.

Around the same time, there was a steep rise in the unauthorized immigration of Mexicans. From 1970 to 2010, the numbers of Latin American immigrants, primarily from Mexico, increased from less than one million in 1960 to nearly nineteen million in 2010.[9] (Incidentally, these numbers began to decline in 2007, well before any talk of "building a wall.") The upshot is that since 1970, the total foreign-born population has more than quadrupled; people born outside the United States now approach 14 percent of the population. Immigrant communities are now part of just about every major American city. They have also made inroads in rural communities, where they were previously wholly absent.

Most of this immigration has come from people born in Asia and Latin America instead of Europe. Most of them are not white but brown. The US Census Bureau now predicts that the United States will no longer be majority white by 2045, and among children at every age below ten, whites are already a minority.[10] For many white Americans, this reality is extremely threatening. Almost half (46 percent) say that the prospect of the United States' becoming a majority nonwhite nation would "weaken American customs and values."[11]

The 1960s

The same generation that grew up under the WMC establishment also did much to bring it to an end. A variety of movements rooted in the 1960s sought to challenge that establishment, demand an expansion of civil rights, and call for freer individual expression.

Most relevantly, the 1960s saw civil rights for African Americans enacted into law. The Voting Rights Act, Civil Rights Act, Fair Housing Act, and a series of Supreme Court rulings all brought the Jim Crow era to an end, but more than that, these new laws acknowledged a long legacy of racism and categorically unequal, unconstitutional treatment. They implicitly, and sometimes explicitly, committed our society to try to do better.

Likewise, just about every other group whose status was less than equal in this society began to demand full equality. Women, Latinos, the LGBTQ community, Native Americans—during the '60s and into the early '70s, all these communities saw major milestone events in their efforts to secure equal rights. They all challenged a society built on the preeminence of the WMC establishment.

These changes had an impact in other areas as well. During the 1960s, the nation saw deep racial unrest as well as violent protests associated with the Vietnam War, particularly against the draft. In reaction, many Republicans sought to refashion their party as defending what Richard Nixon called "the silent majority"—those who rejected assaults on the government and the cultural establishment, calling them un-American, and saw the changes that came in the wake of the '60s as illegitimate and foolhardy. For their part, many northern Democrats decided that votes from members of these minority groups counted just the same. They therefore took up the mantle of equality and pushed against an unjust status quo.

Because of these changes, the United States is dramatically more equitable than it was fifty years ago. Yet it is also true that, in every case, real equality remains elusive. The overwhelming, and overwhelmingly diverse, response to the death of George Floyd in 2020 (and of a litany of other victims) makes all too clear that the battle against racial injustice rages on. Same with the Me Too movement. Same with the demands of transgender people for recognition. For members of these tribes, the changes have not gone nearly far enough.

The Contemporary Tribal Alignment

Again, there is much more to say about any one of these changes, but it is enough for my purposes to say that since the end of the 1950s, the United States has changed dramatically with respect to culture, economics, and politics. And in just about every respect, those changes continue. But not everyone looks at them in the same way. Our society's tribal alignment, our current division into *us* and *them*, turns predominantly on whether you regard those changes as generally good or generally bad.[12]

For many, our nation's growing diversity and its increasing equality for women, racial and ethnic groups, other religions, and people who are not heterosexual are positive, even if they are inadequate. This is especially true for those who are members of these groups, that is, those who have benefited directly from these social changes. Many white Americans, as well, laud these changes as moral progress. A more diverse, equitable society is a society that more genuinely lives up to its ideals. This is especially true of young white Americans who have grown up in a far more diverse society than their elders did and have no nostalgia for a society they never experienced.[13] All these groups are more likely to be Democrats than Republicans.

Others see these social changes as negative, if not disastrous. If you are old enough to remember the 1950s and '60s, you may recall an economy where the United States was king of the mountain, where everyone (even without a college degree) who wanted a job could find one, and where living standards rose almost inexorably. If you are that old and also white, Christian, or male, and especially all three, then you may well recall a society in which everyone knew the rules and knew how to operate within them—and in which your position was, relatively speaking, better than it is now. These changes have left many of these people all at sea. Their accustomed ways of speaking and acting are no longer operative, and sometimes they are spurned. Just as importantly, these individuals see "new" ways of speaking and acting as inferior at best, bearing witness to a country that is diminished from what it once was. At worst, they see these social changes are immoral, reflecting a nation that has lost its religious and ethical moorings. All these individuals are more likely to be Republican. Alan Abramowitz notes that in 2016, "fully 81% of Trump supporters, compared to only 19% of Clinton supporters, believed that 'life for people like them' has gotten worse in the past fifty years."[14]

This split is manifested, and reinforced, over and over again in our society. It is reflected in our big permanent tribes—like those based on geography, religion, and especially race and ethnicity—but the separation is just as clear in the little tribes that we belong to and reaffirm with our everyday choices. Overall, the vast majority of tribes in America serve to point all of us in either one direction or the other, connecting us to one partisan *us* and reflecting our alienation from the partisan *them*. All this explains the state of American politics right now.

The Economy

Of course, much of this feeling of life getting better or worse is a product of one's economic standing. Mark Muro was lead author of a Brookings study of the 2016 election that looked at voting patterns and economic production. He and his colleagues found that while

Hillary Clinton won fewer than five hundred counties in the United States, those counties accounted for almost two thirds (64 percent) of the nation's GDP.[15] Donald Trump, on the other hand, won more than five times as many counties, but they generated 36 percent of the nation's economic production. Reviewing the 2020 election results, the Brookings group again found very similar patterns. While Joe Biden won slightly more counties than Hillary Clinton, and Trump in 2020 slightly fewer than in 2016, the economic disparity had increased markedly. The counties that Biden won made up 71 percent of the nation's GDP. Moreover, those counties that Biden won were not only more productive but also "tended to be far more diverse, educated, and white-collar professional, with their aggregate non-white and college-educated shares of the economy running to 35% and 36%, respectively, compared to 16% and 25% in counties that voted for Trump."[16]

Those who have benefited from the new economy, who are mobile and content to be so, who have marketable skills and a solid 401K: those people are more likely to vote Democratic. For Trump voters, on the other hand, many of whom live in communities that never fully emerged from the Rust Belt decline, there are good reasons to think that life has gotten worse. They see factories closed and a Main Street bereft of stores and businesses, and they conclude that it is not just the economy that has left them behind; it is the politicians as well. They resent their loss of status and don't believe they have done anything to deserve it. Those people are far more likely to vote Republican.

This split between rural and small-town voters, on the one hand, and city voters on the other (with suburban and exurban voters being the point of transition) has created a society that is more geographically polarized around party than at any point since 1860.[17] And you might recall what happened in the United States during the 1860s.[18]

Religion

This feeling of decline for "people like us" is by no means limited to economics. It also refers to the declining standing of the former WMC establishment. Economics aside, many of these rural areas also continue to mirror the conditions and norms that prevailed decades ago—a community that remains largely white and Christian, one in which parents work hard, families stay together for generations, and everyone prays together before the family dinner. These rural communities likewise identify as Republican, and the many Trump flags and signs that dotted yards throughout small-town America before, during, and after the 2020 election speak to this fact.

As I noted, in the 1950s most people—Democrats and Republicans both—professed and practiced Christianity. The culture at large reflected this common faith in ways that are now significantly diminished and, in some cases, gone forever. Public displays of Christian symbols were far more frequent, stores used to close on Sunday, and the phrase "under God" was added to the Pledge of Allegiance. People were more likely to say "Merry Christmas" as well. Now, especially among white Christians, there is deep partisan division.[19] There are still many Christians who are Democrats; they remain the plurality of the party. Yet far more Republicans continue to believe that the United States is a Christian nation, that the United States has a special place in God's providence, and that the Bible and God's commandments are the true and proper foundation for human law. For these citizens, the past was better because our society strove to live up to the special blessings God had bestowed on us. It was better when prayer was part of the school day, when children obeyed their parents (and for that matter every adult), and when everyone recognized that homosexuality was wrong because God told us it was.[20]

Evangelicals are right to say that the United States has moved away from many of these beliefs and practices. Yet they go further: they believe that the cultured elite now spurns and denigrates anyone who still holds to those beliefs. They view this new world and conclude that Christians like themselves are the beleaguered ones in our society. In fact, in 2017, shortly after Trump's first effort to institute a ban on Muslim immigration, a Public Religion Research Institute survey showed that Christian evangelicals believe that Christians face more discrimination than Muslims.[21] They were the only religious group to say so. For the rest of the nation, this outlier status confirms that this group of Christian evangelicals is out of touch with reality. For evangelicals themselves, their isolation confirms that they are indeed under siege.

Because of this feeling, the tribe of white evangelicals identified with, and maintained unyielding support for, Donald Trump. Ralph Reed, leader of the Faith and Freedom Coalition, had this to say about then-president Trump: "There has never been anyone who has defended us and who has fought for us, who we have loved more than Donald J. Trump. No one!"[22] On the other hand, for those who understand Christianity differently, those who practice a different faith, those whose identity is denigrated by evangelicals (for example, who identify as LGBTQ), and those who are among the "nones" (since 2008, the fastest-growing faith designation in the United States)—for all these people, the likelihood that they will be Democrats has increased markedly.[23]

Race

Finally, there is the decline of whiteness, both as a percentage of the total population and in terms of its dominance in American life. When the United States was prevailingly white, so, too, was American politics. Since the civil rights movement, most African Americans have voted Democratic, but even as late as 1976, "the percentage of nonwhite voters in both parties was very low. In the Republican party it was about 5% and in the Democratic Party it was about 15%." As society became more diverse, one party changed, and the other did not: "In 2012, the percentage [of nonwhites] for Democrats had increased to over 40% while the percentage for Republicans still hovered at or below 10%."[24]

As the Republican Party stayed predominantly white and as Republicans began to present themselves, with Nixon, as defenders of the "silent majority," those in the two parties have manifested stark, even oppositional, differences regarding race relations. Among white Democrats, 78 percent believe that the bigger problem for the nation is "not seeing discrimination where it really does exist." For white Republicans, 77 percent believe that problem is "seeing discrimination where it does not exist."[25] Similarly, "about seven-in-ten Republicans and Republican-leaning independents (71%) say white people get few or no advantages in society that black people do not have. By contrast, 83% of Democrats and Democratic leaners say white people benefit a great deal or a fair amount from advantages not available to black people, while only 16% see little or no such advantages." A poll from June 2020, after the murder of George Floyd, produced similar results: "Generally, Republicans were less inclined to say that any group in America faces high levels of discrimination. . . . But significantly more Republicans than Democrats thought there is discrimination against Christians and white people."[26]

Behind these assessments of who, exactly, is suffering from discrimination lurks a more or less explicit sense of racial resentment. Republicans are more likely to see other races and ethnicities as threats to their way of life. For many, this feeling of racial resentment is tied to feelings of anger and betrayal about their economic condition. Part of the explanation for why things are the way they are stems from the distrust and negative stereotypes that inevitably follow our perception of *them*. But for Republicans more than Democrats, racial and ethnic minorities and their representatives overstate their particular disadvantages. In fact, more Republicans than Democrats believe that those groups receive special breaks and support while their own communities are disrespected and neglected.

Much has been made of the fact that while whites with a college degree supported Hillary Clinton over Donald Trump by 30 points, among those white Americans without a college degree, Trump beat Clinton by 40 points.[27] Such a vast disparity would appear to demand an explanation. According to Abramowitz, though, this difference is less important than it seems. In fact, if you isolate racial resentment as a variable, there is no meaningful difference between those Trump supporters who went to college and those who did not. The amount of racial resentment is equally predictive for both groups: "White voters with high levels of racial/ethnic resentment voted overwhelmingly for Trump regardless of education, and white voters with low levels of racial/ethnic resentment voted overwhelmingly for Clinton regardless of education."[28] The only difference between the two groups is that many more people who did not go to college feel racial resentment. Still, college or no, if you do indeed feel such resentment, you are much more likely to be a Trump voter.[29]

Here is another example of the impact of racial resentment. Robert Pape is a professor of political science at the University of Chicago and director of the Chicago Project on Security and Threats. He analyzed the characteristics of the individuals charged for their actions during the January 6 insurrection. Many of his findings were atypical for a political protest. For example, those arrested were not preponderantly young. There were more professionals than is common. The majority were not from red states, and most did not have any previous association with any right-wing extremist group. One variable, however, set them apart: "By far the most interesting characteristic common to the insurrectionists' backgrounds has to do with changes in their local demographics: Counties with the most significant declines in the non-Hispanic White population are the most likely to produce insurrectionists who now face charges."[30] Those who were receptive to the lie that the election was stolen, and who were so angered by it that they came to Washington and illegally entered the Capitol building, were more likely to come from places where the percentage of whites is declining, along with their concomitant economic, political, and cultural hegemony.

To be clear: racial resentment is not exactly the same thing as racism. With few exceptions, Americans don't think of themselves as racists, and most would never explicitly avow racist thoughts. Recall, though, that bias is not conscious. It is the product of thoughts that we are not, and cannot be, fully aware of. That means that we all harbor attitudes toward *them* that are negative and that impact our actions. When *them* means African Americans, then racism is the effective result. In the movie *Hidden Figures,* the white supervisor (played by Kirsten Dunst) and Dorothy Vaughan (played by Octavia Spencer) are washing their hands in the newly desegregated ladies' room. "I don't have anything against you," the supervisor says. Vaughan replies, "I know." Then, after a pause, she adds, "I know you believe that." That's the point. What you believe about your attitudes and actions, and the nearly inescapable messages that are conveyed to others by those very same actions, are not the same—for any of us. With respect to racial resentment, Abramowitz's data, not to mention the overwhelming paucity of nonwhite people at every Trump event, speak at least as loudly as Trump and his supporters' strenuous and no doubt often sincere denials.[31]

Where we are from, our religion, our race, our ethnicity—these are tribes that we are often born into and that we can leave only with difficulty, if at all. And in ways seen before only during our own Civil War, these permanent tribes have all been split in two, and in each case, the identities line up into two coherent and reinforcing partisan tribes. That fundamental difference accounts for politics in the United States today.

Little Tribes

As I have said, tribes are not simply these permanent identities into which we are born. There are also little tribes that we all belong to, the tribes that we choose as ways to signal our identity to ourselves and others. Many of these tribes manifest the all-consuming alignment of partisan identification as well. Our partisan tribe likely aligns with where we shop, what we buy, and what entertainment we choose.

Of course, everyone knows that Republicans watch Fox and Democrats watch MSNBC. The split is far wider and deeper than that. Republicans are more likely to get their coffee from Dunkin', while Democrats go to Starbucks; more Republicans drive a pickup with a US nameplate, while more Democrats drive a Prius or a Subaru; Republicans shop for groceries at Walmart, while Democrats go to Trader Joe's; Republicans follow NASCAR, Democrats follow the NBA, Republicans eat lunch at Chick-fil-A or Cracker Barrel, and Democrats eat at Chipotle.[32] In contemporary American society, partisanship is signaled with just about every choice we make and in every dimension of our daily lives.

Again, my claim is that our nation's ongoing tribal alignment is not really about partisanship. Partisanship functions more as a marker; it signals to ourselves and others how we view changes in our society over the last fifty to seventy years. These changes are not only political or economic but are also, and perhaps primarily, cultural. The split is thus just as likely to be reflected in these little tribes. Cracker Barrel is full of décor and signage that reflect days gone by, and the menu is not that different from what was offered in the 1960s. Chick-fil-A is closed on Sundays, the way most businesses were a generation ago. Ford pickups harken back to an era when the vast majority of the cars on the road were made in the United States. Country music continues to feature more white performers than any other form of popular music, just as it always has. "America runs on Dunkin'" reflects a time when coffee was just coffee, without any French or Italian modifiers. That tag line, too, subtly distinguishes Dunkin' customers from the latte-drinking Starbucks folks who don't get their hands dirty at work. On the other hand, if your commercials show mixed-race or gay or lesbian couples walking or riding bikes in nature or sitting down for dinner in an urban setting, the brand connection to the Democratic tribe is stronger than it is to the other half. Creating and nurturing a tribal identity is a well-established advertising objective and can serve as a quite successful business model.

Of course, some brands seek to transcend any partisan alignment and appeal to both sides. In the current climate, though, that approach has its own difficulties. Sports fans are often wildly united in their support for their team, and sports radio will scrupulously strive to avoid politics. Still, tribalism reemerged with a vengeance when former San Francisco quarterback Colin Kaepernick decided to kneel during the national anthem and when, to protest police violence in Kenosha, Wisconsin, the Milwaukee Bucks boycotted a 2020 NBA playoff game. Similarly, even though Americans unite to celebrate words like "freedom" and "democracy," they do not necessarily mean the same things or think of them in the same way. Republicans are more likely to applaud religious freedom and the Second Amendment, while Democrats are more likely to mention political equality and the right to protest.[33]

It is certainly true that none of these alignments is complete. There are always minorities, holdovers, and outliers—people who don't fit the mold or who don't know or care that there is a mold. Some atheists voted for Trump; some evangelicals voted for Biden. So, too, with choices about coffee, computers, bands, fast food, and everything else. (Driving on the Ohio turnpike last summer, I saw a Subaru with a gun rights sticker prominently displayed.) Yet the more these tribes line up, and the more one's friends and neighbors line up with them, the harder it is for anyone to be the exception: the stronger the current, the more mental energy it takes to paddle against it, and the easier it is to simply float along. To note one striking example, research by Jacob Brown shows that as a neighborhood becomes more Democratic or Republican, even longer-term neighborhood residents are more likely to change their registration to the dominant party.[34] In contemporary America, the partisan tribes of Republicans and Democrats have become the only tribes; any other tribe, big or little, either falls in line or falls into irrelevance. As a result, the current is very strong indeed.

Trump: Tribal Politics

One more point here. To be sure, this tribal alignment of American society has been going on for decades, and its current condition long predates Donald Trump's arrival on the political scene. It is just as true, however, that he has been astute at recognizing this condition and exploiting it. In his 2016 campaign, with the slogan "Make America Great Again," he explicitly referred to "the late '40s and '50s" as a time that he seeks to return to. This was a time when, he said, "we were not pushed around, we were respected by everybody, we had just won a war, we were pretty much doing what we had to do."[35] In other words, greatness refers to our society before so much changed; America was great when the economy was rolling along and when the culture affirmed Christian values and beliefs, whites dominated the cultural, political, and economic realms, gender roles were set and binary, and the traditional family was the cultural lodestone. In the words of *New York Times* columnist Ross Douthat, the slogan conveys the desire to "protect a once-dominant majority, to restore its privileges and reverse its sense of cultural decline."[36]

Trump did not merely harness the energy of those who reject the changes in American society. Ever since he took the escalator in Trump Tower to announce his candidacy, he has poured gasoline on the long-smoldering fire of nostalgia and resentment. The evidence is legion, but consider one especially dangerous way station on the road from tribalism to violence: the dehumanization of one's opponents. Trump created playground nicknames for anyone who stood in his way. He repeatedly referred to people at the Mexican border as "animals" and "an infestation," to the media as "crazed," "corrupt," and "bad people," to those Republicans who opposed him as "human scum," and to Democrats as "savages." Relentlessly, chronically, Trump's words and behavior foster tribalism and its resultant animosity. His advent into national politics has accelerated and exacerbated the danger tribalism represents to our democracy.[37]

Aligned Tribes Are Especially Vicious

I have already said that this kind of tribal alignment is constitutive of civil wars, so it's clear enough that I think it's a bad thing. But why? What exactly happens when a person's many tribes are no longer cross-cutting but align into one, when one identity overwhelms and subsumes every other? Again, inclinations become vices when they overwhelm our sense of who we want to be, and our tribal instinct becomes vicious when favoritism toward *us* bleeds into animus toward *them*. If this is true, then we should see something similar when tribes align. We would expect to see the same kind of favoritism become an untoward desire for *us* to win and *them* to lose; in-group bias; schadenfreude; dehumanization toward *them*; and a move toward enmity and ultimately violence. In fact, that is exactly what we see. In every case, partisan tribal alignment is more likely to produce the vicious effects of tribalism than just strong partisanship alone.

Lilliana Mason's research shows that while a strong partisan is biased and angry, "when partisan and ideological identities move into alignment, that alignment is capable of motivating even more bias, activism, and anger."[38] Even those individuals whose policy preferences were strongly held and who conformed, without exception, to one party or the other were not as intense in their emotional investment as were those partisans whose identities were aligned.

Aligned tribes are also separate tribes. As each tribe reinforces an overriding sense of *us*, it also leads to less interaction with *them*. Aligned partisans are even less likely to have friends or even contact with the other side. Their family and friends are likely of the same tribe, consume the same media, and frequent the same places. As a result, alignment leads to more extreme positions and a more unshakeable commitment to them—and to increased ignorance, distrust, and negative stereotyping about the other side. Both Democrats and Republicans know that they see the world differently, that they like different things and go to different places. But this sense extends beyond culture to a basic understanding of what it means to be an American. Both sides increasingly believe that the other party cannot be trusted, that their very goals undermine the well-being of the nation. Ultimately, as I have noted, this separation leads increasingly to enmity and even an openness to violence.

All the vicious effects associated with tribalism become stronger the more one identifies with the tribe. When all of one's tribes coalesce into a single identity, however, the effect is even more powerful. When one's tribes are in alignment—when one's race, religion, and ideology all conform to and buttress one's partisan identity, when one's family and friends share that same identity, when the places you shop, the products you buy, and the entertainment you choose all reinforce one fundamental sense of identity and of belonging—then tribalism becomes even more powerful and the effects even more vicious.

The Democratic Vice

When our society lines up in two tribes, conflict becomes less measured and less rational. We view our opponents with animosity and disdain, seeing them as less human than we are. Our sense of common identity and purpose, our sense that we are all Americans, evaporates in the all-consuming heat of *us* and *them*. *They* are no longer merely my opponents but, ever more frequently, my enemies. The relevance of the issue at hand, let alone the best interest of the nation, diminishes and even disappears; the only calculus is *us* winning and *them* losing. When our tribes align into two mega-tribes, we lose the ability to constrain our conflict. When that happens, the opposing failures of democracy—tyranny and civil war—both emerge as more genuine threats.

3

TRIBALISM AND MADISON'S PRECAUTIONS

Man's capacity for justice makes democracy possible; man's capacity for injustice makes democracy necessary.
—REINHOLD NIEBUHR

Tribalism is acute right now in American society. It is impossible to hide from that fact. Yet the idea that tribalism is a distinctive problem for democracies goes back at least to the very beginnings of American political thought and practice. The Founders were well schooled in the history of republics, both ancient and (for them) contemporary. They saw that history as a series of experiments in how to organize a society politically—and believed that those experiments demonstrated that democracy was precarious at best. At worst, it was ephemeral.

In a free (that is, democratic) society, the tribal instinct that is endemic to human nature grows and multiplies. As it does, conflict and animosity grow as well. Unchecked, this conflict frequently festers until society ultimately dissolves. Even the most ardent advocates for democracy therefore viewed the lessons of history with trepidation. John Adams was one of those advocates, but his comment is not unusual: "Democracy never lasts long. It soon wastes, exhausts and murders itself. There was never a democracy that did not commit suicide."[1] The question before the Founders in Philadelphia was whether it was possible to develop political mechanisms and institutions that were both sustainable and democratic.

Montesquieu and the Small Republic

Writing in the early eighteenth century, Montesquieu was one of those who took up this question, and for that very reason, he was one of the most important resources for the Founders. His discussion of the need to separate the executive, judicial, and legislative functions, and to create mechanisms whereby each could check the power of the other, was fundamental to the Constitutional solution. But Montesquieu also worried about why so many democratic republics had failed and wondered whether there was any way to avoid that fate. Looking as well to the lessons of history, he came to one relevant conclusion: large republics don't work. He wrote, "It is natural for a republic to have only a small territory; otherwise it cannot long subsist."[2] It is not easy to sustain a democratic republic, Montesquieu argued, but if you are to have a fighting chance at success, that republic must be small.

Evoking the ancient examples of Athens, Sparta, and Carthage, Montesquieu argued that a small republic was better able to sustain itself. Small republics were more homogeneous in terms of ethnicity, language, and occupation (that is, more people were involved in farming or fishing or mining, say). Such commonalities helped republics build and sustain a sense of common identity and purpose. A small area and population, along with a strict regimen of education for all, held out the best hope for a free and sustainable republic.[3]

The new US Constitution sought to create a nation that was both large and democratic. That is one reason why many Americans, called the Anti-Federalists, were against ratification. The Anti-Federalists were a motley group, unified by their opposition to the Constitution and little else. But it is fair to say that many believed that Montesquieu was right, that a large republic would endanger the liberty so dearly won in the Revolution. The best hope for American democracy was outlined in the Articles of Confederation: a union of nearly autonomous states and little to no central power. Of course, the Anti-Federalists acknowledged that many (most) of the American states were much bigger than Athens or Carthage. For this reason, direct democracy of the kind they had in ancient Greece was not feasible; the Anti-Federalists therefore accepted the necessity of a representative assembly. They believed that as long as the terms were short, the government would remain responsive. Besides, even the largest states were still more cohesive and manifested greater commonality than a government for the entire nation ever could.[4] Anyone who supported the ratification of the new Constitution therefore had to take up Montesquieu's argument.

Publius and the Large Republic

The Federalist Papers were a collection of eighty-five essays written by Alexander Hamilton, James Madison, and (minimally) John Jay under the pseudonym "Publius." It is widely regarded as the single most important representation of American political thought. Publius (in all three of his visages) was, like the other Founders, very aware of the legacy of failure associated with democracies. Echoing Adams, Publius (Madison) acknowledges in Federalist 10 that "democracies have ever been spectacles of turbulence and contention; have ever been found incompatible with personal security or the rights of property; and have in general been as short in their lives as they have been violent in their deaths."[5] Both Publius and Montesquieu wanted to figure out how to create the conditions under which a republic would be sustainable, but Publius rejected the idea that this problem could only be solved with a small republic.

In fact, Publius argued that Montesquieu's answer was exactly wrong. Not only was a small size not essential for maintaining a republic, but a large nation actually offered the better prospect to that end. In Federalist 9, Publius (Hamilton) disputes the idea that smaller is better. Publius says, "It is impossible to read the history of the petty republics of Greece and Italy without feeling sensations of horror and disgust at the distractions with which they were continually agitated, and at the rapid succession of revolutions by which they were kept in a state of perpetual vibration between the extremes of tyranny and anarchy."[6] If the city-state is the best solution we have, Publius says, we might as well give up. Second, most of the states under the confederation (Publius mentions Virginia, Massachusetts, Pennsylvania, New York, North Carolina, and Georgia) are not even close to the size of the ancient city-states. So if you, resident of New York, really believe that Montesquieu is right, then you should be advocating the splitting up of your state into little city-states. (This suggestion, Publius knew, would go nowhere.) Finally, Publius says that Montesquieu is really on his side. The philosopher proposed a confederation of republics as the best combination of nation and democracy: it can defend itself against enemies foreign and domestic. Anti-Federalists responded that there was more nation and less confederation in the new Constitution, and they argued that the old confederation worked fine in this regard. (They were correct to claim, after all, that it was a confederation that won the war.) Yet it is also true that Montesquieu himself admitted the inherent vulnerability of the city-state.

In Federalist 10, Madison continues Publius's argument in his own terms, and it is here that we get the distinctively American analysis of, and solution to, the problem of tribalism. Publius refers to factions rather than tribes, but his definition makes clear that he is talking about precisely the same thing: "By a faction, I understand a number of citizens, whether amounting to a majority or a minority of the whole, who are united and actuated by some common impulse of passion, or of interest, adversed to the rights of other citizens, or to the permanent and aggregate interests of the community."[7] "Some common impulse or passion" covers a lot of ground. Some of those passions will be deep and abiding, like one's livelihood. In his classic work *The Process of Government*, Arthur Bentley makes the very same connection. "Factions," he says, "are visible in group attachments of all kinds--kinship, ethnic, racial, religious, occupational, and national, and they are powerful in political life."[8] But Madison's use of the word "impulse" implies that factions can also be short-lived. The combined power of Beyoncé fans or collectors of Hummel figurines will not rend the republic, but whenever citizens join together in pursuit of a common impulse or passion, they become united into an *us* and become less interested in the interests of others, or the nation as a whole.

For Publius, too, the impulse to unite into factions/tribes is an indelible part of human nature: "The latent causes of faction are thus sown in the nature of man." But it is especially a problem for democracies. It is why democracies so often fail. These words begin Federalist 10: "Among the numerous advantages promised by a well constructed Union, none deserves to be more accurately developed than its tendency to break and control the violence of faction. The friend of popular governments never finds himself so much alarmed for their character and fate, as when he contemplates their propensity to this dangerous vice." In democracies, people are free, and therefore factions will grow like weeds: "Liberty is to factions as air is to fire." Free people will inevitably form and express different opinions, recognize and advocate for different objectives, and will inevitably come to coalesce with others who think the same.

Madison also knew, as we have seen, that these factions—these tribes—lead inevitability to conflict. Factions have "divided mankind into parties, inflamed them with mutual animosity, and rendered them much more disposed to vex and oppress each other than to co-operate for their common good. So strong is this propensity of mankind to fall into mutual animosities, that where no substantial occasion presents itself, the most frivolous and fanciful distinctions have been sufficient to kindle their unfriendly passions and excite their most violent conflicts." Publius is very clear. Factions/tribes are an inescapable feature of human nature and thus human society. Unchecked, they make democracy almost impossible to sustain. The citizens of this new democratic nation were right to be worried. Yet, Publius insists, the new Constitution has sufficiently addressed this problem, and that is one outstanding reason why the nation should approve it.

The Science of Politics

Control of factionalism comes structurally. It is a product of what Publius in Federalist 9 calls the "science of politics"—namely, the clear-headed assessment of history and human experience. And this assessment, this science, causes Publius to argue that Montesquieu has got it exactly wrong. A small republic does not help constrain the problems of faction. In fact, it makes them worse.

In the first place, moving from a direct democracy to a representative republic improves the prospect that you will secure better, more educated leaders who are less likely to lose sight of the nation's best interest. More importantly, Publius says, if you want to overcome the effect of tribalism, you should make more tribes. By expanding the republic, you create the conditions for more factions to emerge. It becomes less possible for one majority to emerge, let alone dominate. Just as most people have lots of tribal memberships that push and pull them in different ways, a large republic has more (and more diverse) interests and perspectives, lessening the likelihood that any one unifying principle or interest or industry will emerge. What's more, even if such an occasion for tribal unification were to present itself, greater geographical distance would make it harder (in the eighteenth century, anyway) for a majority to organize. Thus, not only do the factions check and balance each other, but alignment becomes both less possible and less actionable. What Montesquieu saw as a handicap, and even a deal breaker, Madison saw as the best possible foundation for democracy.

For what it's worth, there is evidence to support Madison's argument. Researchers Sonia Roccas and Marilynn Brewer used survey data from the United States and Israel to examine how individuals negotiate the various groups they belong to, seeking to understand how that diversity impacts their sense of identity as well as their relationships with others. They conclude that "individuals who live in a multicultural society . . . are likely to have more complex representations of their multiple identities than individuals who live in a monocultural or a stratified society."[9] In other words, Roccas and Brewer's research lends support to the idea that tribal alignment is more difficult if people belong to many tribes and easier if the society is united around one prevailing identity.

One should not overstate Publius's claim here, however. Expanding the number of tribes makes it less likely that tribes will align or that one tribe will dominate, but it does not make those scenarios impossible. And Publius knows that. An expanded republic was just one example of what he calls in Federalist 51 an "auxiliary precaution" against one dominating faction. There are other such precautions, of course. Most relevant was the idea of creating checks and balances within the government, an idea that the Framers took from Montesquieu. This innovation, as well, was grounded on a more realistic notion of human nature, especially the nature of those who would like to lead. Politicians are naturally ambitious. By embracing that reality instead of denying it, the Constitution used it to control government and keep the nation free. As Publius says, "Ambition must be made to counteract ambition."[10] Still, all these innovations were prudent but not foolproof. They were actually not even sufficient. These republican solutions to a republican problem were, in Madison's own words, "auxiliary." The only way to truly preserve a free society was to sustain a culture of individuals who could live up to it. That required virtue.

Montesquieu led the way here as well. Seeking to learn from history how republics prosper and die, Montesquieu considered the most important example of both in his *Considerations on the Causes of the Greatness of the Romans and Their Decline*. He argues that because sovereign power in a democracy rests with the people, the people must maintain an ardent sense of patriotism and a shared commitment to the public good. That commitment means that all citizens need to be willing to engage in public affairs, including government and defense. What is more, popular rule requires that all citizens be more concerned with the public good than they are with their own. Montesquieu concludes that the fall of the Roman Republic was ultimately a moral failure: the rise of wealth and inequality led to the decline of any sufficient public commitment. He writes, "The grandeur of the state, in general, constituted the greatness of its particular members; but as affluence consists in conduct, and not in riches; that wealth of the Romans, which had certain limitations, introduced a luxury and profusion which had no bounds."[11]

Montesquieu argues that democratic government places very serious burdens on each and every citizen. He believed that each individual needed to place her concern for the republic above her concern for herself and her family, and that included spurning any inordinate accumulation of wealth. "Self-renunciation," he calls it.[12] He even compares the commitment of a democratic citizen to the commitment a religious monk has for his order. But this commitment was necessary if the republic were to maintain itself: "Everything therefore depends on establishing this love in a republic."[13] Developing this kind of commitment demanded a rigorous system of civic education, but it also required that people knew each other and shared the same sense of place and identity. In Montesquieu's thought, virtue and smallness were inseparable aspects of a sustainable democracy. Faction could only be constrained, and civic virtue could only be achieved, in a small republic. The Founders were aware of this argument too. They too, Federalists and Anti-Federalists alike, looked to the Roman Republic for their moral exemplars, and they knew all about its ultimate fall into tyranny. As Publius, Madison was therefore obliged to address both positions.

The American Conception of Civic Virtue

Without exception, all the Founders wanted a free and democratic society. They believed that they had a unique opportunity to achieve it in this new nation. But they were, again without exception, fearful of democracy. They were fearful that giving people freedom gave them the opportunity to misuse it—to act rashly or unjustly and to be taken in by a demagogue. Again, the Constitution was designed to slow the process down and encourage more thoughtful, dispassionate reflection. With each innovation, the Founders sought to constrain the people's inclination to push too far, too fast, and to let fear and anger overwhelm their sense of reason and judgment. But for all this, they knew that these structural constraints were not enough. A democratic republic still had to depend on the citizens' inherent sense of fairness and judgment.

The Federalist writers flatly rejected Montesquieu's idea of just what level of commitment the nation could demand. Just as they presented a realistic notion of what motivates a politician, they had an equally realistic idea of how much devotion one could expect from regular citizens. They therefore argued against the ideal of classic virtue as Montesquieu and some of the Anti-Federalists defined it. The science of politics made it abundantly clear that human beings are not angels; we are selfish and ambitious. If democracy required the impossible, namely, a love of country that overrode one's love of self and family, then democracy itself was impossible.

But for Publius, the idea that culture could sustain a democracy while being indifferent to virtue was equally unrealistic. Montesquieu's demand for civic virtue was modified: attenuated, to be sure, but not abandoned. It could not be. If citizens are constrained to always make the right, decent, or democratic choice—if they do not have the capacity to, in effect, misuse their freedom—then they are not really free at all. Thus, freedom puts itself at risk. The Founders ultimately had to trust that the people were capable of governing themselves. Here, again without exception, the Founders believed that some amount of civic virtue was necessary, even preconditional, to sustaining a democratic society. In the realistic anthropology that grounded Publius and the Founders, self-interest was simply part of the human condition. While it could be put aside during a crisis (as in the Revolutionary War), it could not be excised. This self-interest *could* be guided and even exploited to achieve virtuous ends. It was not inevitably and completely antithetical to virtue. Self-interest was not enough, though. In Federalist 55, Publius (Madison) concludes with this summation of human nature: "As there is a degree of depravity in mankind which requires a certain degree of circumspection and distrust, so there are other qualities in human nature which justify a certain portion of esteem and confidence. Republican government presupposes the existence of these qualities in a higher degree than any other form."[14] Madison understood that human beings are complicated. They are self-interested and ambitious, but they are also virtuous and patriotic. That understanding reflected the influence of his teacher John Witherspoon, a Presbyterian minister who became president of Princeton University. In Calvinist theology, human beings are both chained to sin and reflect the divine.[15] For a democracy to be both genuine and sustainable, it had to accommodate both sides of this reality.

Speaking as himself in the ratifying convention for that same Constitution in his home state of Virginia, Madison makes the point directly: "Is there no virtue among us? If there be not, we are in a wretched situation. No theoretical checks—no forms of government can render us secure. To suppose that any form of government will secure liberty or happiness without any virtue in the people, is a chimerical idea."[16] Madison was the one who spoke directly about the selfishness at the core of human nature. He was most concerned about tribalism. He recognized the distinctive danger it represented to democracy, and he outlined the structural mechanisms whereby factions could best be kept from aligning into two oppositional mega-tribes. This very same Madison argued explicitly that neither those mechanisms outlined in the Constitution nor, for that matter, any other conceivable mechanisms would be sufficient. Virtue, not just in those politicians selected to lead but in the people themselves, was indispensable.

Madison's influence on the new nation was vast, but he was not the only one who thought this way. In fact, almost without exception, all the Founders believed that virtue was necessary to sustaining a democratic society. It is worth highlighting how universal this belief was.

- George Mason: "No free government, or the blessings of liberty, can be preserved to any people, but by a firm adherence to justice, moderation, temperance, frugality and virtue, and by frequent recurrence to fundamental principles."[17]
- Benjamin Franklin: "Only a virtuous people are capable of freedom. As nations become corrupt and vicious, they have more need of masters."[18]
- Patrick Henry: "Virtue, morality, and religion. This is the armor, my friend, and this alone that renders us invincible. These are the tactics we should study. If we lose these, we are conquered, fallen indeed."[19]
- Thomas Paine: "The sovereignty in a republic [that is, the people] is exercised to keep right and wrong in their proper and distinct places, and never suffer the one to usurp the place of the other."[20]
- Gouverneur Morris: "I believe that Religion is the only solid Base of Morals and that Morals are the only possible Support of free governments."[21]
- Benjamin Rush: "Without [education grounded in religion], there can be no virtue, and without virtue there can be no liberty."[22]
- Thomas Jefferson: "It is the manners and spirit of a people which preserve a republic in vigour. A degeneracy in these is a canker which soon eats to the heart of its laws and constitution."[23]
- John Adams: "Liberty can no more exist without virtue and independence than the body can live and move without a soul."[24]
- Adams again: "We have no government armed with power capable of contending with human passions unbridled by morality and religion. Avarice, ambition, revenge, or gallantry, would break the strongest cords of our constitution as a whale goes through a net. Our Constitution was made only for a moral and religious people."[25]
- George Washington: "It is substantially true that virtue or morality is a main and necessary spring of popular or republican governments."[26]

These Founders disagreed about a great deal, both during the ratification of the Constitution and thereafter, but all of them believed that without some common agreement about standards of personal behavior, democracy cannot last. All of them believed that only a virtuous people can remain free.

Among the Founders, Alexander Hamilton had perhaps the least confidence in popular opinion. Whatever he thought of their virtue, he was convinced that "the people" were not smart enough to recognize when they were being deceived. In the very first Federalist Paper, Hamilton noted that they can be readily misled into giving away their freedom: "Those men who have overturned the liberties of republics, the greatest number have begun their career by paying an obsequious court to the people; commencing demagogues, and ending tyrants."[27] In a letter to Rufus King, Hamilton expressed this same low opinion: "But I as yet discover no satisfactory symptoms of a revolution of opinion in the *mass* 'informe in gens cui lumen ademptum.'" Hamilton is quoting from Vergil's *Aeneid*, where Polyphemus, the Cyclops blinded by Ulysses, is described as "'monstrum horrendum informe ingens cui lumen ademptum'" ("'a dreadful monster, shapeless, huge, blind'").[28]

Even leaving out the part about the dreadful monster, that is, to be sure, not a flattering description of the American citizenry. In Hamilton's description, "the people" is both powerful and blind, capable of wreaking havoc without truly understanding that it is even doing so. With this quotation Hamilton demonstrated both the depth of his own learning and his estimate of the wisdom of those who did not possess it. He does not see any evidence, either, that this problem is going away.

Yet for all that, Hamilton, too, thought that citizens had, and had to have, sufficient virtue to choose the most able representatives. In Federalist 84 (the penultimate letter), arguing against the need for a Bill of Rights, Hamilton acknowledges that the preservation of civil rights in a free society will "altogether depend on public opinion, and on the general spirit of the people and of the government." For all his attention to structural measures, Publius had to ultimately trust that the people—or better, enough of the people, enough of the time—would use their freedom wisely. That meant that for Hamilton, as well, free people had to develop and maintain some level of virtue. It would be significantly diminished from what Montesquieu demanded, but it would nevertheless be genuine, and even substantial.

In sum, these same men who fought to create a new nation, who drafted the features of the new democratic government, and who sought to direct and constrain popular rule, faction, ambition, and self-interest also thought that virtue was indispensable.

Their Virtue and Ours

I am arguing that a recommitment to a set of democratic virtues is one essential way to address the problem of raging tribalism. It is certainly relevant therefore to show that the people who founded this nation insisted on the very same thing. But even if one grants that the Founders understood virtue to be a necessary condition for sustaining a well-ordered democracy, it is not clear what exactly they meant by virtue, what specific virtues they saw as most important, and how answers to those questions might inform our own efforts. There, I confess, the example of the Founders becomes decidedly less helpful.

In terms that confirm Publius's point about diversity of interests within the new nation, the ideas about virtue that emerged out of Puritan New England, for example, were not the same as those of the slaveholding aristocrats in the South. Beyond this obvious point, the Founders did not mean the same thing because there were competing conceptions of where virtue comes from, what it entails, and how that conception related to the new nation.

A majority of the Founders understood virtue to be virtually synonymous with Christian faith, as shown above in the quotations from Benjamin Rush and Gouverneur Morris. John Jay, the other member of Publius and first chief justice of the United States, was likewise an ardent Christian and, late in life, served as president of the American Bible Society. John Adams, too, frequently spoke of religion and virtue simultaneously, following long roots in the Congregationalist and ultimately Puritan tradition. Yet others looked not to revealed religion but to the innate sense of sympathy we all have for our fellow human beings. James Wilson, for example, who was born in Scotland and followed the thinking of David Hume, Francis Hutcheson, and Adam Smith, believed that natural law was accessible to every human, placed there by the Creator. For Wilson, the fact that we all feel the stirrings of conscience proves this to be true. Jefferson, for his part, was also sympathetic to the Scots but was most enamored of the Greeks. In fact, he called himself an Epicurean. He saw happiness as the end of human life and virtue as the only way to achieve it. Still others (again especially the Anti-Federalists) looked to classical republicanism as articulated by Montesquieu and exemplified in the heroes of the Roman Republic. Historian James

Kloppenberg acknowledges that three competing and complementary conceptions of virtue were operative at the time of the founding: those based in Christianity, in classic (Roman) republicanism, and in the Scottish Enlightenment. He concludes that "these different intellectual and cultural patterns tended to rearrange themselves, or even to merge, rather than remaining altogether separate."[29]

The prospect of unmerging these intellectual patterns is not one I want to pursue. Nor do I think it germane. I have tried to show that the Founders were very worried about their new democracy and saw virtue as an essential means for maintaining it. It is prudent for us to take their worries and their charge seriously. That said, the Founders' understandings of virtue were complicated and not always in complete accord.

More to the point, they and their conceptions of virtue operated in a much different world. Again, virtues are social agreements that reflect not just the indelible features of human nature but also the specific conditions of any society at any point in time. We are Americans (not to mention human beings), no less than they were. Just like them, we too are worried about the effect of tribalism on democratic society. Yet the world of 1787 is not ours. Our conception of virtue cannot be exactly the same, either. Like the Founders, we have to affirm and agree to some conception of virtue that can help us sustain our democracy, but we must find out for ourselves what that means. In what follows, I try to lay out the virtues that I think are most useful right now—virtues that are both ancient and, in many cases, informed by science. These virtues can help all of us step back from the breach of tribal conflict and reestablish a common commitment to our democracy.

PART 2
Democratic Thinking

Democracy, of course, means that sovereignty lies in the hands of the people. We choose our own leaders. Democracy therefore assumes that virtually everybody has access to common sense and that this access is sufficient foundation on which to affirm that right to rule. (If that assumption is wrong, then democracy is not only illegitimate but doesn't make any sense.) Therefore, just as democracy places power in our hands, it presumes that all of us, or at least the vast majority of us, have the capacity to use it. But sovereignty doesn't just mean that we *have* the capacity; it means that we are willing to employ that capacity carefully and thoughtfully. It is true that we all sometimes (or often) fail to live up to this demand. Our decisions do not always manifest thoughtful consideration, the weighing of different candidates and their positions, and their likely impact on the well-being of the voter, her family, and the general commonweal. There is no law that says we have to do that. We are free to choose not to vote, not to participate. However, when we fail to live up to our role as sovereigns, though, we endanger our democracy, and the more of us so fail, the more endangered it becomes.

The democratic thinking virtues of humility, honesty, and consistency help us live up to our responsibilities. Most important, they help us identify tribalism's threats to our democracy and offer ways to help us overcome, or at least mitigate, those threats.

4
HUMILITY

The spirit of liberty is the spirit which
is not too sure that it is right.
—LEARNED HAND

Humility is certainly not an obvious place to begin.[1] It might well be the most unpolitical virtue there is. Of all the people in some district—city, state, whatever—the candidate decides that she is the one person who should occupy some office. Obviously, she believes that voters should choose her over her opponent. What is more, she believes that people should gladly give her money and devote their free time to listening to her talk and helping her win. In his 2016 convention speech, Donald Trump famously said, "I alone can fix it."[2] Many people quite reasonably heard that as evidence of raging narcissism. Yet the difference may simply be that Trump was willing to articulate the thought. Most office seekers see themselves as uniquely qualified for a role; otherwise, they probably would not run in the first place.

So it isn't just that humility doesn't fit with democratic politics; it appears to be antithetical to the entire enterprise. There is no getting around this. But if we are to move beyond the tribalization of American life, we must recognize and seek to mitigate the in-group bias that inevitably accompanies it. Humility is one essential virtue that enables us to do so.

Hume: Humility Is a Monkish Virtue

When people think of humility, they most often think of religious faith. This is not surprising. Painting with a broad brush, just about all religions profess that human beings should recognize their profound smallness, as well as their individual failures and weaknesses, before the Almighty. And with this recognition comes submission to God's will (the very word *islam* means "submission") and the concomitant diminishment of the individual ego.[3] At its most extreme, this diminishment (to the outsider, anyway) can look like self-denial and even self-abnegation. Whether that view is accurate or not—sometimes it is, and sometimes it isn't—this is precisely how Enlightenment philosopher David Hume understood the term. And that is precisely why he did not like it.

Hume's moral philosophy, while deeply influential, was also idiosyncratic and iconoclastic. It does not fit neatly into any taxonomy. For my purposes, it is enough to say that like the Utilitarians who were his contemporaries, Hume judges the moral worth of an act based on whether it serves society. And given this standard, humility fails. In his *Enquiry Concerning the Principles of Morals*, Hume wrote: "Where men judge of things by their natural, unprejudiced reason, without the delusive glosses of superstition and false religion," they "reject" humility, as one of a "whole train of monkish virtues."[4] That "train" includes not just humility but also celibacy, fasting, penance, mortification, self-denial, silence, and solitude. All these behaviors are *de facto* the manifestation of false religion. To call them "monkish virtues" makes it clear that Hume has a particular model of Christianity in mind. But the point is that for Hume, the religious value of humility, and for that matter every other car in this train, is irrelevant. The question is whether it has any discernible value in the world, in human society, and Hume is confident that it does not—neither to the practitioner nor or to anyone else. These "monkish virtues . . . neither advance a man's fortune in the world, nor render him a more valuable member of society; neither qualify him for the entertainment of company, nor increase his power of self-enjoyment." In sum, humility doesn't increase your happiness or anybody else's, doesn't help anybody, and doesn't improve anything.

Yet it's not enough to say that these alleged virtues don't make human society better. Hume says that they make the individual worse.

Humility and all these other virtues "stupify the understanding and harden the heart, obscure the fancy and sour the temper." Hume therefore concludes that we can "justly . . . transfer them to the opposite column, and place them in the catalogue of vices." In short, these alleged virtues don't make us virtuous at all. They only make us stupid and a drag to be around. The sooner human society relegates humility (and for that matter the false religion that lauds it) to the scrap heap, the better.

As you no doubt expect, I am going to argue against this point of view. I am going to show that humility is not a vice; it is rather a necessary means for countervailing the tribalism that is particularly destructive to democratic society. But the kicker is that I am going to make that argument by appealing to a monk.

St. Bernard: Humility Comes from Knowing the Truth

St. Bernard of Clairvaux lived in France in the twelfth century. He was the founder of the Cistercian monastic order. Bernard was not only a saint but a doctor of the church, which means he is regarded as having made important contributions to Catholic theology. Bernard's most famous work is *The Twelve Steps of Humility*. The twelve steps go in either direction: down toward sinful pride, or up toward God and deeper humility. (Incidentally, Bill Wilson took this work as a template for the twelve steps of Alcoholics Anonymous. Even more incidentally, St. Bernard of Clairvaux is not the namesake of the dog breed; that St. Bernard ran a hostel in the Alps.) All those monkish virtues that Hume decried—silence, chastity, self-abnegation, and so forth—Bernard defends with rigor. He sees them as essential means for developing a deeper relationship with God. Moreover, the Cistercian monks were known for following the rules more stringently than other orders. In short, Bernard's understanding of virtue and the kind of faith he practices are precisely what Hume abhors.

I have no interest in describing, let alone defending, everything that Bernard wants the humble monk to be doing. (For one thing, Bernard was also a big fan of the Crusades.) Frankly, if push were to come to shove, I would line up with Hume. But in one fundamental respect, I think Bernard is absolutely right. For at the core of Bernard's theology is the idea that humility grows naturally from knowing the truth about ourselves.

For Bernard, pride is the product of false belief: "When pride fills your mind, you can no longer see yourself, you can no longer feel yourself such as you are actually or potentially."[5] This is why pride is at the root of our sinfulness and our estrangement from God. Bernard defines humility, on the other hand, as "that thorough self-examination which makes a man contemptible in his own sight."[6] Pride is simply unjustified; it rests on a misapprehension of who we are. Self-examination causes us to realize that we are enslaved to sin and damnable in the face of God's righteousness. And it is on that foundation, that truth, that humility can and must be developed.

"Contemptible." "Damnable." Well, Bernard isn't sugarcoating it, is he? To be clear, I am not suggesting that we all follow Bernard's example; I do not think that it improves our democracy for us all to see ourselves this way. But Bernard is right to say that humility begins with knowledge—in particular, self-knowledge. If we start with Bernard's understanding of that truth, a truth he would call Christian and Hume would call false religion, humility leads to a recognition of our worthlessness. When that accurate understanding of ourselves is grounded not in Christian theology but in scientific evidence, the extremely negative self-assessment recedes into the distance but still leaves us with a diminished sense of ourselves. We still come to understand that we have less reason to be prideful about who we are and what we think, and humility again emerges as a more appropriate, more informed, more realistic response to that understanding. For us as well as Bernard, humility remains an appropriate response to greater self-awareness.

For democrats, that self-awareness begins with our recognition that we are all tribal and therefore biased. All of us are disposed to see the world as we want it to be rather than how it really is. Again, our attachment to our tribe causes us to want our tribe to win; beneath our conscious awareness, we give more weight to information that supports our side. We find reasons to discount information that supports the other side and to discredit those who present it. The more attached we are to our tribe—and the more our tribes are in alignment—the more powerful this effect can be. As I have shown, that accounts for the present condition of our society and our politics.

Hume says that humility is vicious because it undermines our ability to "judge of things by their natural, unprejudiced reason." But once we recognize that we are all tribal and that tribalism leads inevitably and inescapably to in-group bias, then we must acknowledge that "natural, unprejudiced reason" is, strictly speaking, impossible. Our ability to judge is compromised by our tribalism. If that is true, then tribalism, not humility, is the vice. Indeed, humility emerges as one essential means by which we constrain its effects.

Now, in fairness to David Hume, you could argue that he knows all this, too. He just calls it something else. In his *Enquiry Concerning Human Understanding*, Hume acknowledged that "in general, there is a degree of doubt, and caution, and modesty, which, in all kinds of scrutiny and decision, ought for ever to accompany a just reasoner."[7] There is room to argue about Hume's description here: modesty, for example, often refers to a manner of dress that understates one's sexuality, or to a desire to avoid bringing attention to one's self or accomplishments. Is that the best word to describe what Hume has in mind? And how exactly are doubt, caution, and modesty different from humility? It may well be that for Hume the only difference centers on the religious connotation of the latter and the reasonableness of the former. If so, then while Hume thinks Bernard's religious humility is bad for human society, he would nevertheless agree that we can never be too sure about our reasoning or our opinions. Therefore, as far as our reasoning goes, at least, Hume might well agree that something very like humility is a good idea.

Some researchers reflect a similar distinction. They call this scientifically informed version *intellectual humility*. In what follows, you will note that most of the research I cite uses this more specific term. Since I am arguing that humility is a virtue associated with democratic *thinking*, perhaps I should too. But I don't think the distinction is as stark as Hume or others want to make it. Research on the nature and viability of this distinction is ongoing and preliminary.[8] But for now, I would argue that humility, whether intellectual or general, is built on the very foundation that Bernard identified: an honest and informed assessment of ourselves.[9] This assessment, this awareness of the truth, leads us to diminish our opinion of ourselves and what we think and to modify our behavior accordingly. It leads us to be more circumspect regarding what we believe and more open to the views of others, to the possibility that we might be wrong, and to the near certainty that we are not seeing the whole picture. For what it's worth, those who choose the more specific term recognize this same foundation. An "interdisciplinary group" of philosophers and psychologists developed this definition of intellectual humility: "*Recognizing that a particular personal belief may be fallible, accompanied by an appropriate attentiveness to limitations in the evidentiary basis of that belief and to one's own limitations in obtaining and evaluating relevant information.*"[10] The evident consistency between this definition and Bernard's strikes me as important and leads me to stick with the general term. (But if you still want to call it intellectual humility, I am not going to argue with you.)

Humility and Social Utility

Hume says that the problem with humility is that it has no social utility. It doesn't make the individual a better or more successful person and doesn't contribute anything to society. But that is exactly wrong. In fact, scientific evidence shows that humility makes you a better thinker, a better person, and a better democrat.

Hume says that humility "stupefies the understanding." But that is not true. In fact, all evidence points to the conclusion that humility makes you a better thinker. Samantha Deffler and her colleagues asked subjects to rate a series of statements (e.g., "In the face of conflicting evidence, I am open to changing my opinions.") to determine their intellectual humility.[11] Then they gave the participants three tasks. First, they read forty statements on four well-known controversial subjects: "same-sex marriage . . . use of drones, legalization of marijuana, and implementation of the common core curriculum." For each topic, ten statements were in favor and ten were against. Next, participants were asked how familiar they were with certain historical figures and events. Some of them, like the Boston Tea Party, were real, while others (like "Hamrick's rebellion") were made up. Finally, participants read another list of sixty statements. They were asked to identify which statements were on the first list and which were new, and then report their confidence in their answers.

Those participants with high humility read the statements more carefully, including those with which they disagreed. They therefore were better able to identify the statements in the second list that were new. One can conclude that an abiding sense that other opinions are worth hearing makes you better able to hear them. Relatedly, humble people were better at telling the difference between the real and bogus topics than participants who scored low, suggesting that they had a more accurate sense of both what they knew and what they didn't. Finally, awareness of their fallibility meant that humble respondents were less confident about the answers they gave that were wrong. That is, they were not only right more often than those who were not humble, but they also had a more accurate sense of when they were not right. In sum, humility is associated with more careful reading comprehension, especially of opinions that one does not agree with, and a more accurate accounting of what one does and does not know.

Tenelle Porter looked at the behavior of high school students. After a similar test to determine their baseline humility, the students who scored higher in humility were again shown to be more open to alternative opinions and to facts they didn't know. Paying more attention to those alternatives enabled them to do better in the class and end up with better grades. Porter concluded, "We found that the more intellectually humble students were more motivated to learn and more likely to use effective metacognitive strategies, like quizzing themselves to check their own understanding. They also ended the year with higher grades in math."[12] Grades aside, openness to new facts and alternative opinions and a genuine engagement in learning are likewise commonly associated with general intelligence. And here too, these desirable attributes are associated with intellectual humility.

Recall that David Hume concluded that humility is a vice; it makes you a "sour" person nobody wants to be around. Here, again, the evidence points in precisely the opposite direction. Those manifesting high humility are regarded by others as friendly and warm, show more empathy,[13] and are more respectful of all people, including those who disagree with them.[14] What's more, these humble people aren't mealymouthed or obsequious, let alone self-abnegating. On the contrary, humble people seem to profess a higher-than-average sense of physical and mental well-being.[15] They appear to be both emotionally healthier and more comfortable in their own skin.

Then there is the servant-leader model, the basic thrust of which is that leaders who share power and work to put employees in a position to succeed are better managers and achieve better outcomes.[16] A cottage industry has grown up around the application of this idea to corporations, but for my purposes, the point is that for practitioners, "humility forms the essential backbone of the servant leader."[17] Here, too, the definition of humility centers on an acknowledgment of one's limitations and the corresponding value of listening to others. As before, humble leaders are more open to hearing the opinions of others, even when those opinions differ from their own. They are also better at evaluating the arguments and evidence that they hear. This willingness to listen causes subordinates to grow and develop the skills that make them more reliable and valuable employees and more invested in the organization.[18] All this can lead to innovations that improve the company's competitiveness. Humility, in fact, distinguishes CEOs of highly successful organizations.[19]

As if all that were not enough, evidence is also strong that people who are humble tend to have better and more successful romantic relationships. Humble people can listen with respect and openness to criticisms from their partners. Studies have found that these abilities lead to more satisfaction in both partners as well as a greater likelihood of forgiveness.[20]

All these findings are relevant, of course. For that matter, I hope they are persuasive—that they make you want to develop your own humility. But again, my broader argument is that we democrats have to become better at dealing with the effects of raging tribalism. These findings demonstrate that humility is especially useful in that regard. People who practice humility are more open to the possibility that they might be wrong. People who know the truth about their own limitations are more likely to be interested in other people's perspectives and less likely to disparage or denigrate those holding different views. They are also more open to other views and treat people with those views more respectfully. Finally, those higher in humility more accurately distinguished between real and bogus topics, suggesting that they were less likely to be taken in by someone seeking to ratchet up and otherwise exploit a person's tribal identity.

However, none of this should imply that humble individuals are less likely to have political views or do not have much confidence in their opinions. A four-part research study by Tenelle Porter (again) and Karina Schumann reaffirmed the finding that "intellectual humility was consistently linked with greater respect for and openness to the opposing view."[21] But those participants were just as engaged in politics and just as committed to their position as those who were not humble: "Those higher in intellectual humility did not differ from others in the strength of their political views. . . . Despite being aware of the limits to their knowledge, those higher in intellectual humility did not have less confidence or lower self-esteem relative to less intellectually humble participants."[22] People who are humble have opinions. They are confident in them and willing to express them, but they are also able to genuinely listen to and consider the opinions of others.

In every respect, humility makes the person who has it better at managing the conflict that is endemic to democratic society. Humility understood this way does indeed render the practitioner of this virtue a more valuable member of society, and more specifically, of democratic society.

Now consider the opposite: those without humility. People who are unwilling or unable to recognize the limited and compromised condition of their knowledge are more closed-minded in their views and more likely to insist on their correctness. They show more disregard for other people and for their opinions.[23] They are more likely to overreact during conflicts and to stay resentful. If they're the ones who were in the wrong, they refuse to admit as much. Instead, they blame their victims.[24] In sum, if anyone is stupefying the understanding and souring the temper, if anyone is a drag to be around, it is the person who lacks humility, not the one who has it.

One additional point here. One manifestation of our tribal bias is that even when we all agree that some virtue or trait is desirable, we are more likely to see it manifested by our tribe members, not by those in the other tribe. We are more likely to judge those who are like us as more honest and smarter than those in the alternative group, for example. Humility (and the bias that creates the need for it) is no different. Our tribe is far better able to appreciate and listen carefully to those with whom we disagree. It is the other guys and gals who are both biased and prideful.

In fact, research does not show much, if any, correlation between what tribe you belong to and how much humility you manifest. In other words, while all of us belong to tribes that lead us to expect that those in our tribe are the humble ones, the fact is that humility appears to show up in every tribe you can name. That means that despite what tribe members might believe, there are, for example, prideful Christians and humble atheists. (Indeed, there is no apparent correlation between humility and religiosity.[25]) And there are arrogant, strident, and disagreeable Republicans and Democrats.[26]

Still, even if the numbers of humble people are distributed randomly, it would be better for our democracy if there were more of them. Yet this shows us precisely what we are up against: the same biases that compromise our ability to know the truth and develop humility also compromise our ability to know that that ability is compromised. Developing humility is a way to counteract bias, but our biases lead us to believe that we are humble already. We should not expect it to be otherwise; again, all virtues are, by definition, difficult. But if we start with the truth about ourselves, if we never forget that our beliefs are always compromised, if we understand that humility is wanting on both sides of the partisan divide, then we will be better able to diminish our dogmatism and, with effort, increase our humility, thereby lessening the vicious effects of raging tribalism.

"Not Too Sure That It Is Right": Humility as a Golden Mean

It would be nice to be able to leave things right here. Unfortunately, it is not quite that simple. Politics doesn't just require an ego; political action requires—rests on—the belief that you are right. Your values, your assessment of the world, your notion of justice, your policy choices, and your objectives: all of these you judge to be more correct, and to lead to a better outcome, than those of your opponent. The strength of one's belief is often of a piece with how committed someone is, too. No one goes to the barricades being pretty sure that they are right. Those who do could be wrong about objectives, facts, or both, but they don't think so. On the contrary, they are certain—intellectually and morally. And whenever someone acts politically such that they put themselves at risk, to the degree that they do, this certainty needs to be there. The more intellectually humble you are, the more you are open to the possibility you could be wrong, and the more open you are to the alternative views of others, the easier it is to lose that certainty, and with it, the will to fight. Humility, in other words, can enervate us. It can take away our sense that we really know what is right and wrong, and as a result it can undermine our willingness to commit to change.

In the next chapter, I argue that Russia uses a "firehose of falsehood" to make its own citizens and others so uncertain that people don't know what to believe. In this position, we are left unable to act. That is the objective of this form of propaganda. When enough people feel this way, democracy itself is undermined. Humility can bring us to that same end—but in this case, the problem comes from within. If we focus exclusively on the fact that the world as we perceive it may be different from the way it really is, and if we spend all our time wondering whether our opponent might be right after all, those thoughts can likewise bring us to indecision and ultimately to inaction. That makes democratic politics much harder to sustain and makes the case for humility that much weaker.

So while humility is a good thing for any person, let alone a democrat, to affirm and strive for, it is also quite possible for a democrat to become too humble. How do you know when you've crossed the line? Even if you accept that humility is a good thing, how do you make sure that you don't have too much of that good thing?

Consider the epigraph that opens this chapter. In the words of Judge Learned Hand, "The spirit of liberty is the spirit which is not too sure that it is right." Judge Hand gave this speech for the "I Am an American Day" celebration at Central Park in New York in 1944, during World War II. One and a half million people came for the event, but Hand was talking directly to 150,000 newly naturalized citizens. His objective was to tell these new American citizens that the liberty they sought depended on them, not on the Constitution or the laws. To maintain a free society, they must themselves instill and defend "the spirit of liberty." Hand admits that he cannot define what that means. He can "only tell you my own faith." With that, he says the line that opens this chapter.[27]

The operative word in Hand's statement is "too." If humility renders our confidence in our own convictions so tenuous that it is enervating and brings us to a state of inaction, then that "spirit of liberty" is not sure enough. Democracy only works if we are confident enough in our point of view, and the experiences and intelligence behind them, to act: to go out in the political world and vote, to advocate for a candidate, to run for office ourselves, or to protest. Too little certainty, and too much apathy, imperils democracy. But if we are so sure that we are right that we move to arrogance, leading us to belittle and even despise those who think differently and to regard compromise as a betrayal, then that is a spirit too sure. And again, the more people manifest that spirit, the more our democracy is jeopardized. The only solution to this dilemma is to find the correct middle ground—to be sure enough to act, but not so sure that we become strident, unyielding, and pigheaded. There is nothing easy about this. On the contrary, it is a habit of mind that runs counter to our most fundamental instincts. But every political actor, which is to say every democratic citizen, must work out how to achieve this balance. It is yet another example of the unique burdens that democratic society places on all of us citizens.

When we think about virtue as a balancing act, as the midpoint between two extremes, it is impossible to avoid talking about Aristotle. It is not that he would affirm that humility is a virtue, let alone believe that it has a place in politics. On the contrary, Aristotle thought that pride—the pursuit of honor among one's peers—was an essential dimension of any virtuous man, let alone a political leader. And there is virtually nothing in ancient Greek thought—Aristotle's or anybody else's—that resonates with the idea that humility is a virtue. But Aristotle's entire ethical system rests on the notion that virtues lie between two vices. Courage lies between recklessness and cowardice, generosity is found between stinginess and extravagance, and so on. Now the right balance, the right spot between excess and deficiency, is neither simple nor obvious. It depends on the circumstance and on whom you are engaging. Honesty means one thing when you talk to your adversary, another when you talk to a child, and still another when you talk to a friend. We must work to discern those ever-changing, never fully known or knowable circumstances and find the balance between the vicious extremes within them. Aristotle called this balance the *golden mean*. The person who could both determine where it lay and act accordingly was acting prudentially, and only that person was truly virtuous.[28]

Again, Aristotle did not think much of humility. For that matter, most would agree that he was not much of a democrat. Nevertheless, his model fits our current circumstances precisely. Regarding the place of humility in democratic society, I take Judge Hand to be saying that we must strive for our own golden mean, finding democratic humility between timidity on the one hand and stridency on the other.[29] As Aristotle insisted, that right spot between those two vices, the right degree of humility, is different in every circumstance and challenging to find. A Facebook post with no apparent attribution or proof, one that fits in nicely with our tribal identity, merits one kind of certainty; a video in which a police officer kills a suspect after kneeling on his neck for eight minutes and forty-six seconds merits another. But those are the extremes. More often, drawing these kinds of distinctions is fraught with difficulties. It requires knowledge that is difficult to attain, let alone assess, and frequently that knowledge may simply be unavailable. But attaining and assessing information is part of the democratic thinking that our sovereignty demands, no less than expressing our own point of view even as we maintain an underlying sense of our own fallibility.

We should fight for what we believe in, work hard, and invest ourselves, all in order to move society closer to our vision and to defeat those who think otherwise. But even as we do all this, we should nevertheless do so with the abiding recognition that we are no less biased than those opponents, that it is possible that we are wrong, and that our opponents might even have something to teach us.

5
HONESTY

You submit to tyranny when you renounce the difference between what you want to hear and what is actually the case.
—TIMOTHY SNYDER

In his essay "Politics and the English Language," George Orwell said that political language "is designed to make lies sound truthful and murder respectable."[1] That is not an auspicious way to start a chapter on honesty, but there is no use ignoring it. From time immemorial, politicians have demonstrated that Orwell has a point. They are shamelessly inconsistent. They spin. They answer the question they want to answer instead of the one asked. They beat talking points into the ground. And often . . . they lie.

Now there are lots of ways to lie, so I should be clear about what I mean. When I say that politicians lie, I mean that they misrepresent themselves: they present an opinion or judgment about reality as true when they either know or genuinely believe it to be false. When people do that, they are lying. But such a thing is obviously difficult to determine. Suspecting a politician (or anyone else for that matter) of lying is one thing; calling someone a liar is something else.

Sometimes we can demonstrate that a politician lied. We can discover evidence that directly contradicts a claim that a politician made. Donald Trump said he had no knowledge about a payment to Stormy Daniels, but a secretly recorded conversation shows that that is false. Trump's statement was, indubitably, a lie.[2] But this much confidence is rare. More often the most we can do is increase our confidence that someone is lying. For example, we must rely on statements by others (rather than taped evidence) that the person in question knows what he or she is saying is untrue. In the famous example of Anita Hill's testimony in the Senate hearings on the nomination of Clarence Thomas to the Supreme Court, it is impossible to avoid the conclusion that one of the two was lying.[3] Just about anyone who lived through that event has made up their mind, but it is difficult to be certain which one of them was telling the truth.

Most frequently, we see evidence of a lie when a politician judges the same words or actions differently depending on the party of the person in question.[4] Senate Majority Leader Mitch McConnell justified his refusal to bring up Merrick Garland's nomination to the Supreme Court (after the death of Justice Antonin Scalia) because the country was so close to a presidential election. At the time, Barack Obama had ten months left in his term, and the 2016 election was more than eight months away. The people, McConnell argued, should have a say in who gets to select the next Supreme Court justice.[5] When the circumstances changed and a Republican president was in office, McConnell was asked what he would do if a seat were to open up on the Supreme Court with a similar timeframe. "Oh, we'd fill it," he replied.[6]

Of course, that is precisely what happened. Ruth Bader Ginsburg died on September 18, 2020, and Amy Coney Barrett's nomination hearings began on October 12, twenty-two days before the 2020 presidential election. (In fact, even before the hearings began, millions of people had already voted.) McConnell, and for that matter just about every other Republican senator, either rationalized or ignored the rank contradiction between what he had said in the first instance and what he said in the second. Such complete reversal is certainly evidence that neither McConnell nor any other Republican senator genuinely believed the justification they first offered. And if they did not, then they misrepresented themselves. They lied. There was audible laughter from the audience when McConnell answered that question. One might surmise that that laughter derived from the breeziness, the indifference, with which the then majority leader opened himself up to that very conclusion.

But here again, increased confidence, even extreme confidence, is not certainty. Accusing another of lying requires a judgment about what a person knows or truly believes. That is a very difficult thing to be certain about, which makes this whole conversation much more difficult.

First, I refer you to that noted philosopher George Costanza: "Jerry, just remember, it's not a lie, if you believe it."[7] Professor Costanza is absolutely right. If you believe a falsehood to be true, you are not lying. Of course, you are not helping; you are not bringing any light to a world that is too dark altogether. But you are not lying.

I accept that this quote is funny, but it is not merely funny. In fact, considering our current tribal alignment, it is actually quite depressing. Under the best of circumstances, believing our own lies is easier than we all like to think it is. As I have shown, tribalism leads to in-group bias, which causes us to believe something as true or false based on whether it benefits or undermines our tribe. But, again, partisanship right now does not mean loyalty to just any tribe. It is to THE tribe. And when tribes align, the malignant qualities of tribalism only increase, including the in-group bias that causes us to believe things that are not true. All of this is to say that while it is always difficult to demonstrate a lie, it is especially difficult right now.

Lying for Good Reasons

Before Pearl Harbor rendered the whole question moot, Franklin D. Roosevelt was struggling to find clandestine ways to help Britain as it fought against the Nazis, virtually alone, for its very survival. Roosevelt, along with most military leaders, believed that American entry into the war was inevitable, and that it would be far better to do so before Britain was defeated. But popular opinion about supporting Britain was mixed at best. Many thought it was already a lost cause. And there were plenty of America Firsters, and even quiet Nazi supporters, in the nation and even in Congress who were less than terrified at the prospect of German success. Roosevelt's ability to help was thus limited and had to remain secret.

In September 1941, a few months before Pearl Harbor, a US destroyer, the *Greer*, exchanged fire with a German U-boat. In a fireside chat, Roosevelt recounted this event to the American people: "I tell you the blunt fact that the German submarine fired first upon this

American destroyer without warning, and with deliberate design to sink her."[8] This is quite a damning account. Roosevelt was describing what he called "piracy." But it was not true: the *Greer* had tracked the submarine to assist a British seaplane dropping depth charges. All this had happened before the U-boat fired on the *Greer*, and Roosevelt knew that. In no uncertain terms, Roosevelt lied. To be sure, Roosevelt was content that his actions were justifiable and ultimately in the United States' best interest. Given the context of a desperate Britain and the looming threat of a fallen Europe, Roosevelt admitted to a friend, "I am perfectly willing to mislead and tell untruths if it will help win the war."[9] But while Roosevelt's lie might well have been justified, a lie it was.

The *Greer* incident is one example of what Joseph Nye, doyen of political science, calls a "group-serving" lie as opposed to a "self-serving" one.[10] In other words, the president knew he was lying but did so in pursuit of some greater good. As a result, the moral assessment of Roosevelt's actions is different than it would be if he had lied primarily to advance his reelection prospects, for example. Of course, as Nye acknowledges, this distinction is rarely pure. Even though Roosevelt had just been reelected, he could not ignore popular opinion. Roosevelt even mused about the possibility that his clandestine support (in this case and others) might lead to his impeachment.[11] All of this is to say that Roosevelt's decision to hide and misrepresent his choices was certainly driven, in part, by his own political prospects. Moreover, politicians (like all of us) use this prudential reasoning far more often than the situation warrants. Our appeals to the greater good are often nothing more than window dressing to justify to ourselves a decision that we were going to make anyway, one that serves our own self-interest. Still, that does not change the fact that sometimes such circumstances do indeed exist.

Finally, even when politics is working well, there is a duplicity at the heart of it. Consider this remark from Roosevelt's contemporary Reinhold Niebuhr, a Christian philosopher: "The respective parties are bound to contest elections as if the future of the nation depended upon their victory, but they must nevertheless have a reserve conviction that this is not true, that the nation will be safe in the keeping of either party."[12] Elections are routine dimensions of democratic political life. Routinely, then, politicians act as if something is true even though they know, and for that matter *should* know, that it is not.

That sounds an awful lot like misrepresenting yourself. Yet Niebuhr says that this reserve conviction is not merely morally acceptable but essential. Whenever a politician speaks this way without that reserve conviction, he says, "the future of the nation is not safe, no matter which party rules."[13]

For all these reasons, demanding that politicians never lie is not simply impossible but is probably a bad idea to boot. Calling for an ethics of honesty in politics might well appear to be a foolish enterprise—but I am going to call for it anyway. I still insist that honesty is a demand that we must make on politicians, and for that matter, on all of us democratic citizens.

Hannah Arendt: Truth Through Communication

In her essay "Truth and Politics," Hannah Arendt starts with a comment that recalls Orwell's: "Truth and politics," she says, "are on rather bad terms with each other."[14] Again, it would take enormous naivete to think otherwise, and Arendt was anything but naive. As we saw with Henri Tajfel in chapter 1, Arendt's philosophical thought was grounded in her own hard experience as a European Jew during World War II. In her case, she was forced to escape from Germany and then from Paris, staying one step ahead of the Nazis. Arendt knew well the depravity to which politics can descend. What is more, she knew that defeating the Nazis was more important than unwavering fidelity to the truth. Yet Arendt did not leave the matter there. She also argued that despite the disrespect politicians often show to the truth, democratic politics is not really possible without it.

None of us, Arendt says, perceives the world in exactly the same way. Your experiences, your history, your desires, your values: none of these is identical to mine. But it goes deeper than this. Our senses, our brains, and our bodies mediate the reality we experience. As a result, for each of us, whatever we experience, it is uniquely ours. As far as epistemology is concerned—that is, the study of what we can know and justifiably believe—we are all, in a limited but inescapable sense, on our own. The other fact that follows from our distinctiveness is that the way we experience the world is necessarily abstracted from, necessarily different from, the way the world really is. There is a world, a reality, out there—that fact is one of the propositions upon which democracy rests—but it is not identical to the way in which any of us perceive it. Many people were introduced to this concept when, in 2015, a dress that was either blue and black or white and gold became, for a short time anyway, "the dress that broke the internet."[15]

Arendt says that because all this is the case, and because it cannot be otherwise, we need one another. More specifically, we need to talk to one another. It is only through communication between individuals—communication where we present, discuss, and evaluate our different perspectives—that we can come to best understand the world. For Arendt, it is through communication that "truth reveals itself."[16] But if that communication is going to work, we must start with the shared commitment to convey our beliefs truthfully. The less committed we are to this goal, the less genuine our communication becomes, and therefore the less productive it is. If that commitment is entirely absent, there is really no point in arguing at all.

What does all this have to do with democratic politics? Quite a bit, actually. Democracy is about living together and not killing each other even though we have deep and abiding disagreements. If we are to maintain the peace, we have to strive to work through those disagreements, even as we accept the fact that most of the time, they are not ever going away. We do that through procedures and institutions that are, likewise, built on argument. The rights delineated in the First Amendment to the US Constitution, including speech, assembly, and the petition of grievances, all presuppose the idea that we can argue for our point of view and that this effort can, sometimes at least, change people's minds. Elections, too, are about politicians presenting their points of view. Citizens evaluate those arguments and make a choice. It is certainly true that citizens frequently do not make objective evaluations; they simply follow their partisan identity and then come up with reasons that make it seem as if that is what they are doing. (I say more about this in chapter 10.) But none of this changes the fact that argument is the premise of our political system. It is the essential means by which citizens work constructively through their disagreements and make choices.

So, too, in government, in the legislature or town hall, politicians argue with each other. For all the logrolling, arm-twisting, and rank self-interest, that process is nevertheless grounded in debate, in the civil and reasoned presentation of and rejoinders to arguments. That process therefore requires those same commitments. Without them, democratic procedures become pointless, and democratic politics becomes nothing but a means of securing power.

Arendt acknowledges that in politics, the bar for truth must be set low. But that does not mean that we can throw the bar away. Because a democracy requires a shared commitment to truth to sustain itself, lying undermines and threatens democracy. The degree to which a politician (or any one of us, really) lies, what he or she lies about, and to what ends and for what reasons—all of this matters. While it is true that politicians routinely misrepresent themselves, it is also true that democracy requires from all of us some shared commitment to truth.

Lies and Democracy's Enemies

Does this still sound a little abstruse? Too idealistic and disconnected from the partisan struggle in which we find ourselves? It isn't. In fact, the idea that a commitment to telling the truth is necessary to sustain democracy finds support most relevantly, and most threateningly, in the fact that democracy's enemies routinely seek to undermine democracy by undermining truth. Arendt herself was all too familiar with this effort. She saw firsthand how totalitarian governments undertake to undermine one's sense that reality can be understood and to foster a sense of hopelessness and despair regarding the truth. Likewise, all this demonstrates a considered, systematic effort to undermine democracy itself. She wrote,

> Mass propaganda discovered that its audience was ready at all times to believe the worst, no matter how absurd, and did not particularly object to being deceived because it held every statement to be a lie anyhow. The totalitarian mass leaders based their propaganda on the correct psychological assumption that, under such conditions, one could make people believe the most fantastic statements one day, and trust that if the next day they were given irrefutable proof of their falsehood, they would take refuge in cynicism; instead of deserting the leaders who had lied to them, they would protest that they had known all along that the statement was a lie and would admire the leaders for their superior tactical cleverness.[17]

Arendt was not only correct; she was prescient. This strategy of securing authoritarian power by undermining the very possibility of truth remains operative at this very moment.

The interference of the Russian government in the 2016 presidential election is well established and accepted by almost everyone not named Donald Trump. The Russians' objective was to use social media, especially Facebook, to sow false information and stoke the fires of partisan enmity. As for the 2020 election, a National Intelligence Council report concluded that Russia again sought to interfere, but this time through "the use of proxies linked to Russian intelligence to push influence narratives . . . to US media organizations, US officials, and prominent US individuals, including some close to former President Trump and his administration."[18] But interference in US elections (through social media or otherwise) does not fully account for the provocative actions of the Russian government. Through modern media outlets Russia Today (RT) and Sputnik, the Russians employed a different set of means to undermine the ideal, and even the possibility, of the truth. This effort, too, is ongoing.

RT is Russia's international cable TV network. With the same combination of highly produced visuals, breaking news, and talking heads, it is much like CNN. Sputnik is more of an online platform, again featuring news and commentary, that is more like BuzzFeed. Both receive funding from the Russian government, and both model the new softer model of Russian propaganda. The motto of RT is "Question More." That motto is an accurate description of the objectives of both initiatives, but it is also important to understand that it is not merely accurate: it is pernicious.

Soviet Propaganda Was Built on Lies

In the former Soviet bloc, the prevailing model was that propaganda was designed to denigrate the West and its ostensible ideals. By pointing out the failures of capitalism and democracy, the alternative of Soviet-style communism appeared as a less unappealing and perhaps even viable alternative. Often this argument was grounded, to some degree at least, in truth. To note one famous example, the Soviet bloc routinely and correctly argued that African Americans in the

Jim Crow South were not truly free. Their second-class status—as citizens and human beings—manifested the rank hypocrisy behind America's claim to affirm universal human and civil rights.[19]

I saw this argument for myself. In 1980, as a college student, I traveled on a day visa to East Berlin and wandered into a bookstore. My friend found a textbook for teaching English to East German schoolchildren. Inside was a lesson centered on the fact that less than a mile from the beautiful US Capitol building in Washington, DC, were neighborhoods that were predominantly African American and extremely poor. The lesson was that the condition of these neighborhoods belied American claims to racial equality and equality of opportunity and that these claims were used to hide the reality of capitalist power and racist exploitation. The claim was overstated, perhaps, but it was not wrong. As I walked the streets of East Berlin, seeing bullet holes everywhere from a war over three decades before, I knew that the argument in this book was rank propaganda. But because I had also been to DC, I also knew there was truth behind it.

The other traditional form of propaganda was also built around a kernel of truth, but the edifice that was constructed was an elaborate and false counternarrative. The KGB called these efforts "active measures"—disinformation campaigns that presented claims as true when they were indisputably false. One notable and notorious example: in the 1980s, the KGB asserted that the United States had invented AIDS as a weapon. The claim made use of the fact that in the '70s, evidence emerged that showed that the United States had indeed conducted biological warfare research early in the Cold War. This, along with fear surrounding this new and terrifying disease, created the platform for an elaborate rumor campaign. The Soviets turned to the East Germans for help in spreading this disinformation: "The East Germans were told specifically to employ a 'scientific approach' and produce disinformation contending the AIDS virus had been developed at Fort Detrick, Maryland, from where it spread to the general population through human testing."[20] The subsequent effort included an extensive and coordinated media campaign, in which this false claim was presented as truth with, according to Peter Pomerantsev, "po-faced seriousness, broadcasting interviews with fake scientists, providing fake evidence, all intended to keep up a façade of factuality."[21]

In the very specific terms I outlined above, this was a lie. The elaborate, coordinated effort, along with uncovered evidence, makes it impossible to sustain the idea that somehow the Soviets genuinely believed their claim to be true. But that was the former model. Contemporary and ongoing Russian propaganda is less interested in spreading lies; it is more accurately described as spreading bullshit.

Contemporary Russian Propaganda Is Bullshit

In his essay *On Bullshit,* Harry Frankfurt argues for a distinction between a lie and bullshit. A liar, Frankfurt says, wants "to lead us away from a correct apprehension of reality; we are not to know that he wants us to believe something he supposes to be false."[22] But for this very reason, "the teller of the lie submits to objective constraints imposed by what he takes to be the truth. The liar is inescapably concerned with truth-values. In order to invent a lie at all, he must think he knows what is true."[23] If hypocrisy is the homage vice pays to virtue, a lie includes an implicit awareness of, and thus concern for, the truth. All of this describes very well the Soviet bloc campaign that the United States government had invented AIDS.

Bullshit, on the other hand, is "indifference to how things really are."[24] The bullshitter "does not care whether the things he says describe reality correctly. He just picks them out, or makes them up, to suit his purpose."[25] In sum, the liar is more aware of, and more concerned about, the truth than the bullshitter is. And that makes the bullshitter worse: "Bullshit is a greater enemy of the truth than lies are."[26] Again, the Soviets used propaganda to lie. Today's Russian propaganda is more properly understood as bullshit. Pomerantsev writes that if "Soviet measures went to great lengths to make their forgeries look convincing, now the Kremlin doesn't seem to care if it is caught: The aim is to confuse rather than convince, to trash the information space so the audience gives up looking for any truth amid the chaos."[27] The strategy is not to present a specific lie, let alone to convince you of it. Rather, to use the words of Christopher Paul and Miriam Matthews of the Rand Corporation, the objective is to present a "firehose of falsehood."[28]

RT and the Firehose Strategy

In 2017 and 2018, Gordon Ramsay and Sam Robertshaw conducted content analysis of 11,819 articles on the English-language sites of RT and Sputnik (3,815 from RT and 8,004 from Sputnik) using a digital content analysis tool. This tool made it possible for them to assess a heretofore overwhelming amount of data.[29] What is more, this effort

took place during an extremely important event in Russian-British relations: the poisoning of Sergei Skripal and his daughter, Yulia.

In the 1990s, Skripal worked for the GRU, Russia's intelligence agency. He was also acting as a double agent for the UK's intelligence services. Arrested in 2004, he was sentenced to thirteen years for crimes against the state. In 2010, he was exiled to Britain as part of a spy swap. (He now holds Russian and British citizenship.) On March 4, 2018, Yulia was visiting from Russia. While they both sat on a park bench in Salisbury, England, they were poisoned with a Novichok nerve agent. Both ultimately recovered, but only after many weeks in the hospital. The British concluded that two Russian agents were behind the attack.[30]

Naturally, this story received extensive coverage on both RT and Sputnik. Content analysis by Ramsay and Robertshaw confirmed that fact. But more importantly, their work identified 138 distinct narratives that sought to explain what had happened to the Skripals, why the Russians were not responsible, and who, instead of the Russians, had reason to commit this crime. The researchers concluded:

> The sheer number of 138 separate narratives provided by sources—and often presented as fact in the editorial text of RT and Sputnik articles—. . . suggests a willingness, if not intent, to represent as many competing or contradictory explanations of events as possible. . . . In particular, the consistent portrayal of Western governments as untrustworthy partners (in contrast with "honest, reasonable" Russia—as the most frequently recorded narrative in this study attests), driven by dishonest or hypocritical goals and both dangerously aggressive and simultaneously weak and unstable, suggests that the emergence of these groups of narratives may have been a conscious editorial strategy.[31]

By presenting so many questions and different possible explanations for this singular event—Were the Skripals really poisoned? Do we really know what the agent was? And what nation or rogue agent really has a motive for this act?—RT and Sputnik sought not to convince the listener of a particular falsehood but to lead her to the conclusion that the truth was impossible to know. Anybody who said otherwise, anybody who jumped to conclusions and blamed the Russians—they were the ones acting in bad faith.

The efforts of the Russian government to poison those they don't like, and the "conscious editorial strategy" of RT and Sputnik to deflect and obfuscate the truth of the matter: all of this has become little more than standard operating procedure. In 2020, it played out again in the very same way.

Alexei Navalny is an activist who has posted videos on social media that document that raging corruption within the Russian government, including a tour of a billion-dollar home that Putin is building for himself on the Black Sea.[32] That video has been viewed over one hundred million times; Navalny had become quite a thorn in the side of the Russian kleptocracy. Government agents therefore planted the very same nerve agent, Novichok, in Navalny's underwear, and on a flight from Tomsk to Moscow he became violently ill.[33] He was put into a coma and ultimately flown to Germany, where he recovered. German scientists confirmed that Novichok was in his system. While still in the Berlin hospital, Navalny posed as a representative of Russia's Security Council and telephoned an agent who confirmed that he had been responsible both for the poisoning and for covering up after its failure. After he recovered, Navalny flew back to Russia and was immediately charged and convicted of violating parole and insulting a veteran. His arrest prompted demonstrations by hundreds of thousands all over Russia. He was sentenced and remains in prison as of this writing.

All of this is despicable, of course, but for my purposes the relevant point is that after these events took place, RT responded on cue with the very same "firehose of falsehood," questioning every aspect of this story. RT writers argued that there were "many 'interest groups' in Russia and outside the country that could be interested in removing Navalny from the political stage."[34] They pointed out that his poisoning could not have been caused by Novichok, quoting the developers' claim that Navalny would not have survived it. They therefore insisted that it must have been some other poison—and some other poisoner.[35] RT also simultaneously referenced the contradictory claim that many other countries have access to Novichok.[36] Finally, they appealed to the claim that Russia was really the victim in this story, noting that "when it comes to Russia, the mainstream Western media operates in a self-contained pit of rumor, fear, braggadocio, bulls**t, and propaganda."[37]

One might question the viability of this strategy. Are these claims not rendered less effective at sowing doubt by the very fact that they have become so predictable? Perhaps so. But there is no disputing the strategy itself. RT's objective is not to present an alternative perspective on the truth; rather, RT aims to make it virtually impossible for the viewer to assess and evaluate so many competing claims. The viewer will give up, unable to know what or who to believe. Moreover, the argument is that any claim to know what really happened, especially if that claim involves Russia, is really hiding some cynical and self-interested purpose.[38] Peter Lavelle, host of *Crosstalk,* RT's self-described "flagship program," offers this very defense: "The paymaster determines a lot. . . . Are you telling me Murdoch [Rupert Murdoch, owner of a number of media outlets in the United States and Australia, including the *Wall Street Journal* and Fox News] doesn't control the editorial line of his publications? No one can escape who pays for what."[39] Lavelle's message here is that everyone has an agenda and nobody is on the level: if you are committed to the ideal of truth, indeed, if you think *anybody* is committed to that ideal, then you are a sucker—and you are probably not going to get paid.[40]

What was true in Arendt's day is true now. Lies buttress the hold totalitarian governments have over the people living under them. They leave the citizenry exhausted and cynical, unable to rouse themselves even to conceive of something better, let alone demand it. By directing these propaganda efforts outward, as part of their never-ending competition with democratic societies, authoritarian governments seek to cultivate this same sense of cynicism and powerlessness, thereby facilitating the destruction of democracy as a viable alternative.

Trump and the Firehose Strategy

These strategies, and their underlying assault on the truth, were also repeatedly manifested by former president Trump. Throughout his presidency, Trump made over thirty thousand false and misleading statements. This total is genuinely breathtaking; during the 2020 campaign the number jumped to an average of more than fifty such statements a day.[41] But you will note that that accounting does not refer to these statements as lies. This is because, again, it is virtually impossible to be certain that the president did not genuinely believe that what he was saying was the truth. Responsible journalists understand that and therefore limit their conclusions to what they know: that the president regularly, doggedly, relentlessly said things that were not true. I would argue that some of these misstatements were both repeated by the president so many times and noted as false so many times in the media that there are only two reasonable conclusions: either the president is indifferent to the truth, in which case he is a bullshitter, or he knows that he is saying things that are not true and is therefore a liar. But either way, in terms Hannah Arendt would surely recognize, his untruths undermined American democracy.

It is also true that the president used many of the same strategies associated with the new Russian propaganda. More than two thousand times during his presidency, Trump referred to news reports that he did not like as "fake news" and to journalists as "the enemy of the people," "dishonest," "corrupt," "low life reporters," "bad people," "human scum," and "some of the worst human beings you'll ever meet."[42] All of this served to buttress his claim that the mainstream media was driven not by any commitment to the truth or journalistic integrity but rather by a partisan agenda to undermine him and his administration by any means necessary. Just like the Russians, Trump's version of bullshit sought to disparage the idea that journalists are genuinely committed to the truth, even undermining the idea of truth itself, and to paint himself not as the perpetrator of lies but as the victim. In McKay Coppins's words, "When the press as an institution is weakened, fact-based journalism becomes just one more drip in the daily deluge of content—no more or less credible than partisan propaganda. Relativism is the real goal of Trump's assault on the press, and the more 'enemies of the people' his allies can take out along the way, the better."[43] And as with the Russians, Trump's effort was likewise calculated and deliberate. Off the record, and just after the presidential election in November 2016, CBS and *60 Minutes* journalist Lesley Stahl asked Trump why he continued to berate the press even after his victory. Trump replied, "You know why I do it? I do it to discredit you all and demean you all, so that, when you write negative stories about me, no one will believe you."[44]

Trump's insatiable—one might well say pathological—inclination to say things that are not true finds its *pièce de résistance* in his insistence that the 2020 election was stolen. This effort, too, was systematic. Its foundation was laid months before the election. As soon as it became clear that the COVID-19 pandemic would necessitate

changes in election procedures, including increased opportunities for mail-in voting, Trump began to insist, without any evidence and even against the wishes of Republican Party leaders, that such changes were nothing more than opportunities for Democrats to steal the election. Throughout the summer of 2020, Trump repeatedly claimed that "the only way we're going to lose this election is if the election is rigged."[45] Once the election was held and Biden was declared the winner, the president not only refused to accept the results but repeatedly insisted that, in fact, he had won "by a lot!"—and that Biden's apparent victory was really the product of elaborate, coordinated corruption and fraud. Not just the election but the nation itself, Trump said, was being stolen before our very eyes.

On January 6, 2021, the day of the insurrection, Trump reiterated all these claims at a rally of his supporters.

> All of us here today do not want to see our election victory stolen by emboldened radical-left Democrats, which is what they're doing. And stolen by the fake news media. That's what they've done and what they're doing. We will never give up, we will never concede. It doesn't happen. You don't concede when there's theft involved.
>
> Our country has had enough. We will not take it anymore and that's what this is all about. And to use a favorite term that all of you people really came up with: We will stop the steal. Today I will lay out just some of the evidence proving that we won this election and we won it by a landslide. This was not a close election.[46]

These untruths resulted directly in an insurrection that threatened the very core of American democracy. As we all know, within minutes of Trump's speech, the people listening did what he told them to do: they marched to the Capitol. The events that followed are a direct result of the president's words, both that day and for months previous. The gleeful denunciation by the president of the democratic demand for honesty led to the most antidemocratic act in the United States since the end of the Civil War.

Since I excoriated his lack of honesty with respect to the Merrick Garland nomination, perhaps it is appropriate to reference what Senate Majority Leader McConnell said about these events. On the very evening of the insurrection, when the Senate reassembled to complete their interrupted work, he said, "Self-government, my colleagues, requires a shared commitment to the truth and a shared respect for the ground rules of our system. We cannot keep drifting apart into two separate tribes with a separate set of facts and separate realities with nothing in common except our hostility towards each other and mistrust for the few national institutions that we all still share."[47] I have nothing to add to this. It affirms very well the fundamental democratic principle that there is an objective world that we all strive to navigate and understand, as well as the notion that honesty is one essential means by which our society might mitigate the effects of tribalism. I would only note again that virtues are difficult things. They only become relevant when difficult circumstances make them so. Honesty that is chosen or rejected because of a prior calculation of partisan advantage is really not much of a virtue at all.

Unconscious and Conscious Lies

Both bias and lying exist to preserve the self in the face of a perceived threat. After hundreds of thousands of years of human evolution, those behaviors continue to manifest themselves universally. That, in itself, is good reason to believe that they are both part of a successful survival strategy. Be that as it may, it is also true that the current conditions of human existence render them both problematic. Both subvert the possibility of genuine argument; both undermine the pursuit and even the ideal of the truth; both make democracy harder.

But bias is unconscious. Lying, by definition, is conscious and deliberate. We live in a time where tribalism threatens our democratic foundations. It is therefore especially important that we understand this difference. False beliefs arise inevitably from our biases. This is true for all of us. Again, when we lie, we know that what we are saying is false. Democracy is better off when we strive to limit ourselves to the falsehoods we genuinely believe.

Democracy is full of endemic, inescapable difficulties. Committing to the truth, and maintaining that commitment even as one strives to maintain partisan advantage, is only one of them. But as if that balancing act were not difficult enough, it is also true that there are now, and have always been, those who work to exploit these competing goals for their own advantage. They use lies to undermine democracy. Systematic bullshit like that produced by RT and Sputnik, on the one hand, and the former president, on the other, reflects the fact that right now this battle is pitched. If nothing else, telling the truth conveys to the world which side you are on.

6

CONSISTENCY

These are my principles, and if you
don't like them I have others.
—ATTRIBUTED TO GROUCHO MARX

Consistency doesn't sound like much of a virtue. Calling someone consistent is like calling someone neat. Or punctual. It calls to mind someone who is a perhaps a little priggish and even boring. Certainly it's not the most laudable tribute one can offer. Then there is that famous quotation from Ralph Waldo Emerson. Whenever one brings up consistency as something worth pursuing, one frequently hears the rejoinder, "A foolish consistency is the hobgoblin of little minds."[1] Leave aside the fact that people offering this rejoinder are often way too pleased with themselves. The sentiment behind it provides that one extra reason to not take consistency seriously as a virtue. As you will see, I do take it seriously—but not, perhaps, in the way you might expect. My argument is that demanding consistency of ourselves is one essential way to help us reduce the power of our biases and thereby become better democratic thinkers.

Emerson's Foolishness

Start with Emerson's insult: "the hobgoblin of little minds." So what is a hobgoblin? It is a kind of small fairy creature. Did you know that?

Do you care? Probably not, but that only serves to make Emerson's point. Hobgoblins don't exist; therefore thinking about them at all is a waste of time, diverting us from more worthy pursuits. Emerson thinks consistency is a hobgoblin because anyone who seeks it is focusing on the wrong things, chasing the wrong goal. A little mind letting itself be led astray by things that don't matter.

And who possesses these little minds? In the rest of the quote, Emerson says that the hobgoblin of consistency is "adored by little statesmen and philosophers and divines."[2] It appears that Emerson, like Hume, had a similarly low opinion of people like St. Bernard. But these are just exemplars. Anybody who is married to an ideology, such that she will follow it wherever it goes and give it pride of place over her own hard-won experience, practices a foolish consistency and thereby diminishes herself.

This quotation comes from Emerson's *Self-Reliance*. The title references the worthy goal that we Americans *should* be pursuing, and his argument is that consistency doesn't help us achieve it. In fact, it gets in the way. If we are to live authentically, we must find the courage to trust ourselves above all else. Each day, we should confront the world anew and express the truth as we see it. *Inconsistency*, at least as the world sees it, is the almost inevitable by-product of a life lived with that kind of authenticity. Here too, as with Hume and humility, Emerson appears to say that not only is consistency *not* a virtue, it's really more like a vice.

Living this kind of life means that the self-reliant person is going to be different. By failing to conform, she will stick out, and her behavior and choices will confuse and upset other people. She will, inevitably, be misunderstood. Yet that is the price of living authentically. "Pythagoras was misunderstood," Emerson says, "and Socrates, and Jesus, and Luther, and Copernicus, and Galileo, and Newton, and every pure and wise spirit that ever took flesh. To be great is to be misunderstood."[3] Blazing your own trail is a necessary condition of greatness, and if you are up to that challenge, you must also be prepared for the likelihood that most people will misunderstand you.

Most people would agree with that conclusion, I think. But what does that have to do with consistency? While both greatness and inconsistency can cause one to be misunderstood, Emerson does nothing to show that there is some necessary relationship between the two. In fact, there isn't one: people can be inconsistent without being self-reliant. As I noted in the last chapter, a bullshitter is quite inconsistent, saying whatever serves her purposes at the moment, utterly indifferent to self-contradiction. But there is nothing great about that kind of inconsistency. Nor does Emerson say anything about how all the great human beings he lists were inconsistent. Unconventional, they certainly were. Trailblazers finding their own path: absolutely. But most would argue that they were neither foolish nor inconsistent. Regardless, if you are going to associate inconsistency with greatness, that claim would seem to require more support than none at all.

Emerson has a "get out of jail free" card in all this, of course: the word "foolish." With this modifier, Emerson says that it is not consistency per se that keeps us from self-reliance and greatness; it is *foolish* consistency. But what accounts for the difference? When is consistency foolish, and when is it not? Maybe it is one of those things you know when you see it. When consistency is lauded by "little statesmen and philosophers and divines," you can be confident that it is foolish. Maybe. That isn't much of an argument, though. But note that by adding the qualifier, Emerson is effectively (if quietly) admitting that not all consistency is foolish. Yet doesn't this require some elucidation as well? What about consistency that is not foolish? Is it even possible to be consistent and wise? To be consistent *and* self-reliant? And what would that look like? Emerson doesn't address those questions either.

Clearly, as famous as this quotation is, it just doesn't get us very far. It is surely not sufficient reason to denigrate the ideal of consistency. Nevertheless, there is an important point that unites Emerson's objective and mine. For Emerson, self-reliance means that we strive to see the world for ourselves and reject the lazy categories that make our thinking both diminished and false. Tribalism, and the bias that trails inevitably in its wake, is its own kind of laziness. When we are beholden to our tribe, bias overwhelms our ability to evaluate the world accurately and thereby make sound decisions. Biased thinking is inaccurate thinking—compromised, weakened, distorted thinking.[4] If we consistently follow our tribe no matter where it goes, without even a sliver of independent thought, that kind of consistency reflects the operation of a little mind.

But if this is the right way to understand self-reliance, then consistency does not merely manifest the problem. More relevantly, it is a means for addressing the problem. The quest for consistency can help us diminish the power of our tribal identities, overcome or at least moderate our biases, and help us develop a better functioning democracy. This kind of consistency is decidedly not foolish; it is an essential democratic virtue.

Who Is the Hypocrite?

Let's go back to the fan who ardently follows some sports team. This person really wants her team to win. In fact, her identity, even her sense of self, is caught up in the success of her team. This fan also wants to believe that her tribe consists of the good guys or gals. Like all of us, she wants her tribe to be worthy of her allegiance and to reflect well on herself. The ardent fan is therefore more inclined to look the other way, or explain away, the negative actions of those whom she supports. If someone on her team commits a cheap foul, say, that action undermines her feeling of superiority. Depending on her level of commitment, this disconnect between her desires and this ugly truth can feel like a betrayal and even cause her physical discomfort.[5] When this happens, our fan's brain automatically comes up with ways to diminish the pain she feels. In many cases, the simplest reaction is simply to ignore it. Forget that it ever happened. Alternatively, the fan is more likely to say that that person was caught up in the moment or was reacting to something that happened earlier. It was a one-off. Could have happened to anybody. No big deal. Anyone who follows the NFL and has had a conversation with a New England Patriots fan about their team stealing signs or deflating footballs has seen this evidence firsthand. On the other hand, if you are a Jets fan, the fact that the Patriots stole your team's signs only confirms your feeling of superiority. (Moral superiority, anyway; superiority in the division is another story.) And you are not about to ignore it. What is more, in this case, no Jets fan is asking questions about context or explanations. They are not interested in nuance and are quite ready to render a categorical judgment. The whole Patriots team is a bunch of cheaters. They play dirty. And so on.[6]

The point here is that there is nothing unique about Patriots or Jets fans. Anyone who invests their identity in group loyalty—whatever the group—behaves the same way.[7] This effect is called *ultimate attribution error.*[8] It means that when we perceive some action that we judge to be negative, we come up with different explanations for that behavior depending on whether the person in question is part of *us* or part of *them*. This is just one more way in which our tribal identity leads to in-group bias and thereby compromises our ability to think accurately. It has been demonstrated for just about any group category you want to name. Not just sports teams but gender, ethnicity, religion, and, not incidentally, partisanship.[9]

How Do We Explain What Mike Did?

Jamie Barden is a psychology professor at Howard University. He selected college students who had a strong partisan identity for a research study. He told them the story of Mike, a political fundraiser. At an evening event that he organized, Mike had too much to drink, left for home, and got into a serious accident. Then, about a month later, Mike made a speech railing against the dangers of drunk driving. How did the students account for this difference between what Mike said and what he did? Was it because Mike is a craven hypocrite who was only looking for partisan advantage and who didn't really believe a word he said? Or was it because his experience had changed him and he now took the matter much more seriously?

Again, the students in the study already had a strong partisan identity. In the tale, so did Mike. Half the students were told that Mike was a Republican; for the other half, he was a Democrat. When Mike's partisan identity was the same as the student's, 16 percent thought he was a hypocrite. But if Mike represented the other party, that number increased to 40 percent. The research subjects found it much easier to condemn Mike when he was one of *them*. In that case, he was a hypocrite, a person devoid of principles, a flip-flopper. When he was part of *us*, the students found reasons to explain, or perhaps explain away, his apparent hypocrisy. The contradiction between Mike's words and his actions resulted from his changing his mind and developing as a person. Barden concludes, "Factors extraneous to the target's actions, namely whether a perceiver matches or mismatches the target's group membership, can significantly affect the amount of hypocrisy ascribed to the target."[10]

A factor is extraneous if it does not properly belong in our decision-making process; it inevitably increases the chances that we will end up making a bad decision. Ultimate attribution error is thus one of those dozens of biases that all human beings exhibit, and it is especially associated with tribalism. As with any bias, this one compromises our thinking. It causes us to make less accurate judgments. And because our social identities are right now ever more aligned into two competing tribes, *us* and *them*, this bias and all other associated biases have become all the more powerful.

As I have noted repeatedly, biases are endemic and mostly unconscious. We cannot stop them from happening, but we can develop strategies that help us diminish their effects. These strategies are called *metacognitive*. They help us think about how we think. There are lots of examples of metacognitive strategies. A student might, for example, determine that her reading comprehension is not as good if she is in a reclined position as opposed to upright in a chair. Other strategies are more directly concerned with our biases. Of those strategies that educators and researchers have investigated to determine their effectiveness, the "most well attested in the literature"[11] is called *consider the opposite*.

Consider the Opposite

In 1979, researchers Charles Lord, Lee Ross, and Mark Lepper selected undergraduates for a classic study.[12] Half the students believed that capital punishment had a deterrent effect on criminality and therefore supported it. The other half rejected the deterrent argument and were therefore opposed. The researchers gave each student the results of two research studies. These reports were made up but carefully designed to lend equal support to both sides. As you would probably expect, the students found that the study that conformed to their already-established opinion was far more convincing than the other. The authors concluded that "the same study can elicit entirely opposite evaluations from people who hold different initial beliefs about a complex social issue."[13]

But this was not the most striking result of this study. As part of their evaluation, the researchers asked the students to reflect on how reading the two reports changed their opinions. You might expect—or at least hope—that the students would come away from the research with the sense that the question of whether capital punishment deterred crime is more complicated than they first believed it to be. They might decide that they should therefore approach the issue with a more open mind. That is not what happened. Instead, exposure to research that was designed to undermine the students' certainty ended up strengthening it. The researchers concluded that the students viewed the countervailing research through biased eyes, and as a result, the reports had only reinforced their bias: "In so doing, subjects exposed themselves to the familiar risk of making their hypothesis unfalsifiable . . . and allowing themselves to be encouraged by patterns of data that they ought to have found troubling."[14] In Emersonian terms, the students were exhibiting the most foolish sort of consistency, attending to conflicting information but, despite that encounter, ending up even more convinced that they were right all along.

The researchers themselves were distressed by this result. Years later Lord, Lepper and this time Elizabeth Preston wrote, "for those who value social science evidence on complex and important social issues, the way in which Lord et al.'s (1979) subjects evaluated new evidence seems less than optimal."[15] (That is how a social scientist expresses distress, anyway.) So in 1984, these researchers tested whether they could mitigate such "suboptimal" effects. The students were selected just as before and given the same set of summaries of bogus research articles. Some students (the control group) were asked to be as objective and unbiased as possible, to think of themselves as judges or jurors. In the other group, the researchers described the process by which bias develops and then gave these students the following instruction: "Ask yourself at each step whether you would have made the same high or low evaluations had exactly the same study produced results on the other side"[16]—that is, if the study had produced results that supported the opposite partisan position. In short, the researchers offered these students a metacognitive strategy of considering the opposite, pushing them to think beyond the confines of their preestablished biases.

It worked. In every case, the students in this latter group displayed less attitude polarization than the students who were simply encouraged to be impartial. The research confirmed the importance of a metacognitive strategy: "Many biases . . . are the result of inadequate cognitive strategies rather than inadequate motivation."[17] Since this study, research has sought to best way to frame that strategy, to achieve the most effective and longest-lasting "debiasing" effects. But for my purposes, the point is clear. Considering the opposite is one way to diminish the effect of partisan bias. It makes us think better.

The Opposite Is the Other Tribe

So what does all this talk of ultimate attribution error and metacognitive strategies have to do with consistency? Well, "the opposite" in question here is of course *them*, the other tribe. Consistency therefore doesn't mean following one's tribe without concern for evidence. In fact, that is quite consistent with what Emerson meant by a *foolish* consistency. On the contrary, for a democrat, consistency means striving to judge any action on its own terms, irrespective of its impact on our tribal identity. Consistency requires that we ask ourselves one question when we come to a judgment about some political action: Would we come to the same conclusion if a member of the other party had undertaken that same action? Consistency means that we judge the situation the same if it is the same. If some behavior is wrong for a Democrat, it is wrong for a Republican. If some policy was unfair or illegitimate in a previous administration, it is wrong in the current one.

Since Plato, at least, the idea of justice has centered on giving someone their due, giving them what they deserve. The *Institutes* of Justinian, a codification of Roman law from the sixth century, defines justice as "the constant and perpetual wish to render every one his due."[18] To say that this objective is "constant and perpetual" is to say that justice is not arbitrary or selective. It requires that where two cases are the same, they should be treated the same. They should result in the same outcome.

Understood this way, consistency emerges as one indispensable manifestation of justice and a means for helping ensure it.[19] Engraved on the front of the Supreme Court of the United States is the phrase "Equal Justice Under Law." Justice that is not equal, that doesn't treat the same crime in the same way, is not justice at all. Treating acts and the individuals who commit them equally is constitutive of justice—and impossible without it. During the building's construction, some suggested that the engraving should simply read "Justice Under

Law." But then Chief Justice Evan Hughes defended the inscription by referring to the oath of office that incoming justices take. The oath says that the justices will "administer justice without respect to persons, and do equal right to the poor and to the rich." That, Hughes said, "is the essence of equal justice under law."[20] If the point needs any more clarity, that is why every statue of Justice is blindfolded: justice is not influenced by any extraneous matters.

Of course, no one disputes how difficult this goal is to achieve, nor how our nation's history abounds with failures to achieve it. It is almost certainly true that a full and complete achievement of this kind of blindness is beyond human capacity. We are biased and cannot *not* be so. But the motto and statue reflect an ideal we must always pursue, one that serves to guide and critique our actions, even as we know that we will always fall short. Considering the opposite, asking whether we would make the same decision if the question involved the other tribe, treating tribe membership as an extraneous criterion, and holding ourselves to the standard of consistency: all of this is part of how we hold ourselves and our decisions to the standard of justice, the standard of treating everyone equally and giving everyone their due.

For the students in Barden's study, consistency requires that they ask themselves whether they would judge Mike's actions in the same way if he had been a member of the other party. Would the Republican students have been as likely to call him a hypocrite if he were a Republican, or as likely to justify his actions if he were a Democrat? If we cannot answer such a question affirmatively, then our decisions are inconsistent. And when that is the case, when we give in to our tribal biases, our judgments undermine democracy and justice and can properly be called vicious.

Consistency in Politics

The virtue of consistency helps us think about our thinking—or better, to judge our judgments. If we know that we are biased and are likely to have a compromised view of reality, then consistency can help us limit that effect. And regularly seeking consistency means that we are taking our biases seriously and striving to mitigate their role in our decision-making. In his book *Unjust,* Noah Rothman, editor of the conservative journal *Commentary*, demonstrates how the quest for consistency can lead us to better, less biased arguments and a better democracy: "White nationalism is perhaps the primordial form of identity politics in America, and its program is social justice for white people. . . . Conservatives cannot reject the identity politics practiced by their adversaries while simultaneously adopting a style of it for themselves."[21]

It would be foolish, in precisely the sense that Emerson means it, to insist on consistency regardless of the circumstances. No two situations are exactly the same; they all manifest little differences. Do those differences matter? Do they give us legitimate ground to come to different conclusions? Sometimes. And arguing whether the circumstance in question is one of those times leads to one of the oldest arguments there is. "It's the same thing!" "No, it's not! It's totally different!" But just as importantly, the ground is always moving under our feet, especially in politics. The least we can say, and the minimum standard to which we can hold our elected representatives, is this: the virtue of consistency requires that any democrat articulate what it is that makes the cases different, and why that difference is important enough to override apparent similarities.

In 1927, while serving as Chancellor of the Exchequer (what Americans call the Secretary of the Treasury), Winston Churchill wrote an essay entitled "Consistency in Politics."[22] There, Churchill acknowledges that politicians must confront constantly changing circumstances. The political calculus of today can lead you to very different conclusions than it did yesterday. But Churchill says that while a politician's policies, and the pursuit of those policies, must change, a politician nevertheless can remain consistent. In fact, it is the most legitimate way to do so: "The only way a man can remain consistent amid changing circumstances is to change with them while preserving the same dominating purpose." Churchill's argument is that in the maelstrom of politics, consistency is not obvious. Circumstances change, and when they do, pursuing the same objectives, standing up for the same values, can sometimes require tactics that might appear to be inconsistent, when they might actually reflect the best possible consistency. The best of Great Britain's prime ministers, Churchill says, did exactly that.

None of these problems go away because we all affirm the goal of consistency. If anything, it makes them more prominent. But that affirmation does set the terms for the argument, and it is therefore likely to make that argument more productive. In contemporary American politics, any such common affirmation seems to be beyond the pale. For a strong partisan, as for anyone whose identity is strongly associated with one's tribe, one's party is not an extraneous factor: it is the only factor. For those partisans, the only outcome that matters is that their side wins. "Politics ain't beanbag," they say, and it never was. Anybody who argues otherwise is operating in an unreal world and certainly not the world we find ourselves in right now. These partisans are therefore inclined to spurn the virtue and practice of consistency. I don't expect that I have argued them out of this position, and I expect that what I am about to say will only increase those reactions.

Help from the Other Side

Our biases are unconscious. We do not consciously experience them, and we often quite sincerely affirm that they are not even there. We can accept that tribalism undermines democracy, and that considering the opposite is a useful metacognitive strategy for us to mitigate tribalism's effects, but we must also recognize that the deck is stacked against us. We can therefore use all the help we can get, even if that help is coming from an unwelcome source. If it is true that we are congenitally unable to perceive our own biases, then it is also true that others are far better able to perceive our biases than we are—and vice versa. Therefore, if consistency is indeed a democratic virtue, we need those on the other side.

We all know at some level that the way we perceive the world is different from the way the world is. We all have seen optical illusions that cause us to think something is the case when we can be shown that it really is not.[23] But it is extremely difficult to sustain that knowledge. As with the blue/black, white/gold dress, we cannot help but believe that the color we see is objectively *the* color. Our senses, we believe, simply and directly convey to us the world as it is. It's called *naive realism*. In almost precisely the same way, we know we are all subject to bias, but we forget this too. We think—again sincerely—that our evaluation is fair-minded and impartial. We think we are being objective and that therefore our judgments are sound and reliable.

But when we view the actions of others, and especially those in the other tribe, our reaction is exactly the opposite. We are naively skeptical.[24] We cannot know what is going on in others' heads, but we see their actions and we have some insight into their self-interest. Thus, we have no problem attributing their decisions—the very decision that they regard as objective—as really being driven by how they want to see the world and what they want to be the outcome.

Justin Kruger and Thomas Gilovich looked at married couples, debating teams, and teams playing video games and darts, asking them about how their partner, their teammate, and (in the latter cases) those on the other team would judge the importance of their contribution to the endeavor at hand. The researchers' "robust" finding was that in every case, "people consistently expect others to be motivationally biased." In every case, individuals expected that others they worked with, even those with whom they were cooperating (or were even married to!), would judge their participation in a way that was self-serving. They were especially likely to expect bias, however, when they were judging the actions of those on the other team. All of this is to say that we find it easy—if anything, we find it a little too easy—to perceive bias in others. That trait is especially pronounced when we are talking about *them* rather than *us*. Now again, those on the other side cannot know the internal thought process that led to our choice, and therefore they may see bias even when we have worked hard to mitigate its effect. This means they might well be mistaken, but that does not change the fact that others are more aware of our biases than we are. Self-interested explanations about which we are unconscious are far more apparent to them.

We know that our biases undermine our ability to perceive the world accurately. We know that we are unconscious of their operation and that even with metacognitive strategies, it is difficult for us to control those effects and impossible to overcome them. What is more, we know that tribalism has exacerbated our in-group bias. This has led to a downward spiral of distrust and animosity that makes it harder for us to sustain our democracy. If all this is true, then becoming aware of our biases and their operation helps us to become more aware of their impact on our thinking and makes it more possible for us to act consistently. German philosopher Immanuel Kant famously said that to will the end is to will the means.[25] If you really want a goal, you have to also want the steps that you need to take in order to achieve it. In this case, if we really want to achieve consistency, then we ought to seek out those strategies that can help us achieve that end. We should value those who have a perspective we do not have. We should therefore welcome the criticism of others.

Anybody who follows politics right now will likely view this proposal as driving right past farfetched and into ludicrousness. It's true that the prospects are dim for a useful exchange of helpful information with those we view with an antagonism verging on enmity. But it is not impossible. Of course, both parties have to be interested in such an exchange; it hardly works for one party to do all the criticizing or all the listening. (I say more about reciprocity in the chapter on charity.) This quest for consistency requires the other thinking virtues, too. Both parties have to start with the humility to recognize that all of us are subject to bias. They must likewise commit to reflect their opinions as honestly as they can. It might well be that for politicians and pundits, all the incentives point the other way, and therefore such a level of commitment is just not in the cards. But perhaps two old friends chatting over a cup of coffee might be able to. It would be difficult, to be sure, but the effort alone would constitute one little act that seeks to improve our democracy. And with enough such little acts, we might actually do so.

PART 3
Democratic Acting

As I've noted above, if honesty, humility, and consistency are virtues are that improve our democratic thinking, we can think of moral virtues as the means by which we improve our action. These action virtues come after the thinking virtues just as action should follow thoughtful consideration.

Again, the cardinal virtues are temperance, courage, justice, and prudence. Two of these four virtues are particularly important for understanding how a democrat ought to behave, especially right now: courage and temperance. Though they pull us in opposite directions—indeed, *because* they do—we need both to best achieve democratic action.

7
COURAGE

Courage is not simply one of the virtues but
the form of every virtue at the testing point.
—C. S. LEWIS

No one is going to argue about courage being on this list. Different societies don't always conceive of this virtue in exactly the same way, nor do they always point to the same kind of hero or exemplar, but there is not a culture, past or present, that does not value it. Every human life has risk. Every human being feels fear. Every human being also believes that there are ideals, values, and goods that are worth defending. When people recognize risk but choose to act anyway—act such that they seek to preserve that ideal, value, or good—that is courage.[1] Rushing into the heat of battle or into a burning building are the classic manifestations. But so were the actions of health care workers who served patients dying of COVID-19 when no one really knew what they were dealing with. In every case, individuals saw the risk to their well-being and safety, and even their lives, and they accepted that risk in order to achieve some greater good.[2]

Aristotle talked about courage like this. I have already mentioned his concept of the golden mean, the idea that virtue lies between two extremes, two vices. The concept is never clearer than when he is talking about courage. As he does repeatedly, Aristotle connects a virtue to one aspect of human endeavor. In this case, he focuses on battle as the place where both this virtue and its excess and deficiency are displayed. Someone who has too much confidence, or who creates or exacerbates danger when it is not necessary to do so, is not courageous but reckless. The risk is so great, and the prospect for success either so small or so trivial, that their action is more foolhardy than brave. Conversely, someone with too little regard for the good they claim to serve, and too much regard for their own safety and security, is a coward. Courage lies in the middle: it requires recognition of risk along with a willingness to accept it for the sake of a good that is not impossible to achieve.[3]

So defined, most would argue that it is myopic and false to consider courage only in the context of war. At the minimum, this concept of courage demands that we expand our concept of battle.

In 1961, the Freedom Riders rode buses into the segregated South to break state segregation laws (and test a Supreme Court ruling affirming integration). Every time their bus came into a station, they knew that they would be subject to arrest and quite likely physical attack. They could well have lost their lives. In truth, it is amazing that no one did. One bus was firebombed with the passengers on board and the exit door blocked; it was only fear that the gas tank would explode that caused the rioters to disperse and made it possible for the Freedom Riders to get out. In Birmingham and Montgomery, Alabama, they were attacked by mobs with bats, iron pipes, chains, and hammers. Several were admitted to local hospitals. After these harrowing events, each member of a second group of riders, led by Diane Nash, left a last will and testament before departing. These riders were arrested in Mississippi and sent to the infamous Parchman State Penitentiary. There, they were treated to much of the brutality for which the prison was known. But still, the riders kept coming. By the end, they numbered over four hundred.[4]

Many of the Freedom Riders did indeed consider themselves soldiers. To that extent, they fit within the constraints of Aristotle's definition. But they were soldiers of nonviolence. They had no weapons, and they never struck back against the mobs attacking them. This is not war in the sense that Aristotle (or almost anyone else) would conceive of it, but the riders' actions surely confirm that courage is not limited to the battlefield. Not only did the Freedom Riders display courage in exactly the sense Aristotle intended, but their actions truly epitomize the virtue.

The level of courage that these Americans displayed is rare. Most of us must simply stand in awe. But courage is not only manifested in such extreme circumstances. While all courage requires risk, not all courage requires risk to life and limb. And while all courage seeks to preserve some good, sometimes that good is not another's life but a social ideal.[5] In a functioning democracy, the risk is rarely that extreme, but courage is still required. Some call it social courage, moral courage, or civil courage. Of course, my inclination is to call it "democratic courage," but whatever you call it, the idea is that courage is not only manifested by heroes in heroic situations. It is also found in the little acts that makes democracy go.

Everyday Courage

Democratic courage is reflected, to one degree or another, in most political acts. Putting up a sign or bumper sticker; signing a petition; writing a letter to the editor; canvasing door to door; protesting. These acts require you to make a choice and present it publicly to your fellow citizens. There is some measure of risk in any such act.

One risk centers on the fact that you can be wrong. Neither the standard definition of courage, nor the democratic version, requires that you act for the right reason. You can be wrong about the end for which you act and still act courageously. There were certainly courageous Nazis, Confederates, or whatever other wrong side you want to name. Indeed, for all their villainy, one can even admit that those individuals who took over the planes on 9/11 met all the criteria for courage. In each case, the "greater good" they fought for was a moral scandal, but those actors recognized and accepted the danger inherent in their service to it.

Again, in democratic politics the risk associated with being wrong is not as great. But this risk is unavoidable; it simply has to be lived with. While the world is infinitely complex, politics requires that we make discrete choices—this candidate or that one; yes or no to this referendum—and make that choice based on limited information. We don't really know the candidate we choose, and unless we are policy analysts, we don't likely know everything about an issue put before us. (For that matter, referendums are often worded in ways that are designed to confuse voters). If we live long enough, and are involved in enough choices, all of us will come to recognize that the person or side we supported so ardently really was not the best choice.

On the other hand, recall Learned Hand's admonition in chapter 4: "The spirit of liberty is the spirit that is not too sure it is right." Of course it is easy to be too sure, to feel no need to hear, let alone engage with, any opposing position. And for Hand—and let's be honest, for us as well—that really is the more relevant danger. But courage is the midpoint, and that means there is also the possibility that we find ourselves so unsure, so overwhelmed by how much we do not know, that we don't act at all. We withdraw from the choice—even withdraw from politics altogether. In this case, our lack of certainty leads us to cowardice. In a democracy, we must recognize that we could be wrong but nevertheless must make the best decision we can with the information we have. The act of making that decision anyway, despite the risk of being wrong, is one more way in which democratic citizenship requires courage.

There is also the possibility that when you act in public, you risk making a fool of yourself. The courage that most of us must summon when we perform in public or give a toast at a wedding is operative in politics as well. In 1970, Maggie Kuhn was forced to retire at the age of 65. With a group of friends who were similarly treated, she founded the Gray Panthers, an organization dedicated to advancing the rights of older Americans. After the unwelcome end to her professional career, late in life, Kuhn became a novice and entered the hard and unforgiving world of politics. Her advice to her peers acknowledges the fear that comes along with such an entrance, but she insists that if one is to act politically, that fear must not stop us from speaking out. "Leave safety behind. Put your body on the line. Stand before the people you fear and speak your mind—even if your voice shakes. When you least expect it, someone may actually listen to what you have to say. Well-aimed slingshots can topple giants."[6]

Finally, speaking out, expressing your opinion, also entails the risk of retribution from those who don't agree with you. During the 2020 election, there were lots of stories about raised middle fingers; political signs being torn down; cars scratched; rocks thrown through windows; people coughing on other people, raising COVID-19 fears; and hard feelings between neighbors and family members.[7] Such actions are hardly unknown in our history, but in the recent presidential campaign, not to mention the aftermath of the election, they were more extensive and more severe than they had been in decades. The amount of courage needed to soldier on despite this risk is therefore likewise higher. Yet even under the best of circumstances, that risk exists. If you have ever been berated by someone at the door or on the phone for presenting your political view, you know that it is not always easy to get right back to doing it again. (All the more so when that person is related to you or lives across the street.)

The willingness to accept these risks and act anyway is democratic courage. It is part of what is required from us to make our democracy work. Of course, the risks associated with putting up a sign are minimal, and so too is the courage manifested by such an act. That is why I call it *everyday courage*. It is on the far end of the spectrum. And when democracy is working as it should, this is as it should be. But as the risk increases, so does the courage the act requires. The Freedom Riders exhibited extreme courage. In recent years, so have protesters in Hong Kong, Egypt, and a host of other countries. For all these actors, and many more just like them, the risks they took were anything but everyday.

Democratic Courage and Anger

What leads us to courage? What makes it possible for human beings to overcome the very powerful drive to avoid ridicule and embarrassment, let alone harm to life and limb? Researcher William Cuff investigated this question, and his answers will not surprise you. The most frequent feature shared by brave people is a concern for others. Tenacity, the idea that these people "do not give up easily," is a close second. In addition, courageous people tend to be resilient in the face of loss and have some sense that their lives are spiritually meaningful. Cuff also found that brave people can point to affirmation, either from others close to them (I believe in you!) or from themselves (I can do this!).[8] Research also confirms that people are more likely to be brave when that feeling is activated. That activation can come from friends, self-talk, and even from reading about other people's bravery.[9]

Still, all this only makes one predisposed to courage. At the moment of action, something must move that person to be brave.

And almost always, this comes from our emotional reaction to what we are seeing. The common understanding of democratic courage frequently references a strong and motivating feeling of anger. Silvia Osswald, Dieter Frey, and Bernhard Streicher call it "an integral component."[10] This is hardly surprising. Regardless of whether it led us to do something courageous, all of us can recall an emotional reaction to seeing a group singling someone out for abuse, a person in power treating someone unfairly, or some stranger mocking another because of who they are. We all have an innate sense of justice, and any time we see it violated, anger is almost an inevitable reaction. Similarly, if you are in one partisan tribe and you see someone torching a police station, or in the other and you see someone parading the Confederate flag in the Capitol Building, then something you think is important and valuable is being denigrated and belittled. Any such demonstration is liable to make you angry—and it is that anger that spurs us to courageous action. To be precise, sometimes that spur isn't anger, exactly. You can't really get angry at a virus or a fire. But you can feel a strong emotional and negative reaction toward something going on. That strong emotion drives you to react and to strive to stop it.

As tribal alignment draws us ever more into two separate and antagonistic tribes, partisan animosity rises. And since that animosity is always connected to a group of people (as opposed to an inanimate object), the feeling that rises along with it is always properly understood as anger. The more separate the two tribes become, the more opportunity for anger. In fact, as our partisan tribes become mirror opposites of each other, practically everything that that other tribe stands for, admires, likes, and values runs counter to our own preferences, values, and so on. Even ostensibly common commitments like patriotism, the responsibilities of citizenship, and in some cases, religious faith are expressed so differently that they only serve to manifest our division. Because we are so polarized, to act in one way is often simultaneously to act against the other. It is extremely difficult, given these circumstances, for any of us *not* to get angry—and as this anger rises, so too does courage.

Again, over the last four years, and especially during the 2020 campaign, we saw repeated examples of this. Two groups menacing each other during protests, campaign events, even school board meetings. Confrontations starting with ugly words, quickly escalating into threats and often genuine violence. As I noted in chapter 1, the deep instinct of defense and aggress causes many of these actions to foster a counterreaction and thus escalation. All those actors almost certainly believed that with their actions, they were defending something important. In short, the context is driving more and more of us to anger, which leads more of us to act courageously.

If this were all there was to it, if the new normal means that all of us see anger toward the other side as routine, if the democratic courage required of us is always more than the everyday variety, if we chronically risk aggression from the other side whenever we express a political point of view—if all this is true, then it would be very hard to argue that we need more of it. But polarization brings with it another kind of risk and another opportunity for courage, a kind of courage we absolutely could use more of right now.

Courage Within Our Tribe

Increasingly, we are far more likely to live in a social world lined up on one side or the other of the partisan divide. Many of us have no more than a few friends (and few opportunities to engage with anybody, friend or not) who are members of the other tribe. In this kind of society, it is all too easy for us to caricaturize and stereotype the other tribe, to belittle their opinions and point of view and to malign the things that are important to them. It becomes easier to think, believe, and say things that are at best overstated and at worst untrue. As we move away from democratic thinking to democratic action, we strive to put into practice the virtues of humility, honesty, and consistency. That requires both the courage to think critically about our own thinking and the courage to practice these virtues, especially when we are with those in our own tribe.

Tribalism is a natural human tendency. But the more powerfully it impacts our sense of who we are and what is important, the more it increases the power and liability of our biases. We reach conclusions more quickly, but those conclusions are more likely to be false. Yet while tribalism is natural, critical thinking is not. Challenging our assumptions, even those we hold most dear; recognizing that we have biases and striving to identify and even think past them; taking seriously points of view that we are so readily inclined to dismiss;

striving for consistency in the application of our principles: none of this is easy. In fact, questioning, let alone leaving aside our former foundations, can be unsettling, disagreeable, and even frightening. Like any form of courage, then, critical thinking presumes a risk. The disposition to do so anyway requires discipline and, yes, courage, especially if we are to challenge assumptions within our own tribe.

What exactly is at risk in such a situation? Quite a bit, actually. Whenever we find ourselves in situations like these it is usually with people we know. They are our coworkers, neighbors, friends, and family. With some, you have a relationship that you want to maintain. With others, especially neighbors or family, they are relationships that remain even when you don't necessarily want them to. Either way, the more attached we are to one tribe or the other, the more our many identities line up into one mega-identity, and the more our family, friends, and neighbors affirm the same identity, then the more likely everyone in that situation will reflect the same opinions and beliefs. Yet the more these things are true, the more we have invested in that identity and in those relationships, then the more we have to lose if something were to jeopardize them. In short, in speaking up to our own tribe, we risk ostracism; in our current context, that is a great risk indeed.

Ostracism

Tribalism reflects the very human need to belong, to be liked, to be part of a group. Ostracism exploits this aspect of our humanity. When someone is ostracized by the group, that person is singled out and then either physically excluded—sent away—or ignored. Sometimes this act is explicit, and the person is verbally rejected. More often it is not. In the latter case, the ostracized person starts with a vague feeling that something is wrong and then gradually comes to understand that the other members of the group are no longer communicating with them. Whether it be face-to-face conversations or phone calls, emails, or texts, contact ceases.

For the group, this is a powerful and effective strategy. Ostracism is a way of keeping order and maintaining a shared sense of cohesion and solidarity within the group. To the individual and to the group, ostracism says: "We do not tolerate that sort of behavior." It is so adaptive that according to Kipling Williams, ostracism "has been observed in almost all social species (e.g., primates, lions, wolves, buffalos, bees)."[11] It is also observed in just about every culture and group throughout human history. Individual spouses and family members, as well, will frequently resort to "the silent treatment" to convey their displeasure.

For the one on the receiving end, this rejection is an extremely negative experience. As I have noted before, this feeling has its roots in the earliest days of our species. Imagine how frightening it would have been to be abandoned by your tribe, alone and defenseless on that African savanna. Our reaction echoes that same deep-seated feeling. People who have been ostracized report feeling sad and angry. They say they have diminished feelings of control and self-esteem. Subjects who were ostracized as part of a scientific study manifested reactions similar to someone feeling threatened, including "significant increases" in blood pressure and cortisol levels. Another study showed subjects experiencing "increased activation of the dorsal anterior cingulate cortex . . . a region of the brain that shows activation during exposure to physical pain."[12] Finally, just as with physical pain, the pain associated with ostracism likewise throws us for a loop. We lose our bearings and can find it hard to concentrate: "The blow of social exclusion is much like the blow of a blunt instrument, and it causes a temporary state of cognitive deconstruction."[13]

In his book *Profiles in Courage*, then-senator John F. Kennedy describes the experience of Senator Edmond Ross. Ross was a Republican senator from Kansas. He was a senator of no great renown. "Practically nobody," Kennedy calls him.[14] But he was *the* Republican who voted against the articles of impeachment brought against Andrew Johnson. His one vote meant that the Senate would not achieve the two-thirds necessary to remove Johnson from office. Whether he made the right decision or not, Ross certainly thought he was doing the right thing. Moreover, he knew the grave risks associated with his decision. As he stood to render his verdict, Ross recounted, "I almost literally looked down into my open grave. Friendships, position, fortune, everything that makes life desirable to an ambitious man were about to be swept away by the breath of my mouth, perhaps forever."[15]

The only other point worth referencing here is just how accurate Ross's prediction turned out to be. After the vote, and Johnson's acquittal, Ross "clung unhappily to his seat in the Senate until the expiration of his term, frequently referred to as 'the traitor Ross,' and complaining that his fellow Congressmen, as well as citizens on the street, considered association with him 'disreputable and scandalous,' and passed him by as if he were 'a leper, with averted face and every indication of hatred and disgust.'"[16] The power of ostracism and the pain associated with the rest of Ross's short career only confirm the courage it took for him to make the choice he did. But the same risks are no less operative, and no less painful, in our contemporary politics. In *Why We're Polarized*, Ezra Klein references a recent interview with David Brooks. Brooks is a very well-known, well-respected, and well-compensated conservative, with a long list of bona fides. Yet he said that when he came out against Trump, "Suddenly I wasn't the kind of conservative all the other conservatives were, and so my social circles drifted away. . . . My weekends were just howling silences."[17]

Since so many of us are attached to one partisan mega-identity, getting cut off from that identity would mean becoming an outcast ourselves, and those silences would howl for us, too. That prospect would be frightening to anybody. In short, the costs associated with speaking out to those in our group are profound, and given our contemporary climate, perhaps even worse than usual.

So play this out. Say you're at a party in your neighbor's backyard. You have been here many times before. You know the kids' names, and you know where they keep the cooler with the beer. Someone pipes up about some current controversy. You hear a few murmurs of agreement, and a few quick references to the fact that this issue demonstrates yet again why the other side is so benighted, wrong, immoral, what have you. You waver, but you have heard this rant just one too many times. It's not just that it is wrong. It reflects what to you is a kind of cultish adherence. You don't argue, exactly; you just raise questions. Is it really that simple? What about this argument on the other side? What about this piece of evidence?

Even before you finish, it is immediately clear that you are in a minority of one. The conversation ramps up a little.[18] People dismiss your point of view. Things get a little more heated and a little more personal: "Sometimes I think you like to start arguments." "Why are you always so hot to defend those people?" You also hear rejoinders that are more verbal talismans than arguments (e.g., "my cold dead hands," "trans women are women"). At some point there is an awkward pause. The conversation moves back to more mundane things, but there is a chill in the air, and even before you leave, you have a palpable sense that your friends no longer see you in quite the same way. From then on, it's clear that they are not as interested in staying connected. Emails and texts dry up, and the conversations while walking the dog that used to go on for minutes now conclude after a short and bloodless "hi," and sometimes not even that. You feel it in your gut. You have been ostracized.

Tend and Befriend

What happens next? How do you react to an experience like this? As with any pain, the overriding objective is to make it stop. But how? Some ostracized people choose to join a different group. The feeling that you have been treated unfairly sparks its own kind of anger, and you think you might be better off without your old tribe. In effect, you reject the group that has rejected you. You find another tribe where you can feel like you belong. Williams notes that sometimes people are so bereft and desperate for connection that it leads them to join a cult or some other extreme group.[19]

But these are your friends and neighbors. You have had a lot of good times together. Plus, you drive by their house every day. Even if you wanted to, how possible would it really be to completely separate from them? More likely, therefore, even if you feel an initial sense of rage, it will be followed by a more judicious strategy to get things back to the way they were: what Williams calls "tend and befriend."[20] The ostracized individual initiates interactions that seek to diminish bad feelings and demonstrate that she is committed to, and once again acceptable to, the group. She seeks to make it clear that she affirms the group's shared identity. In short, the ostracized person shows that she is contrite and willing once again to conform.

So how might this "tend and befriend" effort work for the one who spoke up at the barbeque? A recent experiment by Kelly Garrett and his colleagues offers one likely account.

The researchers chose subjects who identified as either Democrats or Republicans and told them that the experiment was about completing tasks with other people online. They were asked to make an online profile and then read and interact with other people's profiles, which they could only do by clicking a "like" button. In reality, there was no group. All the other profiles were created by the experimenters, and a computer randomly assigned the subject to either an ostracized group or a control group. People in the control group would receive several likes; ostracized people would receive only one. This was the extent of the ostracism the individual was made to feel. There was no connection to the subject's partisan identity. Moreover, there was no face-to-face interaction associated with the whole enterprise. There was only the small number of likes that the subject received. For all this, the impact was still demonstrable.

Participants were next asked to read a statement that corrected misperceptions commonly associated with their partisan tribe. Regarding the 2016 presidential election, Republicans read a statement that challenged the claim that there was widespread voter fraud, while Democrats were reminded that there was no evidence that Russians had directly altered vote tallies. Then they were asked questions that reflected on the statement they had just read. The answers they gave reflected the impact of feeling ostracized: "Ostracism promoted partisan falsehood endorsement in the face of a message carefully crafted to promote accuracy. When ostracized, both Democrats and Republicans were more likely to endorse party-line falsehoods about election-related issues."[21] In short, those who had felt ostracized unconsciously implemented the "tend and befriend" strategy and were therefore more inclined to endorse a falsehood associated with their tribe.

That feeling of ostracism was generated by what the subject thought was a group of individuals she had not and would not meet, one that had nothing to do with her partisan identity. Nevertheless, this experience led that individual to work harder to mend fences with her partisan tribe. As the researchers noted, "The fact that a short virtual interaction with strangers in an apolitical context can make someone more likely to express support for a false political claim in the face of detailed counter-evidence is striking."[22] One could readily conjecture that this effect would only be more powerful if any of these conditions were changed—as would be the inclination to affirm partisan falsehoods.

It is clear enough that when someone manifests the courage necessary to dispute claims made by their own tribe, there is a genuine possibility that such an act might result in ostracism. To assuage the pain that such a response might engender, the person who was courageous could end up adopting a "tend and befriend" strategy, seeking to rejoin the group rather than separate. But if Garrett and his colleagues are correct, that means that the brave individual who stood up for truth and fairness might very well end up going so far as to reaffirm the very falsehoods that she was responding to in the first place. The risk, therefore, is that courage will only leave the individual and the group further cemented in those same partisan falsehoods. If this is true, if it is even a genuine possibility, then why be brave at all?

Why Be Brave?

Courage presupposes risk. If there are no risks, there is no need for courage. The fact that courage can backfire and lead us to double down on the worst inclinations of our tribal identities is another manifestation of that risk. Serious, to be sure. It ought to give us pause and make us deliberate and thoughtful. If in order to avoid this risk we fail to address our tribalism, both within ourselves and within our fellow tribe members, we spurn one means we have to step back from the abyss and restore our democracy. Without courage, we cannot extricate ourselves from the doom loop. If risk is everywhere, then we must determine which risk we choose and how best to manage it.

If courage can be invested in outcomes that are wrong, even immoral, then that is sufficient reason to conclude that courage as a virtue does not, and should not, exist on its own. Aristotle argued that a person who is only partially virtuous is not really virtuous at all. Virtue is an all-or-nothing enterprise.[23] In the first place, humility, honesty, and consistency require that we think carefully and critically about our beliefs and values. There is no doubt that such an effort requires courage even when we remain only in our own heads. When we do move from democratic thinking to democratic action, we need courage once again to make our commitments to humility, honesty, and consistency genuine. If those commitments wither away in the face of any risk, then they aren't really commitments at all. Still, courage functions better—it is more likely to judge the circumstances and find the proper mean between recklessness and cowardice—if the thinking virtues are operative. If we are humble, honest, and consistent, then we are more likely to better understand, and better respond to, the risks associated with democratic courage.

When we strive to make all these virtues operative, we are more likely to be deliberate about our own biases and about when, how, and to whom we make our objections known. This means that a courageous person should strive to be a self-aware and self-assured individual, one who speaks out but does so in a way that is less likely to cause hard feelings, let alone rupture friendships. (Maybe the person at the neighborhood party pulls aside the instigator to present her case or asks to meet for coffee another time. Maybe she tempers her comment with a dose of humor and self-deprecation.) A person like this, who is brave but not reckless, prudent but not calculating, self-aware but not self-absorbed, is better able to determine whether and how to intervene—how best to affirm the goal that she believes in while maintaining her relationships and identity.

Sometimes individuals simply have no choice: despite the pain of ostracism, they must leave their tribe. But that occasion as well is better understood and undertaken by someone who is honest and humble. To say the least, a person like this is significantly less likely to deal with ostracism by accepting the lies they previously spurned or succumbing to a more extreme group.[24] In sum, attention to all the virtues is the best way to navigate the risks associated with our present condition, risks that are all around us, and from which there is no easy out.

Finally, recall what Madison said about faction: "Liberty is to faction as air is to fire." In a free society, we are going to disagree, and we are going to argue about those disagreements. Hearing opinions you don't like is an inescapable part of living in a democracy. If our democracy is going to function, let alone function well, we have to be able to hear those opinions, both from those in our tribe and those outside it, with some measure of acceptance and self-control. No matter how strongly we identify with our tribe, we all must accept that ostracism is simply not a legitimate response to an opinion we don't like. This search for democratic self-control leads immediately to the next democratic action virtue: temperance.

8

TEMPERANCE

The war against democracy begins by the destruction of the democratic temper.
—DOROTHY THOMPSON

A quick review: Risk is endemic to democratic politics, so we need courage to make politics go. When politics is operating as it should, the risk is minimal, so not much courage is required. (Call it everyday courage.) But there are also political acts that require greater risk and therefore greater courage. That risk can extend to physical danger, even to our very lives, as it did for the Freedom Riders and does right now for protesters in countries all over the world.

Whenever one is confronted with risk, in or out of politics, you need some reason, some motivation, to act anyway. The greater the risk, the more that something is required. And as I showed, in most cases, that something is anger—anger at what is happening or at what people are doing. When we experience this emotional reaction, we are more likely to be courageous. For my purposes, this connection means that just as risk is part of democratic politics, so, too, is anger. It is, in the words of Peter Lyman, "the essential political emotion."[1]

Anger Is Democratic

In the American context, anger is written into our political DNA. The freedoms of speech, the press, and religious exercise, all articulated in the First Amendment, mean that people have the right to say and do things with which many of us will disagree. And sometimes that disagreement will be strong, even vehement. Take the recent example of Nazis marching in Charlottesville, Virginia, in 2017. Their actions and chants made most of us very angry indeed. But most of us accept that as visceral as our reaction might be, as long as that march remained lawful, we had no right to stop them. The point is universal. Anytime a politician talks about assault weapons or abortion, or for that matter practically anytime anyone expresses an opinion about some policy debate, that talk will touch on someone's sense of identity and well-being, and it will make them angry. Politicians know this, and from time immemorial, they have used that anger to spur their supporters to vote, to work on their campaigns, and to give them money. Of course, not every political speech or act will create this anger. Sometimes politicians give speeches in which nothing they say rises above the anodyne or contentless. But when they actually decide to articulate their point of view, someone is going to disagree with it, and insofar as that statement implicates their values and sense of identity, some people are going to do more than disagree: they will react with anger.

This reaction, too, is part of our First Amendment freedoms. The rights to assemble and to petition government for a redress of grievance are grounded in the recognition that anger is the inevitable by-product of governmental action, and a free people must have the right to express that anger. Merriam-Webster defines "grievance" as "a cause of distress (such as an unsatisfactory working condition) felt to afford reason for complaint or resistance."[2] Synonyms for grievance include "injustice, injury, wrong," and all of these words convey "an act that inflicts undeserved hurt."[3] As I will show, the notion of some "undeserved hurt" is at the core of modern and ancient notions of what causes anger. But the point is that the Framers understood that grievances will be the product of government action and decisions, and that some of those grievances, at least, will rise to the level of anger. A free society gives citizens the right to articulate their anger to the government.

The right to assemble concerns the means by which most citizens express that grievance. Think back to protests you have witnessed or taken part in. For some, the event is just an exciting break from the status quo. But most of those participating are marching because they are angry, either about something that has happened or that might happen. Very rarely is the goal to present some specific objective—there is not a lot of opportunity for nuance or detail in a chanted slogan. Instead, most often the goal of a march is to convey one thing: there are a lot of us who are very angry about a certain something. We are organized and we represent countervailing political power.

In sum, from the very beginning of our politics, we accepted the fact that anger is inbred and inescapable. We understand that sometimes, we will become angry in reaction to what others have said or done. We know, as well, that we have the right to express that anger, even as we understand that this act, too, will evoke anger in others. All of this is simply part of what we sign up for when we live in a democracy.

At the same time, limits on that anger are part of our Constitutional rights, too. We *petition* the government for redress. Returning to Merriam-Webster, the verb "petition" means "to present a formal written request."[4] The word "petition" (rather than "demand," for example) sets rhetorical limits regarding the way one's anger can legitimately be expressed. In short, while "request" and "anger" can, with difficulty, go together, "request" and "rage" simply cannot. In the same way, the right to assemble includes the adverb "peaceably." Here, too, the right to express one's anger is only acceptable if that protest stays within the limits of public order. One's civil rights end when that qualifier is no longer operative. Here again, democracy walks a fine line: anger is an inescapable dimension of democratic life, but expression of that anger is only legitimate if it operates within limits.

These limits may not just be prudent for public welfare but necessary to sustain a democracy. In his book *American Rage*, Steven Webster presents evidence that people who are angry, whether it be about politics or anything else, have less trust in government. They also demonstrate less commitment to democratic norms and values—most relevantly, tolerance—and have less respect for minority rights.[5] Angry people are more likely to "mentally retreat" into their partisan identity, showing less openness to other points of view, less friendliness toward the individuals who hold them, and more loyalty to their own tribe. None of these outcomes ought to come as a surprise. Webster's research echoes evidence that I presented earlier. But the point worth emphasizing is that all these behaviors reinforce our anger, which in turn reinforces the behavior. Worse, these behaviors foster and extend the nation's doom loop. Without some way to control its effects, anger feeds on itself and makes democratic society ever more difficult to sustain.

The relevance of this need for control is clear enough. You don't need me to tell you that right now our nation is very angry. As we continue to separate into two tribes, arguments about policy become inseparable from identity. To say that your position on gun control is wrong is to say that *you* are wrong. To fight against my position on climate change is to fight against *me*. We cannot *not* take it personally. And none of us responds to such an assault with equanimity. Polarization breeds anger, which breeds more polarization, and so on. As society has polarized, progressively, chronically, our nation has gotten angrier.

Here, too, we saw more than enough evidence of this in the 2020 campaign. People who supported Donald Trump were very angry: they believed that they had been disrespected and ignored and that their candidate had been treated unfairly by a domineering and corrupt establishment. People who supported Joe Biden were very angry: they believed that Donald Trump had failed miserably to control the pandemic, exacerbated the racial divisions in our society, and scorned long-standing norms and values that help maintain American democracy. A poll conducted just before the 2020 election found that 32 percent of Americans (one in three) said that they were experiencing anger, and those findings were fairly consistent across demographic groups.[6] If that doesn't strike you as a particularly high number, note that the same poll found that slightly fewer people (31 percent) said that they were experiencing fear. In other words, in the middle of pandemic, one more prolific and lethal than anything our nation has seen in one hundred years, slightly more people said they were angry than afraid.

That anger was reflected in the candidates themselves. The disaster that was the first presidential debate of the 2020 campaign revealed a level of animosity virtually unknown in American presidential politics. And in keeping with Webster's analysis, this event fomented even more extreme reactions on the part of the citizenry, which only served to further undermine democracy: diminished faith in the electoral process; yelling matches and fights breaking out whenever the two sides met; the rise of armed protests, orchestrated traffic jams, and partisan "poll watchers." All this behavior finds its acme in the events of January 6, 2021. To my mind, there is little doubt that the insurrection was as irrational as it was undemocratic. But there is even less doubt that those breaking into the Capitol building manifested extreme, unprecedented, and virulent anger.

Democracy requires both that we accept that anger as inevitable and that we manage it, setting external and internal limits for how, when, and where it is expressed. Without those limits, democracy becomes unstable and ultimately unsustainable. For most of us, the evidence is all too clear that we are not toeing that line. On the contrary, anger is tangled up with our tribalism, and as the doom loop progresses downward, its effects continue without pause, and the future well-being of our society becomes ever more insecure. In terms we have discussed previously, we need to find and commit to a golden mean that is especially appropriate to, and useful to, our precarious circumstances.

Aristotle on Anger

Since we are looking for an Aristotelian mean, it makes sense to reference the philosopher himself. Aristotle defines anger as "an impulse, accompanied by pain, to a conspicuous revenge for a conspicuous slight directed without justification towards what concerns oneself or towards what concerns one's friends. . . . It must always be attended by a certain pleasure—that which arises from the expectation of revenge."[7] Anger results, Aristotle says, when someone expresses illegitimate, unwarranted disrespect toward me and mine: "The persons with whom we get angry are those who laugh, mock, or jeer at us, for such conduct is insolent."[8] When that happens, someone undermines my social status unjustly, and that leads to anger. Whenever such an act occurs, my thoughts inevitably turn to revenge—the desire to get back at the perpetrator, to even the score.

Now in the first place, Aristotle's definition echoes the definition I presented earlier: anger is the result of some "undeserved hurt." The eminent psychologist Richard Lazarus presented an almost identical account. Lazarus argued that anger is the product of any assault on one's ego identity: "a demeaning offense against me and mine."[9] But note also that Aristotle reflects the democratic belief that a virtuous person can still be angry. Anger is not inherently illegitimate. Aristotle maintains that it must be managed with prudence, like every other natural inclination, but it is not something that we should always and everywhere strive to overcome.

This was hardly a universal opinion among the ancients. The Stoics, founded in Greece but reaching their zenith in Rome, argued that anger was unmanly and reflected a loss of control. Moreover, they argued that the effort to be angry and in control, to be angry but not too angry, was a fool's errand. The Stoics held that any such impulse must be fought from the outset. In Seneca's words, "The enemy [that is, anger] must be met and driven back at the outermost frontier-line: for when he has once entered the city and passed its gates, he will not allow his prisoners to set bounds to his victory."[10] At about the same time, Jesus said that "whosoever is angry with his brother [some translations include the words *without cause*] will be subject to judgment" (Matt. 5:22). Jesus, too, says that anger is dangerous. Once indulged, it can easily overwhelm our reason and lead us to do things that we later regret. The most prudent and most virtuous strategy is to reject it at the first moment.

Aristotle knows, of course, that anger can cause us to act rashly, leading to a result that is far worse than any apparent slight. Conversely, it can also cause us to nurse our grievances for far too long, becoming either sullen or obsessed, again diminishing ourselves in the process. But virtue is not found in rejecting anger. On the contrary, Aristotle says that "those who do not show anger at things that ought to arouse anger are regarded as fools." Virtue is a matter of showing anger "in the right way, at the right time [and] at the right person."[11] Such an effort, like most of the virtues, is fraught and extremely difficult, but Aristotle says it is more legitimate than suppressing the feeling and not acting on it at all.

The other important point is that by zeroing in on status and disrespect, Aristotle argues that anger is not merely some animalistic response. In fact, he says that animals can't really experience anger. Anger is an emotion, yes, but that emotion depends on an assessment of the situation, and that assessment can only take place within a social context. Aristotle might well be wrong about this. Given that even bees practice ostracism, it would seem that many animals are quite capable of assessing social context. But the point is that for Aristotle our status is socially constructed, and therefore so too is the sense that that status has been disrespected. Because anger is therefore partially a product of reason and judgment, Aristotle believes that reason and judgment can likewise control its expression.

No one would dispute, I think, that unjust slights do indeed make us angry. The fact that people offer "respect" to a competitor (as Donnie said to Conlan after their boxing match in the movie *Creed*), and on the other hand speak of "throwing shade" or feeling "dissed," is evidence of how much Aristotle's description continues to resonate. For that matter, I doubt there is anyone who hasn't lain awake nursing their desire for revenge for some mistreatment.

Still, most would also agree that this is a strangely limited notion of what anger is and how it is engendered. As I have noted, Aristotle has a habit (bad, in my opinion) of restricting specific virtues to specific domains of human life. Just as courage is limited to warfare, anger is all about assaults to one's status. Our modern understanding rejects the idea that human behavior fits into such neat and distinct boxes. On the contrary, as I noted in the previous chapter, we believe that a virtue like courage is manifested and justly celebrated in all sorts of ways. And while we would acknowledge that disrespect toward ourselves and those we love is one cause for our anger, it is hardly the only one. Only if we read Aristotle's notion of "one's own" to include everything that we care about—including our values and beliefs—does it mesh with our understanding. This means that the feeling we get when someone insults us and when that person insults something we highly value (the flag, say, or our faith, or science) is one and the same: it can properly be called anger.[12]

Since Aristotle's understanding of when someone gets angry is limited, so too is his golden mean. A person who is both angry *and* virtuous, that is, one who responds appropriately to a perceived slight, is a person of good temper. The actions and disposition of such a person fall between what Aristotle calls "irascibility" and "inirascibility." Here again, I don't find this framing particularly useful. (When was the last time you heard somebody call someone inirascible?) But whatever its general utility, this model certainly does not serve our specific purpose. Our objective is to find a golden mean appropriate for democratic life.

If anger is part of our democratic DNA, then too little anger means that we are indifferent to our society, to the norms and values that our nation espouses, and to our very human sense of justice and fairness. A person who is never angry simply does not care enough about any of these things. That is the deficiency. But while apathy can certainly be a problem for a democracy, it is not *our* problem. *Our* problem is too much anger. So much, in fact, that it appears to be part of a doom loop that undermines and ultimately destroys that same society. That is the excess. I am calling the mean that lies between these two extremes *democratic temperance*. This form of temperance recognizes that reactions to governmental action and to arguments that belittle our identity or our values are inevitable and even possibly legitimate, but it seeks to control those reactions so that they do not overwhelm reason and cause us to act in ways that damage our humanity.[13] In this case, *democratic* temperance lies between rejecting anger completely and allowing it to consume us all—a point that we can identify between the anger that simply goes with the territory and a level of anger that destroys our society.

Anger Versus Hatred

We need to figure out how to stop the doom loop, how to control the anger such that it stays within the mean, conforming to Aristotle's goal of being angry correctly (or, if you will, democratically). Here again, I want to start by returning to his works.

Aristotle's definition of anger is from his *Rhetoric*. In that same work, he also distinguishes anger from hate. He doesn't say much, but the differences he outlines are useful for this question. I think they help us define the conditions under which anger goes too far.

> We may hate people merely because of what we take to be their character. Anger is always concerned with individuals . . . whereas hatred is directed also against classes: we all hate any thief and any informer. Moreover, anger can be cured by time; but hatred cannot. The one aims at giving pain to its object, the other at doing him harm; the angry man wants his victims to feel; the hater does not mind whether they feel or not. . . . Much may happen to make the angry man pity those who offend him, but the hater under no circumstances wishes to pity a man whom he has once hated: for the one would have the offenders suffer for what they have done; the other would have them cease to exist.[14]

Aristotle says that hatred and enmity can develop from anger, but they are not the same thing, and the latter is not merely an overabundance of the former. Anger is toward an individual, toward some person who treated us unjustly. But hatred can also be toward a group. We all hate thieves, he says, even if we don't know a particular thief and that person never stole anything of ours. Second, he says that anger can recede; time passes and the injury just doesn't seem as important anymore. Hatred abides. It becomes part of who we are, part of our very identity.[15] Third, we seek to cause pain to the person who made us angry as a way to compensate for the pain they caused us. That is the point of revenge. Once that retaliation has taken place, once a sense of justice is restored, anger recedes, and even reconciliation is possible. But with hatred, we are not interested in reciprocity. Using language that is cold and ominous, Aristotle says that we simply want that person or group to "cease to exist."

It is a tribute to Aristotle's uncanny powers of observation to note that neo-Nazis and other hate groups recruit and develop converts to their cause in ways that are fully recognizable in Aristotle's description. Such groups tie their identity directly to those they are not: we are those who hate this group and this is why. They offer a tribe, and an accompanying sense of belonging, to individuals who are without one. As I noted in the last chapter, those who feel ostracized are particularly vulnerable to recruitment. These groups start, moreover, with the idea that there is not and cannot be any meaningful dimension of individuality within the hated group. If a person is Black, Jewish, Muslim, or what have you, then just like Aristotle's thief, that is sufficient reason to hate. "They're all alike" is virtually the calling card of a racist.

In his book *Prisoners of Hate*, Aaron T. Beck lays out the steps by which one comes to identify with a group that hates another group: "First, the members of the opposition are *homogenized*; they lose their identities as unique individuals. Each victim is interchangeable, and all are disposable. In the next stage the victims are *dehumanized*. . . . Finally, they are *demonized* as the embodiment of evil."[16] Just as Aristotle says we want those we hate to cease to exist, neo-Nazis want to rid the world, or at least society, of the groups they have marked. They look to a race war as a way to cleanse society of the hateful element. A reformed white supremacist said, "At some point, I thought that society was so contaminated with liberalism and Marxism that it kind of had to be reset, there was this thing about killing every non-white that I felt was the logical end to our world-scale project."[17]

We are not all Nazis. Most of us do not view the other with that level of hatred. We must admit, though, that Aristotle's distinctions reflect our society's current condition. As I have noted, both sides feel partisan anger and distrust. That anger is not a reaction to any one particular action or grievance. It is driven less by policy differences and more by our stereotyping and dehumanizing beliefs about the other side. In a poll conducted by the Public Religion Research Institute just before the 2020 election, 81 percent of Republicans believed that "the Democratic party has been taken over by Socialists," and 78 percent of Democrats believed that "the Republican party has been taken over by Racists."[18] The other tribe is a group characterized by a different label, an epithet, one that makes its members even easier to hate. Republicans' feelings about socialists and Democrats' toward racists is just like Aristotle's feeling about thieves. He didn't have to meet any to know that he hated them. In sum, for most of us, and especially those of us with strong partisan leanings, anger has (at minimum) become awfully similar to hate.

The effects of this hatred on our democracy are clearly negative and readily apparent. I have covered some of this ground as well. But the point is fairly straightforward: if you think the other side is genuinely loathsome, then you naturally feel more unwilling to accept their victory in any election, or their right to rule as a result. The fate of the nation you love, the values that you are so firmly committed to, would be too damaged, too subject to destruction, for you to just say "Oh, well," and wait until next time. Hatred thus makes us more willing to consider breaking the rules, and even resorting to violence, to keep that from happening. I can't imagine how one can consider the events of January 6, 2021, without feeling a wave of recognition. When anger changes to hate, democracy becomes progressively unsustainable, tenuous, and subject to acts just like that one.

But it is not only at the extremes that hatred undermines democracy. Democratic politics requires coalition building and compromise to operate successfully. If we are to achieve our political objectives, we must work together with those who are different and those with whom we frequently disagree. The motto of the Congressional Black Caucus is this: "Black people have no permanent friends, no permanent enemies, just permanent interests." In democratic terms, this notion of impermanence is precisely the point. In Aristotelian terms, this impermanence is precisely what becomes impossible; hatred leads us to regard our opponents as enemies, and our enemies as permanent. Under such conditions, democratic politics becomes impossible as well.

In their book *How Democracies Die,* Steven Levitsky and Daniel Ziblatt frame the point this way: "Coalitions of the like-minded are important, but they are not enough to defend democracy. The most effective coalitions are those that bring together groups with dissimilar—even opposing—views on many issues. They are built not among friends but among adversaries. . . . When we agree with our political rivals at least some of the time, we are less likely to view them as mortal enemies."[19] Hate, then, is the other extreme, the other specifically democratic vice. The golden mean for a democracy is therefore an anger that does not descend into hatred. Call it democratic anger—and call the virtue that helps us stay merely angry, and keep that anger in check, democratic temperance.

Temperance-Building Habits

Nobody would argue that outright hatred between members of the nation's two political parties is a great recipe for sustaining a democratic society. If nothing else, seen alongside Aristotle's descriptions of anger and hatred, recent events demonstrate how far along the doom loop we find ourselves. But Aristotle's distinctions can also help us identify what we need to do to step back. Anytime anger becomes abiding and effectively permanent; anytime it becomes more than simply an emotion we feel but rather part of who we are; anytime it is expressed toward a group, rather than an individual; and anytime we want to do the other side harm—when any of these things happen, we are no longer merely angry but hateful.

So let's just say that we (enough of us, anyway) agree that things have gone too far. While most of us continue to believe that our feelings toward the other side are justified, even indisputable, and that theirs toward us are the product of ignorance, malevolence, mental illness, or some combination thereof—and for that matter, even if we are correct to think so—we acknowledge that for the sake of our democratic society, we need to step back from the brink. How do we do that? How do we develop the self-restraint that keeps anger from becoming hate? Let me mention two ideas: one thing we can do, and one that we should stop doing.

First, what we can stop doing: we can stop indulging in media that feed into our anger. Websites, social media, talk radio, and television all have plenty of examples of a very successful business model, one that in a previous book I called "partisan infotainment."[20] This kind of media endorses and feeds our feeling of tribal identity. Indeed, that is their product. Such presentations make us feel part of a group, one that is smarter, more patriotic, and more moral than the other one. It does this primarily by making us angry at the other tribe. There is pleasure in this experience, in the feeling of belonging—to being one of the friends in *Fox and Friends*, for example—and in feeling superior, seeing our side get the better of somebody who is part of the other side, to *own* them. And make no mistake: there is pleasure in the anger that we feel toward the other side. Aristotle knew this. This is exactly how hate groups operate: by surrounding the recruit with friends, news, and entertainment (perhaps all three words should be in quotation marks) that all serve to reinforce this feeling of animus and that leave no room for any countervailing feeling or evidence. The more we take in these experiences, the more difficult it becomes to see past this narrative.

Purveyors of this kind of pleasure do very well for themselves. But there are lots of pleasurable experiences that we know are not good for us. This is one of them. In a recent experiment, Hunt Allcott and his colleagues paid people a good amount of money to stay off Facebook, cold turkey, for four weeks. Almost none of the subjects found this easy; some had been going onto the site frequently, even several times a day. But after the period was over, most subjects said they had a better sense of well-being and, more importantly for my purposes, felt less animosity toward those on the other side of the partisan divide.[21]

Facebook is only one platform, of course, and there is no guarantee of similar results if someone were to withdraw from television, say, or talk radio. Facebook's sophisticated algorithms work to connect us with people who are part of the same tribe, though, so for most of us, the "news" and opinions we see on Facebook are no less part of the fabric of tribal reinforcement than other media are. It would be better for all of us if we could diminish our exposure. Being told over and over that those in the other tribe are hateful or idiotic makes it progressively easier for us to believe it. If this appears too difficult, if you feel too invested in one or more of these outlets, you could start by never forgetting that you are being sold a product: you are buying the pleasure that comes from having your tribal identity and your accordant sense of superiority reinforced. (You might also consider that such a product does not need to be associated with the truth for this business model to be successful.)

Those who can limit their consumption of that model would likely find themselves more content. They might also find themselves with some newfound free time. There is something better, something positive, we can do with that time that can further help us develop temperance: we can join a group, one that remains outside the tribal alignment of American culture. Of course, I think that it is a good thing that we Americans devote time and treasure to supporting the candidates and causes we believe in, but in this case, with respect to stepping back from hatred and developing democratic temperance, meeting regularly with people from your own tribe is not likely to have much of an impact. In service of that specific end, therefore, I suggest that you join an organization that is genuinely (and not merely putatively) nonpartisan.[22]

Organizations like these are not particularly easy to find. The partisanization of American life extends far down into the nooks and crannies of our civil society. Neighborhood organizations, churches, and even a host of volunteer organizations all reinforce our preexisting tribal identities. But those alternatives are out there: think adult recreational sports leagues, community bands, animal shelters, literacy programs, or similar nonprofits that depend on volunteers. Whatever the group is, the objective is to find one that brings you into contact with real people who share at least one of the same passions you do—and therefore belong to one of the same little tribes—but who are nevertheless members of the other big partisan tribe. If you have chosen wisely, this one important commonality aside, you will meet people who do not think like you do or believe or value all the same things. They are representatives of the very group that most of us find so easy to hate.

In this context, though, we are meeting such people face to face, as individuals, with aspects of their identity that do not fit neatly within our stereotypes. What is more, in a group, we need to work together. Normally, we must discuss, debate, and collaborate in order to make decisions that help the group achieve a common goal—working on the annual fundraiser, setting the schedule for the coming season, and so forth. While all this is going on, I expect you will find that hate is harder. Once you come to know individuals as individuals and not merely as modular cutouts of the group you don't like, you come to see that, just like you, they don't know everything, they love their families and their country, and they are doing the best they can.

It is worth noting that for those leaving neo-Nazi groups, this kind of experience is precisely what causes them to reject their formerly hate-filled lives. These individuals come to have enough interactions with people from the groups they hate that they can no longer see them as simply one more representative of that group. One former neo-Nazi said, "My change came with just human beings being human beings to me when I needed it the most—they didn't even realize it."[23] Calling these individuals human beings means that they were not necessarily saints. Some probably were, committing to the humanity that they knew (despite all evidence to the contrary) lay under all that hatred. Most were probably no better than the rest of us. Regardless, through such encounters the neo-Nazis could no longer sustain the drivel that lay at the core of their identity. Individuals became individuals, no longer just another Black or Jew or what have you. Once that happened, their group stereotype crumbled before their eyes, and with that, so did the hatred.

For the Hate That Remains

Both of these strategies would no doubt help us move back from hatred and toward a more manageable level of anger. But I fear that they make temperance sound easier than it really is: turn off Tucker Carlson once in a while, find your old cornet from high school, and you are on your way. I don't want to leave you with that impression. Our society is very hateful right now, with dim prospects for improvement. Nor do I want to imply that I am somehow immune to these emotions. Over the past few years, I have confessed feelings of extreme anger, at least bordering on hatred, to myself, my family, and my friends. Whatever side you find yourself on, I bet you could say the same. Our animosity toward the other tribe is deep, abiding, and probably growing. It will take a great deal of self-restraint from a great many of us to arrest that progression. Strategies like those I have mentioned are probably not up to the task. In his first inaugural address, Abraham Lincoln pleaded to citizens in the South, "I am loath to close. We are not enemies, but friends. We must not be enemies. Though passion may have strained it must not break our bonds of affection. The mystic chords of memory, stretching from every battlefield and patriot grave to every living heart and hearthstone all over this broad land, will yet swell the chorus of the Union, when again touched, as surely they will be, by the better angels of our nature."[24] This appeal for democratic temperance, nearly perfect in its eloquence, did precisely nothing to stop the Civil War.

Lincoln's impotent appeal drives home another point. There has always been behavior that can quite predictably, and often legitimately, bring people to feel hatred. To note again the Charlottesville example, what are we to say about those who marched with tiki torches, chanting, "Jews will not replace us"? If such a vile and deeply stupid phrase does not merit hatred in exactly the terms Aristotle outlined, it is hard to see why not. If sustaining our democracy means swallowing such bile with stoic equanimity, then for some, and perhaps most, Americans, that may well be a bridge too far. And because so many of us are inclined to hate not just Nazis but about half of our fellow citizens, we might well be stuck. The doom loop will just keep on looping.

Still, even if we cannot turn completely from hatred to anger, perhaps we can move a little further away from the former. For Aristotle, again, hatred is different from anger because the latter means that you want to cause pain; hatred means that you want to do that group in, to have them cease to exist. Perhaps if we don't cross that line, we are still within the golden mean. At the very least, this might be a way for us to move closer to it.

Revenge Without Harm

Wunsiedel is a small town in Bavaria in southern Germany. Until 2011, Hitler's right-hand man, Rudolf Hess, was buried here. Neo-Nazis had for years gathered annually to commemorate Hess and to march in celebration of the glory of the Third Reich. The march was banned in 1991, allowed to return in 2001, then banned again in 2005. Still, the march continued. Citizens of the town seethed at this annual invasion and tried multiple strategies to rid themselves of it. With the cooperation of Hess's ancestors, they even exhumed his body and destroyed the headstone, all in hopes that the Nazis would go away. It didn't work. Nor did counterprotests or campaigns celebrating diversity in the new Germany. Every year, the march would go on.

In 2014, the marchers were once again met by townspeople, but this time with cheers, encouraging signs, even snacks and drinks. The town had decided to turn the march into an unwitting walk-athon. Locals sponsored the marchers so that with every step, they were raising funds for a German organization dedicated to helping people exit neo-Nazi groups. Instead of screaming at the marchers, they cheered them as they crossed the "finish line" that they had painted in the road.[25]

This is an example of what Serbian activist Srdja Popovic calls laughtivism.[26] The idea is to place the leader or group squarely on the horns of a dilemma: either react to such a lighthearted and absurd provocation, and end up looking ridiculous, or acquiesce, withdraw from the confrontation, and look weak. In this case, it worked. The Nazis have not been back since. Wunsiedel has its town back.

Those of us who hate the people who marched in Charlottesville can only imagine the feelings of those townspeople who had to endure this invasion every year. They were certainly more justified than we are in stepping beyond anger and into hatred. Their nation, after all, knows best of all the pathology of Nazism. Let's be clear, though: their reaction was not driven by kindness. Their objective was to mock the Nazis, to make them feel the sting of ridicule. They no doubt felt some of the pleasure of revenge, of meeting pain with pain, that Aristotle saw as caught up with anger. What they did *not* do is harm the people who were marching. That means that their actions were, by Aristotle's definition, less hateful. The people of Wunsiedel did indeed take a step back.

Also, because this is *democratic* temperance, it is worth noting that in contrast to the typical counterprotest, this strategy was much more effective. The Nazis ended up going elsewhere. Part of the argument against hate, then, is not ethical but practical. What one person sees as defense, another likely takes as aggression. Both sides respond in kind, up the ante, and soon violence becomes a distinct possibility. This very predictable trail does not improve prospects for a well-ordered democracy, but it also does not hold out much hope for addressing the problem. For years, counterprotesters at Wunsiedel had the opportunity to vent their hatred at marching Nazis, but the Nazis kept coming. But when the town chose to channel its anger into nonviolence, when they chose to embrace the desire to inflict pain rather than harm, they were more effective. Of course, such actions will not always work, but they demonstrate a strategy that is more democratic, because it seeks no harm, and more effective, because it is more democratic.[27] Even those of us who feel pulled toward hatred might find enough reason to appeal to democratic temperance and thereby take a step back.

One more point here. In the last chapter, I noted that courage without the other virtues is easily lost. Without a unified sense of virtue, we can end up being courageous for very bad reasons. On the other hand, if we practice the democratic thinking virtues, we are more likely to be courageous in the right way and toward a good end. Just so with temperance. If we understand that we cannot escape our own biases, and if we strive to be honest about what we think is happening and consistent about how our values are applied, we are more likely to keep our anger from becoming hatred and more likely to hold that anger in check. The democratic virtues come as a set. Committing to all of them is the long and arduous task that lies before all of us.

If you think all this is beyond the pale, if you think the ideal of temperance evaporates in such an intemperate time, then hold on to your hat. The effort to move away from hatred is not simply a matter of self-restraint. It is also a matter of giving those whom we oppose the benefit of the doubt. I call that virtue democratic charity. That is the topic of the next chapter.

PART 4
Democratic Belief

Thomas Aquinas is by all accounts the most important interpreter of Aristotle. As I noted above, Thomas agreed with the ancients that the four cardinal virtues were necessary but incomplete. We human beings were called to more. The *theological* virtues—faith, hope, and charity—"surpass" human reason. They make it possible for us to achieve a dimension of both happiness and excellence that we cannot achieve otherwise.

The Establishment Clause in the First Amendment ("Congress shall make no law respecting an establishment of religion") means that legal consensus around matters of faith is not an option. And as many on the right are all too aware, even the quasi-establishment of the former Judeo-Christian cultural consensus is a vestige of its former self. Thomas's theological virtues therefore cannot be part of the agreement that grounds democratic society—but I want to argue that we need faith, hope, and charity to make our democracy thrive, especially right now.

9

CHARITY

With malice toward none,
with charity for all.
—ABRAHAM LINCOLN

Rancor, distrust, even outright hatred: for many of us, this is the air we breathe. Democratic temperance means developing the mastery necessary to step back from that hatred into mere anger. Taking that step is extremely difficult. Democratic charity is another, even more formidable step. It is directed outward, toward those for whom we feel such animus, with the goal of replacing enmity with acceptance and mutual respect. For many, the idea might sound almost comic. Of course, that is precisely why we need it right now—but we must acknowledge that getting there is daunting at best.

Charity as Philanthropy

In common usage, *charity* refers to instances when someone gives away something they have that another person needs. That something can be as simple as a hand down the steps or help loading the trunk. Most commonly, it refers to material needs, such as food, shelter, or money. Charity can also refer to efforts to respond to deficits in education and health care. In such cases, what is given can be time rather than something material: visiting those in hospitals and prisons, for example.

Cultures differ, sometimes widely, in regard to who is entitled to that giving—and when, why, and how, for that matter. But few cultures lack such a concept, and even fewer religions. In Western civilization, the concept of charity long predates Christianity. However, Christianity grounds the modern understanding. Jesus's parable of the Good Samaritan showed that mercy toward the stranger who needed help was far more in keeping with God's will than outward signs of piety (Luke 10:25–37). In fact, the very word *charity* entered Western Europe through the Christian Bible, in which the Greek word *agape* (a love that is focused on the well-being of the other and modeled on the love that God first showed us) was translated with the Latin word *caritas*. (The word *philanthropy*, from the Greek words *philos* for love and *anthropos* for humanity, conveys the same idea.)

Every question associated with this understanding of charity—the who, when, why, and how—continues to invite controversy. These arguments are not germane to my discussion, but there is one basic, even inescapable, feature worth noting. By definition, charity means that there is something I need (which makes me "the needy") and something you have. Some have argued that this imbalance is not only presumed but even maintained and reinforced through charity. Reinhold Niebuhr argued that "philanthropy combines genuine pity with the display of power . . . the latter element explains why the powerful are more inclined to be generous than to grant social justice."[1] Similarly, scholars, writers, and philanthropists alike acknowledge that paternalism and even condescension are always risks associated with any such unbalanced relationship.[2]

As with the broader concept, *democratic* charity is likewise concerned with giving what we have to those who need it. Yet in one fundamental respect, at least, it reflects exactly the opposite point. Democratic charity doesn't start with an unequal relationship. Instead, it reflects the ideal that in a democratic society, we are all equal. Charity is something that all citizens deserve and that all can rightly expect from others; all citizens are both givers and receivers. Moreover, while it is too much to call it love, democratic charity similarly expresses benign (or at least less hostile) feelings toward our fellow citizens. In fact, those feelings are integral to what is being given. What we give is not some material good or even our time, but simply the benefit of the doubt. Democratic charity means adopting the posture, often before we have sufficient evidence, that like me, my opponent is rational, truthful, and a person of goodwill.

The Principle of Charity

The other contemporary idea that is relevant here is the "principle of charity," a methodological concept derived from analytic philosophy. The idea is similar to, but distinct from, the commonplace notion that scholars and students alike should strive to be charitable when approaching a new idea to better facilitate genuine understanding. The interpretive principle of charity seeks understanding, as well, but it does not follow from generous feelings toward a new and uncomfortable idea; rather, it is a necessity that stems logically from that very objective.

Whenever we engage another in conversation, we are using language to bridge the distance between us in order to find out what the other person is thinking, how they understand the world, and what they believe and value.[3] The American philosopher David Davidson argued that for that effort to be successful, communication requires that a listener be "charitable." That means that before the listener tries to evaluate and criticize an argument, she begins by assuming that the person she is listening to is both truthful and rational, and then she seeks to give that argument its most credible, persuasive interpretation.[4]

Understood this way, "charity" goes on all the time, especially with those we know: you ignore incidental mistakes or poor formulations because you know what the other person meant, and you evaluate and respond to it in that sense. But with other languages and cultures, that effort becomes more difficult. The less commonality, the more difficult it is—but for that very reason, the principle likewise becomes all the more necessary. To get anywhere, we have to start with the assumption that understanding is possible. For Davidson, the principle of charity "is the only policy if we want to understand other people."[5] We don't undertake this principle for the sake of the other person; if anything, it is driven by simple self-interest. We want to understand the world as well as we can, and to do that we need to understand other people's perspectives and arguments. The principle of charity is the method best able to help to reach understanding.

Only when this interpretive principle is operative can we properly appreciate when an argument is wrong or even irrational. Disagreement can only be understood once it emerges from a ground of common presuppositions. If you and I disagree about whether a Christian baker has a right to refuse to bake a wedding cake for a gay couple, that disagreement can only be understood on the foundation of a whole host of propositions on which we do agree, propositions regarding the First Amendment, the concepts of marriage and free enterprise, and even more fundamentally, presumptions about the truthfulness and rationality of the person with whom we are arguing. The twentieth-century American Jesuit John Courtney Murray echoed this point: "Disagreement is a rare achievement, and most of what is called disagreement is simply confusion."[6]

The idea that charity is oriented around arguments rather than persons and is driven by self-interest rather than concern for the other: all this quite distant from the story of the Good Samaritan. Much of the swirling debate about the term and its logical necessity I am happy to leave to philosophers. Still, there are important points of continuity here. Arguing across partisan or tribal differences is difficult, too, but democracy depends on argument, and argument depends on understanding. Here, too, argument is more likely to produce understanding if we start by assuming that the other person is rational and truthful. Therefore, the principle of charity is no less essential in this context. If we do not make that assumption, then we rule out the possibility of interpretation and understanding before the conversation even begins. Under those conditions, misunderstanding, distrust, anger, and even hatred are almost certain to thrive.

In the pursuit of mutual understanding, democratic charity also strives to interpret the other's claim in the best possible terms. It may turn out that that assumption was unwarranted. If our objective is to understand, though, then this initial effort is not merely warranted but necessary. If anything, democratic charity is different because it is even more demanding. It assumes not merely truthfulness but good faith, rationality, and commonality: this person is a democratic citizen who loves her country and seeks the best for it, as do I.

With Charity for All

With these distinctions in mind, we can now attend to the most justly famous expression of this idea: Abraham Lincoln's second inaugural address. That speech was given in March 1865, only weeks before the Union victory in the Civil War. Everyone understood that the war, and thus the rending of the nation, was coming to an end. Lincoln used the occasion to turn the nation's attention to the long, hard task of restoring the Union. His speech ended with these words (now carved on the north wall of the Lincoln Memorial): "With malice toward none, with charity for all, with firmness in the right as God gives us to see the right, let us strive on to finish the work we are in, to bind up the nation's wounds, to care for him who shall have borne the battle and for his widow and his orphan, to do all which may achieve and cherish a just and lasting peace among ourselves and with all nations." Of course, there were hundreds of thousands who were going to need charity in the traditional sense—life and limb taken; widows and orphans without support; farms, industries, and livelihoods lost; towns and cities in ruin. Lincoln's words refer to many of these specifically, and he says that all this is part of our common task of binding up the nation's wounds. But that is not the limit of charity; it should, rather, extend to all of us, on both sides of the conflict. After a time of appalling hatred, violence, and cruelty, all Americans should strive to move past their grievances toward the other side, however just and deep those grievances might be. Lincoln says that with the end of the war, malice must be put away by everyone. All deserve, and ought to give the other, the charity of the benefit of the doubt. Only in that way can we hope to restore a just and lasting peace.

A President-Elect's Call for Democratic Charity

On November 7, 2020, in his hometown of Wilmington, Delaware, Joe Biden delivered his first speech as president-elect. In declaring victory, Biden spoke directly to those who didn't support him: "And to those who voted for President Trump, I understand your disappointment tonight. I've lost a couple of elections myself. But now, let's give each other a chance. It's time to put away the harsh rhetoric. To lower the temperature. To see each other again. To listen to each other again. To make progress. We must stop treating our opponents as our enemy. We are not enemies. We are Americans." Biden's words—"We are not enemies. We are Americans"—also recall Abraham Lincoln's first inaugural speech. As I have noted, Lincoln used that occasion to make a poignant, if fruitless, appeal to his fellow citizens to step back from the looming Civil War. Yet the echo of Lincoln's second inaugural is also unmistakable. Both Lincoln and Biden call for a new beginning after a time of extreme division. Both reflect a specifically democratic idea of charity that all Americans ought to strive for: that we all ought to be given a chance, the benefit of the doubt, and that we all deserve the presumptive right to be heard and respected.

As was the case with his first inaugural, it is not apparent that Lincoln's pleas in his second inaugural address changed much. He was assassinated a few weeks later, and as many have noted, animosity between the North and the South only really began to wane with the backroom deal that resulted in the election of Rutherford B. Hayes as president.[7] Southern Democrats accepted this outcome in return for the effective end of Reconstruction, allowing them to establish Jim Crow laws and reestablish a culture in which African Americans lost the very equality that so many, including Lincoln, had died to achieve. So much for a just and lasting peace.

Many have a similar sense of gloom about the times in which we find ourselves. The very idea of charity, democratic or otherwise, toward those in the other tribe might sound noble, but why should we not expect that any such appeal—Biden's, mine, or anybody else's—will prove equally ineffectual? Even if we agree on some basic sense of what democratic charity is, it does not feel any less unreachable to us. As I will note later, Biden's call was not exactly met with ringing affirmation by Trump voters. I do not discount these reactions. Though you hear reckless rumblings, our divide does not yet rival the Civil War. Yet our feelings of animosity are likewise deep and longstanding. To make any progress, we will need to get out of the rut in which we find ourselves. That is one reason why it is useful to think of democratic charity as a nontheological theological virtue. To make that case, I want to turn first to Thomas, and then once again to St. Bernard.

Thomas Aquinas on the Fount of Charity

Again, for Thomas Aquinas, we human beings need the theological virtues because our unaided reason is not enough. It is only with the virtues provided by God that we can fully become what we are meant to be. In fact, for Thomas, charity is the most excellent virtue because charity makes it possible for us to achieve a richer, more perfect expression of all the other ones.

In keeping with the Christian notion of caritas, Thomas says that charity is the kind of love that is devoted to other people. For him, though, that love does not start with other people; it starts with love of God. In fact, we love others for God, because of God, and really, through God. God is the principal object of charity, while our neighbor is met with charity for God's sake. Loving God makes it possible for us to love others in the same way that God loves them: "Charity is friendship first with God and secondly with all who belong to God."[8]

For Thomas, this is the only way that charity can be genuine. We are only able to love others because God first loved us (1 John 4:19). This path makes it possible for us to be genuinely charitable to all whom we might serve. People who need charity are not always lovable on their own. We live, and certainly Thomas lived, in a world where those needing charity included criminals, the mentally ill, the lame and disfigured, and so on. We might well feel pity toward these individuals, but possibly revulsion as well. Charity for all is easier to achieve, and is sometimes only possible, when we love them through our love of God. The charity of some American citizens today reflects this same ideal. They find love of others and the strength of service through love of God. All of us—believers or not—are better off because they are able to do so.

All of this is obliquely relevant to our circumstances. Most of us do not view those of the other tribe with the same distaste we might have for the deformed and diseased, but there is no doubt that all of us find it difficult to feel anything approaching love toward them, either. Democratic charity is a nontheological theological virtue because it asks for more than we can muster on our own. In her book *Talking to Strangers*, Danielle Allen notes, "The best one can hope for, and all one should desire, is that political friendship can help citizens to resist the disintegration of trust and achieve a community where trust is a renewable resource. But to accomplish this, *citizens must set their sights on what lies beyond their reach:* goodwill throughout the citizenry."[9] Call it democratic charity or political friendship, it lies beyond our reach. And in our free society, there is no common faith commitment that we can rely on to overcome that.

If we are committed to democracy, though, and if we judge that the current condition of raging polarization and tribalism undermines and even endangers it, then perhaps Thomas offers us an alternative strategy. I am not suggesting that commitment to democracy could or should take the place of God. For a believer, that is the very definition of idolatry. But if we start with the idea that our democracy needs democratic charity, then we can focus on that need as a way to overlook the unlovable features of those on the other side and at least move away from malice. We give others the benefit of the doubt not because they deserve it, nor because we expect that they respond in kind, but because we are committed to democracy. We find some measure of love for those in the other tribe first, and perhaps only, through our love for democracy.

Bernard on the Foundation of Charity

In chapter 4, I referred to St. Bernard's notion that humility begins with knowing the truth about ourselves, namely, the truth of our own sinfulness. Once we genuinely understand the depth of our own depravity, pride becomes impossible and humility emerges as the only reasonable, legitimate response. I argued that science provides a similar foundation. Research into the workings of the human brain shows that we are all inescapably biased and that none of us perceive the world as it really is. Knowing this truth about ourselves can likewise lead us to intellectual or, as I call it, democratic humility. I return to Bernard here because he believes that this sense of humility is a necessary foundation for charity. It is only after the monk fully understands his own sinfulness that he can genuinely serve others. Here, too, there is a nontheological version of this foundation that might be useful in our current circumstances.

Bernard says that without humility, without sufficient awareness of our own shortcomings (our own "wretchedness," he says), we "are likely to be moved not to ruth [that is, pity] but to wrath, not to condole but to condemn, not to restore in a spirit of meekness but to destroy in a spirit of wrath." Without this self-knowledge, it is not possible for us to know how to be merciful; it is "a thing you cannot know in any other way."[10] It is only when we see that our neighbor is just like us, just as fallen and just as weak, that we are best able to be charitable and practice the virtue effectively. When we know that we are all in the same boat, then and only then may we "know how to act gently toward a trespasser."[11]

The idea that humility is the foundation of charity remains part of Catholic theology. Shortly after beginning his papacy, Pope Francis pronounced that "charity without humility is sterile."[12] As a practicing Catholic, Biden may very well hold the same understanding. But whatever we can say about Biden, it is undoubtedly true that this is how Lincoln understood it. Just like Bernard, Lincoln's call for charity rested on the Christian notion that all Americans have fallen short of God's judgment. Without going into too much detail, there is a trail that unites the two. Lincoln's theology was deeply influenced by Calvinism, and John Calvin, in turn, thought highly of St. Bernard and cited him frequently.[13]

Lincoln plainly believed that slavery was an affront to God. He said as much in the second inaugural: "It may seem strange that any men should dare to ask a just God's assistance in wringing their bread from the sweat of other men's faces." But Lincoln refuses to allow himself or any Northerner the safety and contentment of moral superiority: "Let us judge not that we be not judged." That phrase comes from the Gospel of Matthew, in which Jesus admonishes his followers, "Why do you look at the speck of sawdust in your brother's eye and pay no attention to the plank in your own eye?" (Matt. 7:1–5). The metaphor might be confusing, but the point is simple. Followers of Jesus should concern themselves more with their own sins and less with the sins of others. In sum, all people have fallen short. Knowing that, Lincoln says, ought to make Americans more likely to practice charity toward those on the other side, even the other side of a bloody civil war. For Lincoln, as well, charity begins with humility, and humility begins with understanding the truth about ourselves.

Nontheological Humility, Nontheological Charity

The idea that charity rests on humility follows readily from the Christian concept of sin—everybody is guilty of it, and no one can escape it. But while that is one foundation, it is not the only one. Contemporary research by Julie Exline and Peter Hill lends support to the idea that humility works this way regardless of where it comes from. In three separate studies, their results show that if a person answers survey questions that identify them as humble, charity follows. Humility, more than any other single variable—including religiosity—is "a consistent and robust predictor of generosity."[14] It is not irrelevant to note that humility improved the prospects of generosity regardless of the relationship of the subject to the person being helped. Humble people were more likely to help friends and family, strangers, and even "people who have been unkind to [them] in the past."[15] Again, I argued that the fact that all human beings are subject to motivated reasoning and confirmation bias can be the truth on which humility can be grounded. Just so, recognizing this truth likewise makes it possible to develop a more generous perspective toward those on the other side. Democratic charity can therefore just as readily rest on a nontheological sense of humility about the self.

Democratic charity offers Americans the opportunity to take a step back from hatred and, in Biden's words, give one another a chance. Given that such a step might help us restore a well-ordered democratic society, that effort is worthy. Still, as was true for Lincoln, there is no denying the challenge that it represents. We, too, live in a society with deep and abiding polarization and growing feelings of distrust and animosity. The theological virtues can help us by refocusing our attention away from the other tribe and toward our common commitment to democracy—and by resting charity on a nontheological foundation of democratic humility. Neither of these steps makes democratic charity easy. Both make it somewhat easier.

Charity for Some

Let's say that some of us can get there. Through these steps and others, some good democrats find it possible to reach out to the other side in a spirit of democratic charity, to strive to respect the opinions of those in the other tribe and presume their goodwill, truthfulness, and rationality. What if, after all that, the effort itself is ignored? While I was writing this chapter, my friend E. J. Dionne wrote a column for the *Washington Post*: "Biden Reaches Out. The GOP Slaps Him in the Face."[16] Recounting the same Biden speech along with similar efforts by Biden and his team to clear the air and call for a new beginning, Dionne notes that "with just a handful of exceptions," Republican politicians "refused to stand up against the anti-democratic lunacy of Trump's efforts to nullify the results of a fair election." Any such response is hard to accept with equanimity (remember the defend/aggress model in chapter 2), especially when that response is grounded in "lunacy." It is easy to see how the spurning of Biden's outreach could reinforce and even exacerbate partisan anger and polarization. For Dionne, though, the problem goes further. The rejection of Biden's overtures could undermine his prospects for achieving his agenda and therefore (for him and all who voted for him, at least) improving the nation's well-being. "Anyone advising Biden and members of his party to turn the other cheek and reach out to Republican congressional leaders as though none of this has happened," Dionne writes, "is urging them down the path of political suicide."

From where I sit, Dionne is absolutely right. The silence of so many Republicans in the face of reckless assaults on our democracy (to say nothing of reality itself) is only the latest instance in which they have put their own well-being ahead of the country's. Biden would be well advised to think carefully about when and how to make such overtures in the future. Yet the point is general as well as specific. What should Biden and other Democrats do if these forays into democratic charity are at best ignored, or at worst, taken as an opportunity to undermine a fairly won election? More generally, what does *anyone*—politician or citizen—do when democratic charity goes unreciprocated?

Does democratic charity demand that we should continue to give the other side a chance even when those efforts are rejected? For Dionne, the answer is no: "Those who lack the conviction to sustain [the democratic] tradition by defending rationality and the democratic rules of engagement forfeit their standing to ask the rest of us to believe that they are operating in good faith." In short, if someone has shown you that they do not merit the benefit of the doubt, it is foolish and unproductive to go on giving it to them. That goes for anybody in a similar position. I have no doubt that there are Republicans—again, politicians *and* citizens—who would say that they have made just those kinds of efforts toward the other tribe, namely, Democrats, and have been met with similar rejections. The answer should be framed more generally as well: the pursuit of democratic virtue does not demand that we allow ourselves to be disrespected, let alone exploited.

Now this is not true for all understandings of virtue. For most believers, the burden of virtue or good works obtains whatever the cost or context. Mahatma Gandhi was willing to try *satyagraha*, passive nonviolent political resistance, against Nazi Germany and Imperial Japan, knowing full well that the effort would likely mean untold slaughter.[17] As for Christians, in the Sermon on the Mount (and only shortly before the passage where he says "judge not, lest ye be judged"), Jesus admonished his followers, "If anyone slaps you on the right cheek, turn to them the other cheek also." The disciple Peter asked Jesus how often he should forgive "my brother who sins against me," suggesting, "Up to seven times?" Jesus answered, "I tell you, not just seven times, but seventy times seven."[18] For most believers, then, the point is clear. Whatever the actions of the other, whatever the consequences, God expects unrelenting charity from his followers.

Democratic charity does not rest on theological claims and therefore cannot demand such high, even superhuman, standards. More to the point, unrequited democratic charity does not help sustain democracy. Democratic charity is different from the everyday understanding of the word because the former is, in Lincoln's words, for all: every citizen both gives and receives respect, a hearing, and the benefit of the doubt. That means that anyone striving to live up to it has a right to expect it in return. If I seek to understand you, it is incumbent on you to seek to understand me. Danielle Allen follows Aristotle to affirm the idea of what she calls political friendship. Whatever one calls it, the point is the same: "Political friendship must be reciprocal."[19] If democratic charity isn't for all, if only some give and only some receive, then that charity is not equitable and therefore not democratic. Equality requires reciprocity; reciprocity manifests equality. Without both, democratic charity does not exist.

The absence of reciprocity renders democratic charity impossible. Its absence also means that any such effort is unlikely to achieve

the end we seek. As I noted above, charity in its everyday sense is inherently unequal and, for that reason, prone to paternalism and condescension. If democratic charity lacks reciprocity, if it is practiced by one tribe and spurned by the other, it becomes more like traditional charity. Those who receive it become the needy, and they naturally grow to resent those who give it, doubting their motives and sincerity. On the other hand, when charity is not met in kind, it becomes that much harder to see past the malice that has built up
over the years. In sum, when charity becomes simply one more way for one tribe to distinguish itself from the other, then such charity is extremely unlikely to overcome animosity. It is far more likely to exacerbate it.

Generous Tit for Tat

So now what? If one-sided democratic charity does nothing to stop the doom loop in which we find ourselves, what should we do? I will say more about this in the conclusion, but with respect to charity, we need a strategy that is at once virtuous and strategic, democratic—that is, reciprocal—and still charitable.

We find an answer in game theory: specifically, the prisoner's dilemma.[20] As you might know, the story goes that two people are suspected of being accomplices in a crime. They are held in separate cells. Police offer both individuals the same deal. If you confess and your partner does not, then you will walk away, and he will get the book thrown at him: ten years in jail. If you both confess, you will split that time: five years for both of you. If neither one of you confesses, the judge will find you guilty of littering and sentence you both to six months in jail.

As the prisoner, you have four possible outcomes: ten years, five years, six months, or no jail time. You must make your decision, though, without knowing what your partner will choose. Obviously, the best outcome for both of you is that you both choose not to confess. But while six months is good, freedom is better—so your partner might confess, hoping that you will not. In that case, you would end up with ten years. Thus the dilemma.

If this is a one-time event, prospects for cooperation are nonexistent. However, politics has been called the game that never ends.

What might that mean for the prisoner's dilemma? What if the game were repeated hundreds, or even thousands, of times? In that case, every game tells you something about what the other is thinking, and it might tell you when their thinking has changed. What would be the best strategy then?

Robert Axelrod's Iterated Prisoner's Dilemma is a software program that plays the game repeatedly against the same opponent. He invited academics to develop strategies for winning the game.[21] What strategy ended up with the least amount of time in jail? Always trusting your opponent—in effect, forgiving seventy times seven—turns out to be a very bad strategy. The opponent is all too happy to let you take the rap while she walks out the door. So, too, is a consistently selfish strategy: turning in your partner in crime just makes her more inclined to defect as well, so you both end up serving a very long sentence. Over the long term, one of the most successful strategies was also one of the simplest: "tit for tat." This strategy involves cooperating the first time you meet another agent. After that, you simply always repeat whatever your opponent did the last time the game was played. If your opponent confesses on one turn, you punish them by confessing on the next; if they cooperate (keep silent) on one turn, you reward them by cooperating on the next. This position is very much like Dionne's: whenever a politician reaches out to the other side and gets her hand slapped, she should punish the hand-slapper next time around.

But while this strategy is better than either extreme, it is not foolproof. If the game never ends, then this strategy could well lock us into our current doom loop trajectory. If you retaliate against your opponent and then, the next time, they retaliate against you, politics becomes an endless and unbreakable pattern of unproductive retaliation. The only way to avoid this possibility is to adopt a slightly different and slightly better strategy: "generous tit for tat." Here, the basic strategy of retaliation adds random, periodic, and unreciprocated invitations to cooperation. The player using this strategy would sometimes decide to be generous and extend the opportunity to cooperate, even though she had no immediate justification for doing so—and indeed, even though doing so would put her at immediate and genuine risk of more jail time. Again, in the short term, this is not a good strategy. Over the long run, though, this strategy produces slightly better outcomes: more cooperation, because more opportunities for cooperation are presented, and less time spent in jail for both prisoners.

This evidence shows that when it is possible, when chance or prudence or mere optimism reveals an operative moment, we should periodically seize the opportunity and offer random acts of democratic charity, hoping that this time it might be met with reciprocity. To be sure, that is not a lot to hang your hat on. Even in Axelrod's tournament, the advantage of this strategy only emerges over the long run, and it is all too easy to see any such act disappearing into the maw of all-too-human anger and winner-take-all politics. Still, so far as the evidence shows, it is the best strategy available. We should not continue to practice democratic charity if that practice is not reciprocated. Christian charity may make such an extreme demand, but democratic charity does not. Nevertheless, we should always be open to doing so, always looking for opportunities to give it another try, always hoping that when we do, those actions will be met with a spirit of reciprocity. Any such action is eminently faithful. Thus we are brought once again to a condition that reflects theological virtues, albeit in a nontheological way. That faith might well represent the best chance we have for moving beyond our current impasse.

If democratic virtue demands reciprocity, then we have to find some way to restore the latter as well. That requires some ideal or principle that transcends our tribal animosity, something that makes it possible for us to reach out with generosity to the other and to respond in kind when such a gesture is made by the other to us. Patriotism has long served as that principle. Whatever else we thought, however much we disagreed, Americans knew that everyone feels love and pride in their country, and that feeling was enough to sustain our investment in each other.

Right now, evidence is all too clear that, for many, patriotism no longer works that way. In fact, for many, patriotism is inseparable from tribalism. Because of the work of Donald Trump and his cohort, the term is little more than another way of distinguishing between *us* and *them:* those who support the former president and genuinely love our country, and those who do not. Many in the other tribe hear this rhetorical equivalency and are repelled by it. They say that if that's what patriotism entails, then they are willing to give up the word altogether. Either way, the very idea does more to reflect and reinforce our current pathology than it helps us emerge from it.

Democratic charity refocuses our attention away from ourselves and the recipient and toward democracy itself, and that ideal ought to be one we can all share. Even the relatively recent history of our nation includes two world wars, the attacks of 9/11, a nationwide civil rights struggle, a great depression, and a great recession. During all these crises, faith in democracy was tested but turned out to be justified, when enough of us forgot or at least bracketed our differences long enough to resist a common enemy or commit to a common purpose. Of course, such an appeal will mean little to those Americans who are no longer committed to democracy. For everyone else, though, democratic charity might offer not just a way of sustaining democracy but also a way of honoring our past and the charity practiced by others before us. That might be an expression of patriotism upon which some measure of unity can rest—and thereby the possibility of reciprocity.

10

FAITH (AND HOPE)

In a democracy dissent is an act of faith.
—WILLIAM FULBRIGHT

Way back in the introduction, I outlined a set of propositions upon which democracy rests. Here is that list once again:

- There is a world out there, a reality, that is the same for all of us, even though we all perceive it differently, and that world exists regardless of whether we understand it or agree about it.
- As citizens, all of us have equal standing, and within wide limits, an equal right to live life the way we want, to believe what we want, and to express those beliefs freely.
- People can disagree deeply, even passionately, about those beliefs and still live together peaceably.
- Our all-too-human commitment to our group identity or self-interest does not wholly overwhelm our commitment to reason, fairness, and the goals of liberty and justice for all.
- Despite the difficulties, it is nevertheless possible to genuinely hear arguments with which we disagree, to debate those arguments productively, and (sometimes) to even find ourselves persuaded.

I said that these propositions were democratic answers to questions every society must answer: who we are, what makes life meaningful, how we should live together, and the like. Moreover, I said that democratic virtues both rest on and imply these answers. I hope that point is clear. The virtues of honesty and consistency, for example, are means by which we make reasonable argumentation possible. Democratic humility confirms the idea that we are all human and therefore deserve equal status. Temperance affirms that we can both hear what we don't want to hear and live together peacefully anyway. And so forth.

Still, the answers that democracies put forward are not incontestable. There are good reasons for affirming them, reasons born of evidence both from our own experience and from human history. The latter, incidentally, is exactly what James Madison did as he prepared for the drafting of the US Constitution. He compared the constitutions and laws of dozens of ancient and modern democracies (he called them confederacies), assessed their successes and failures, and argued for his conclusions.[1] That research is one reason why the Constitution has been such a successful document. But as I will recount below, history also presents good evidence for rejecting democratic answers. Ultimately, evidence alone will not prove one set of propositions over another. The propositions upon which democracies rest are a matter of faith.

What Is Faith?

What exactly is faith? This isn't a straightforward matter, but we can't start without some definition. Thomas Aquinas said faith is "a habit of the mind . . . making the intellect assent to what is non-apparent."[2] This definition follows straight from the Christian Bible: "Now faith is the substance of things hoped for, the evidence of things not seen" (Hebrews 11:1). "Non-apparent" means that you are assenting to truths that are not evident in themselves. You cannot prove that there is a God in the same way that you can prove that the earth revolves around the sun. But that does not mean that faith in God is the same as faith in the Easter Bunny. For Thomas, faith is "midway between knowledge and opinion."[3] Even though the existence of God is not evident to unaided human reason, Thomas argues that it can be "demonstrated." (He offers five such arguments.) Therefore, even if faith requires more than reason, faith is nevertheless reasonable. Even if we must ultimately take what Danish philosopher Søren

Kierkegaard called the "leap of faith," Thomas insists that that leap is intellectually justified.

For Thomas, and (for that matter) for most people, God is both the cause and object of faith. Faith in God comes about because of the grace God gives us. Democratic faith, on the other hand, is nontheological; it is not contrary to belief in God, but the former does not require the latter. Even so, democratic faith can likewise be accurately described as a habit of mind, an intellectual assent to propositions that are reasonable but not wholly demonstrable. Just as it is for Thomas, democratic faith means that assent to these propositions requires more than evidence. Affirming that they are true takes more than mere rationality; it takes faith.

All the propositions outlined above are quite inevitably undermined by tribalism. As we have seen, any time we identify ourselves with a group, we view reality with an eye toward defending our group, and we do it at the expense of the truth. What is more, our tribe causes us to become less interested in justice and equality for those who are outsiders. When tribes become polarized into two overarching identities, when society cleaves into two predominant groups of *us* and *them*, those propositions become even more difficult to sustain. The ideal of equal justice, the possibility of argument, the illegitimacy of violence, even the grounding idea that there is a reality out there that is the same for all of us: all these beliefs are threatened when society reaches this level of polarization. So is democracy itself.

Yet there is good evidence that these beliefs are under threat not because of our current condition but because they are unsustainable. In their book *Democracy for Realists*, Christopher Achen and Larry Bartels argue that our tribal polarization is better seen as a perennial feature of our human brains. The propositions I say are essential they see as secondary, even epiphenomenal, to the real story of how democracies and democratic citizens operate. If we are realistic about democracy, Achen and Bartels argue, we must accept a vastly diminished conception of what democracy is, or even what it possibly can be.

Democracy for Realists

Achen and Bartels are out to dispose of what they call the "folk theory" of democracy.[4] This theory, they say, claims that people approach politics as rational, self-interested actors. We want certain things from government, we make judgments about parties and candidates based on their ability to deliver these things, and then we cast our votes accordingly. Politicians, in turn, respond to these judgments and, because they want to stay in office, give the majority what they ask for. Democratic government is thus the product of citizens rationally expressing their will to politicians and politicians, in turn, rationally delivering on that expression.

For Achen and Bartels, just about nothing in this account is accurate. Marshaling a mountain of evidence, they show that most citizens do not follow politics closely. People are remarkably uninformed and uninterested in policy debates and can't tell you which party supports which option. In fact, citizens "often vote for parties whose long-standing issue positions are at odds with their own."[5] All those people who share their political ideology with such gusto, all those edifying websites that help you determine which candidate's position is closest to your own: these might reflect how we want to believe politics works, but the truth is closer to the exact opposite. As Achen and Bartels put it, "Candidate choices determine issue positions, not vice versa."[6] We pick the candidate we want and then adopt their positions as our own, even if we sometimes tell others and ourselves that they were ours all along.

In addition, once those candidates win election and hold political office, citizens are not very good at evaluating their performance. Here again, citizens make judgments that reflect low information and not much considered attention. Did those politicians successfully achieve their promises? Did they do a good job of managing the economy, handling foreign policy, or what have you? Even if citizens are inclined to ask these questions, they do a very bad job of answering them. They make judgments that are at best "myopic" if not genuinely "blind." It is true that citizens consider their well-being and what has happened to it over the last six months or so and make their choice accordingly, "punishing an incumbent when things get worse and rewarding them when things get better."[7] And while six months might not be the best frame in which to evaluate a four- or even two-year term, even such a short-sighted judgment would be legitimate *if* it reflected some effort to connect it to something the officeholder did or did not do. But even that thin connection is simply not to be found.

In a now famous part of their book, Achen and Bartels show that in the 1916 election, support for the reelection of Woodrow Wilson among New Jersey beach townships slipped significantly (about 10 percent).[8] Why did this happen? What had changed to make these voters turn against the president? Was it Wilson's efforts at progressive election reform or his management of America's neutrality before our entry into World War I? No. Achen and Bartels trace the change to a string of shark attacks along the Jersey Shore the summer before the election. The financial impact of these events was severe; they led to a very disappointing summer tourist season. For the people in these communities, then, recent experiences were clearly worse than usual.

Wilson had been governor of New Jersey, so he was well acquainted with the attacks. But the notion that he could have done anything about them as president is dubious at best. (Federal disaster relief was not even an idea at the time.) The residents of the beach communities were not asking those kinds of questions, however. Rather, many residents simply felt that their own personal condition had deteriorated. They therefore chose not to support the president's reelection, and they did this even though the former had precisely nothing to do with the latter.

While the event is dramatic, the authors argue that this democratic myopia—making voting decisions based on some irrational connections between the officeholder and the voter's well-being—repeats itself with "considerable regularity."[9] Sharks, droughts, economic downturns: it doesn't matter. The admittedly depressing conclusion is that there is little to no accountability for what a politician does or does not do, and the decision-making process of the average voter represents, at best, questionable rationality.

People Vote Their Tribal Identities

But even if citizens are uninformed, disengaged, and irrational, many, even most of them, still vote. So how *do* they make decisions? The answer is straightforward and (I would expect) very familiar. People vote the same way that they conduct just about every other aspect of their lives: they follow their tribe. "For most citizens most of the time," Achen and Bartels write, "party and group loyalties are the primary drivers of vote choices."[10] Achen and Bartels see themselves as following and extending what they call "the realist political tradition in the West." Front and center in that tradition is James Madison. Madison's account of factions, presented in Federalist 10 (and recounted here in chapter 3), "prefigures" their own argument about "the group theory of politics—the powerful tendency of people to form groups, the ensuing construction of 'us' and 'them,' and the powerful role of emotion rather than reason in directing group activity."[11] They review the work of scholars in a number of disciplines who "have reinforced and deepened" Madison's insights regarding the tribal core of politics (including Henri Tajfel, whose work was discussed in chapter 1). That research shows that attachment to group can overwhelm independent, rational thought; that we are all inclined to break the world down into *us* and *them*; and that we come to see the latter group as not just different but diminished: less moral, less intelligent, and less human. Though we like to think that there is something more meaningful going on, a competition between ideals and values, politics is simply another manifestation of the underlying and inescapable fact that human beings are tribal animals. Indeed, Achen and Bartels see their subject as "the conceptual limitations of human beings." Even though we "like to think that we are thinking," carefully considering questions of competence and policy, "voters primarily look for politicians who match their identities."[12] As with every other aspect of our lives, most of the time we are just following our herd.

Faced with all this evidence, Achen and Bartels say that we must abandon the folk theory. We are not judging politicians according to their fealty to our positions or, for that matter, to our interests and beliefs. Instead, our votes simply reflect and reinforce our sense of tribal identity. Once we know this, we are constrained to embrace a far more realistic, and therefore far more limited, notion of what democracy is or ever can be. What's more, it has always been this way. We cannot escape our humanity, which means that there is nothing distinctive about our present condition. In a new afterword written after the election of Donald Trump, the authors acknowledge that the world stage reflects developments in democracies that are "alarming." But the alleged "crisis in democracy" is not really new. It is more correct to say that these developments signal the end of a short anomaly in history where, for a variety of reasons, our tribal instincts were in abeyance. According to Achen and Bartels, "the current political environment is probably more typical in the broad sweep of history than the mid-twentieth-century period that contemporary observers often think of as 'normal.'"[13] The wiring in the human brain has not changed meaningfully in one hundred thousand years; democrats can't expect anything different. We must be much more realistic and much less exuberant about the possibilities of democratic government.

Now What?

So where, exactly, does this leave us? On the one hand, the argument that Achen and Bartels present strongly resonates with what I have suggested above. The idea that we human beings are inescapably tribal, that we can't help but divide the world into *us* and *them*, that our commitment to tribe overwhelms our independent reason and judgment, and that this tribalism inevitably manifests itself in politics—all of this is consistent with my own position. I take Madison as something of a touchstone, too, accepting his argument that faction is at the core of politics and that it diminishes what we can really expect from a well-functioning democracy. In all these ways, I am a democratic realist as well.

Yet my agreement only goes so far. Tribalism is an inescapable condition of our existence, but I dispute the claim that our democracy is no more imperiled now than it normally is, or that what we are really experiencing is the end of a peaceful, albeit ephemeral, interlude where tribalism was not such a serious problem. On the contrary, I argue that our times are distinctively precarious, and while I agree that democracy is forever undermined by our tribalistic proclivities, I contend that we now find ourselves in a progressive doom loop. More importantly, I continue to affirm a conception of democracy that at least bears some resemblance to what they call the folk theory of democracy. While I appreciate that citizens are not wholly rational, it is too much to say that all our political choices are bereft of judgment. Finally, Achen and Bartels do not convince me to reject the idea that democracy both requires and is able to sustain a sense of common purpose and common responsibility. It is one thing to say that those propositions are challenging and that we can never fully actualize them. It is quite another to dismiss them as naive and unrealistic.

Where exactly do Achen and Bartels come down on the "thus far but no farther" axis? Late in the book, in a footnote, they appear to leave themselves some wiggle room: "Of course, not everything in politics reduces to power and raw competition among groups and parties. Nonetheless, they are central to understanding policy outcomes."[14] Well, just so. The evidence that Achen and Bartels present is formidable, and I have no doubt that while we can argue the margins, the basic premise is largely correct. That is, a fervent, all-too-human commitment to group identity does indeed drive politics, and that commitment undermines our ability to affirm, let alone live out, the democratic virtues. Still, that is not all that drives it. As Achen and Bartels acknowledge, there is more to democratic politics than the realistic perspective they present. I think there is enough evidence to justify the democratic faith that lies between knowledge and opinion.

What's more, I would insist that in this regard, as well, I am following Madison. For all his concerns about faction and his structural efforts to control its effects, Madison believed that people both deserved and were able to live up to the burdens of self-government. I quote again from Federalist 55: "As there is a degree of depravity in mankind which requires a certain degree of circumspection and distrust, so there are other qualities in human nature which justify a certain portion of esteem and confidence. Republican government presupposes the existence of these qualities in a higher degree than any other form."[15] Madison's conception of human beings, informed by a Calvinist notion of human nature, is in fact far more complicated and nuanced—and even realistic—than the one described in *Democracy for Realists*. Madison reflects the idea that while human beings will never be angels, democratic government is not beyond our reach. First, through careful observation, we have the capacity to design governmental systems that can both direct and mitigate the effects of tribalism. Second, human beings not only must but *can* develop within themselves and their culture a commitment to virtue that can likewise mitigate this most antidemocratic vice.

The Difference Democratic Faith Makes

In chapter 7, I referenced the democratic courage of the Freedom Riders. For most of those who took part, that courage rested on a strong Christian faith. Many of them looked to Jesus as their ideal. Even as they were being beaten, many of them prayed for the strength to endure. But not all of them were Christians. There were Jews and atheists on those buses as well. Still, whatever their *religious* faith, all of them reflected a *democratic* faith—a faith in the propositions that began this chapter. The Freedom Riders believed that all people are entitled to equal rights, and that entitlement must include the right to sit where they wanted on the bus and in the bus depot. They believed that to the degree that that equality was a lie, democracy was as well. They believed that there was in almost every human being, including white people in Alabama and Mississippi, a conscience, an innate sense of justice that could be reached and appealed to. And they believed that their righteous suffering was the best vehicle by which to do that. It would cause people—force people—to reconsider their beliefs and ultimately change their minds. Whatever its religious foundation, that faith is what got the Freedom Riders onto those buses.

That faith continues to push us to make democracy better. At fifteen years old, Greta Thunberg went on "school strike" and spent her days alone outside the Swedish Parliament silently witnessing for government action on climate change. Just one year after her protest began, Thunberg's action resulted in millions all over the planet, many of them students like her, marching for international political action. Speaking before the US Congress, she recalled Martin Luther King's speech at the March on Washington for Jobs and Freedom in 1963. Thunberg said, "I have a dream that the people in power, as well as the media, start treating this crisis like the existential emergency it is."[16] Thunberg's words uphold the proposition that, first, there is a world out there that affects all of us and, second, that people can be reasoned with through arguments and evidence. Most importantly, she affirmed the democratic faith that when someone—even a solitary teenage girl—undertakes a peaceful protest, her actions can change people's minds.

In 2019, Lt. Col. Alexander Vindman served as director for Eastern European, Caucasus, and Russian affairs for the National Security Council, Russia political-military affairs officer for the chairman of the Joint Chiefs of Staff, and military attaché in the US Embassy in Moscow. In October of that year, he responded to a subpoena to appear before the House Intelligence Committee and their inquiry into then-president Trump's actions regarding Ukraine. Vindman was on Trump's famous telephone call to Ukrainian president Volodymyr Zelensky, the one in which he appeared to make US aid to Ukraine contingent on Zelensky's opening an investigation into alleged actions by Joe Biden and his son Hunter. The specifics are not relevant, except to say that Vindman testified that he was concerned that the call was improper and had informed his superiors of that concern. His testimony contradicted the Trump's assertion that he had made "a perfect phone call." In his opening statement before the committee, Vindman thus contradicted his commander-in-chief and risked all the repercussions with which Trump had threatened those who had crossed him. Addressing his deceased father, who had worked so hard to bring his sons to America, Vindman also affirmed his democratic faith. He ended his opening testimony with these words: "Dad, my sitting here today, in the US Capitol talking to our elected officials is proof that you made the right decision forty years ago to leave the Soviet Union and come here to the United States of America in search of a better life for our family. Do not worry, I will be fine for telling the truth."[17] Later, under questioning, he repeated the point, saying that he was willing to testify because "here, right matters."[18] Vindman acknowledged that he was "assuming a lot of risk," but he professed confidence that for all our partisan disagreements, all Americans are committed to reason, fairness, and the goals of liberty and justice for all. That very commitment would ensure that he and his family would "be fine."

Bryan Stevenson teaches at New York University Law School. He also runs the Equal Justice Initiative, a nonprofit based in Alabama that provides legal representation to incarcerated people (most of them Black folks) who were not well served by the American justice system. After decades of working to secure that equal justice for those he serves, with many successes and some failures, he articulated a conception of democratic faith that, as with Thomas, is rational but not wholly rational, a conception that lies midway between knowledge and opinion. "I think my hope is not entirely rational," he says. "It wouldn't make sense for me to be in Alabama if I didn't believe. . . . I have, now, 30 years of amazing things that have happened that reinforced that belief. . . . I can see it's not entirely scientific and rational. But I do think it's entirely well-founded."[19] Assenting to propositions like equal justice under law, believing that everyone in our society genuinely affirms that idea, and orienting your behavior accordingly may not be irrational—there is certainly evidence that makes it reasonable to keep believing. But Stevenson admits that it is not *merely* rational. So it is with all these propositions, and with these three democrats.

These three, like the Freedom Riders before them, are well known and (by most, anyway) greatly admired. We mark their courage and their commitment, their willingness to accept the risks. Greta Thunberg risked being ignored or mocked as a histrionic little girl who just wanted to get out of school. Vindman's testimony jeopardized his position at the National Security Council, his military career, and even his safety. Bryan Stevenson has invested his time and energy defending clients who have already lost every prior attempt to achieve justice. All of them knew this. Yet they professed a democratic faith that made it possible for them to act anyway.

Often, the reason we know about acts like theirs is because they were so successful. Within a year, Thunberg's solitary witness led millions of students all over the world to march. A breathtaking achievement. So, too, we recognize Rosa Parks's protest because it led to the desegregation of public buses in Montgomery, Alabama, and became known as the beginning of the civil rights movement. We know about Gandhi's Salt March because his simple act forced the mighty British government to change its policy, ultimately setting in motion the drive that would lead to Indian independence.

But the raw fact is that most democratic acts are not so successful, and no act is wholly without cost. Vindman's faith was not fully vindicated, for example. His testimony did not carry the day, and the Senate did not agree with him on the president's guilt. Moreover, he did indeed suffer retribution for his actions. Almost immediately after the Senate acquittal, he was fired and escorted from the White House. The president justified the action with this tweet: "Actually, I don't know him, never spoke to him, or met him (I don't believe!) but, he was very insubordinate, reported contents of my 'perfect' calls incorrectly, &. was given a horrendous report by his superior, the man he reported to, who publicly stated that Vindman had problems with judgement, adhering to the chain of command and leaking information. In other words, 'OUT.'"[20] In a *Washington Post* editorial, Vindman called this action part of "a campaign of bullying, intimidation and retaliation."[21] The editorial marked the occasion of his retirement from the military—before his promotion to full colonel—and Vindman said that his testimony was the reason. It had "ended my career." All for obeying a Congressional subpoena and telling the truth.

There are untold numbers of people, lost to history, whose faith was even more tragically dashed. Frequently, we do not remember these people at all. Some of these, of course, were on the wrong side of justice. As with courage, faith can be misplaced. Yet just as many were

not on the wrong side of an issue; rather, they sought through their actions to stand up for their rights, for freedom, and for democracy. But their actions changed nothing. Their act was witnessed by too few, convinced too few, and motivated too few. The prevailing power, including the power of tribal identity and the associated bias, was too much to overcome. Worse, some of these democratic actors did not just fail. Some suffered and even died because of their actions.

No doubt these failures far outnumber the successes that we all know and praise. Reflecting on that fact can reinforce the idea that democratic faith is anything but realistic. The successes, though—few though they may be—are part of human history as well. Sometimes, at least, people actively listen to or otherwise engage a democratic protest. Sometimes, at least, people are convinced by that engagement. The protest causes them to change their minds. And sometimes, at least, people are so convinced that they join with the protesters. In fact, sometimes so many join that history is changed and society ends up more democratic.

Such examples serve as data points, too—no less than the voting habits of those living on the Jersey Shore. These democrats believed that despite the power of group identity, we can remain committed to reason, fairness, and the goals of liberty and justice for all, and that sometimes people can engage with those with whom they do not agree and come away from that experience with their opinions changed. For them, that faith was rewarded. Because they were faithful to these democratic ideals, our society moved just that much closer to them.

Most of us can only look with awe on the courage of the Freedom Riders. We are just as unlikely to display the faith of Thunberg, Vindman, and Stevenson. Just as with courage, though, democratic faith is not and must not be limited to heroes. Democratic courage—even merely everyday courage—is required in just about every democratic act, and so too is democratic faith. When we put up a yard sign or a bumper sticker, when we take part in a protest, or when we frame an argument or cite evidence that runs counter to someone else's point of view, we have faith that those hearing us accept that we have a right, peaceably, to express our own. More, despite the power of human bias, we have faith that they will accept that we are striving to reflect our beliefs honestly. We have faith that they will be open to hearing what we have to say, and finally, that they will accept at least the possibility that their minds can be changed. Virtually any democratic act is, at its core, as a faithful act. Democracy rests on these everyday acts of democratic faith.

Faith and Hope

As we all know too well, right now everyday acts of democratic faith are frequently dashed. The power of tribalism repeatedly overwhelms all these democratic commitments, making the evidence that helps sustain democratic faith as partly, if not wholly, rational harder to come by. Yet throughout history, and throughout the world, it was (and is) ever thus. Those protesting in authoritarian nations surely recognize that they are up against an extremely powerful, potentially violent, and deeply antidemocratic foe. Under such circumstances, faith becomes less connected to evidence and ever less justifiable. Under such circumstances, the point of reference moves to the future, and with that, faith must turn into hope.

For Thomas, hope, like faith, cannot focus on an impossibility. It is not legitimate to hope to be able to fly like a bird. The good that hope seeks is "difficult but possible to attain."[22] But hope must acquiesce to the fact that at this moment, that evidence is "not-seen." More so than faith, it is therefore an act of will. We know that there is little reason to believe that things will be different any time soon, but we still choose to believe that they someday might be. We therefore move our faith from the present to the future. When we do that, faith becomes hope.

Among believers and democrats alike, the line between faith and hope is always thin. Both ask a lot of human beings. Under the best of circumstances, they require assent even though the evidence behind them is hardly definitive (and sometimes, like now, that evidence seems to diminish to a vanishing point). Prospects are daunting, the task arduous, and the path unclear. Moving from faith into hope is how we keep going. For a democrat, hope means we recognize that the propositions of democratic faith are hard to justify right now, and they may not be more easily justified anytime soon. Whatever their current status, however, they remain values and ideals that deserve our affirmation. We continue to fight for them, even though we know that success might not come for years, or decades, or even our own lifetimes. Hope is what makes that fight possible. In the words of Reinhold Niebuhr, "Nothing that is worth doing can be achieved in our lifetime; therefore we must be saved by hope."[23]

We continue to act as if the propositions were true, oriented toward a future in which they may become so. By such hope—indeed, only by such hope—do impossible things happen. Without hope, Jim Crow does not end, the Berlin Wall does not fall, marriage for gay couples remains impossible. With it, the little acts continue, and those acts ultimately move us to become a society that better realizes the democratic propositions.

CONCLUSION

Democratic Excellence

Few will have the greatness to bend history; but each of us can work to change a small portion of the events, and in the total of all these acts will be written the history of this generation.
—ROBERT KENNEDY

Aristotle said that the proper application of virtues—finding the golden mean—depends on our understanding the circumstances in which we find ourselves. Well, we have all lived through the last few years. We know our own circumstances only too well. Because of that indisputable knowledge, calling for a renewed commitment to virtues—and especially virtues like humility and temperance—must appear to many to be deeply inadequate. I understand that skepticism and frankly, on many days, I have felt it myself. We must therefore confront the question of whether now is a time for virtue at all.

A sizeable percentage of Americans believe that the other tribe—that is, the tribe of Democrats—is so deeply immoral, such an existential threat to all that real Americans hold dear, that it justifies subverting democracy. For some, it even justifies violence. We saw some of those people on January 6, 2021. To call for these insurrectionists or their fellow travelers to practice temperance and humility would seem not just naive but even foolhardy. This one act, this antidemocratic tantrum, cannot be viewed as some bizarre and isolated event. It was rather the all-but-inevitable outcome of President Trump's sustained and reckless assault on American democracy.

Donald Trump is not a democrat. He never expressed concern for the norms and procedures, let alone virtues, that make democracy go. And as Trump took over the Republican Party, most Republicans, in office and not, followed along in his wake. His claims of election fraud spiraled well beyond the orbit of reality, and once again, most Republicans gladly went along. The ideal of a free and fair election, the very bedrock of democratic politics, was left gravely wounded as a result. For Trump, democracy itself was far less important than his continued occupancy of the White House. Even now, for many of his acolytes, it remains far less important than their own continued occupancy of their elected office.

My point is not to rehash this event and its causes; it is rather to acknowledge an unavoidable objection to the argument I have presented. Virtue represents a social agreement. A society agrees and affirms that certain habits and behaviors are important, valuable, and help us understand who we are. If some part of the society does not accept this agreement and does not agree that democracy is worth preserving—or that the concomitant virtues constitute obligations we have to each other, or that they are at least ideals that help guide and regulate our conduct—then it is not clear how you have a society at all. Of course, you have people occupying the same landmass, driving on the same roads, and paying taxes to the same authority. For that matter, you can be assured that people will still be concerned with virtue, at least insofar as it applies to other members of their tribe. Still, with nothing to unite those tribes into one identifiable group, there is no society.

As I write, a preponderance of Republicans continues to reject Joe Biden's election as illegitimate. Many are content to spurn even the ideal of democracy, insisting—falsely—that our nation is not a democracy at all. Some are quite willing to subvert democratic norms and even the truth itself to achieve their partisan ends. If all this is true, then why should the other side remain committed to democratic virtue? Those virtues are, and must be, reciprocal. If democracy is valued by one side more than another, and politics has become little more than war by other means, then honesty and humility, for example, can rightfully be understood to be bad politics: it is bringing a knife (or maybe better, a throw pillow) to a gun fight.

For starters, let's acknowledge that a gun fight is not a good idea, either. If our politics is unable to move beyond one relentless, unremitting O.K. Corral, then democracy is already lost. The whole point of democratic politics is to avoid gun fights, to live peacefully amidst our disagreements. After all the very dark moments we have witnessed recently, it might well appear that this is just not possible, that we have sunk too low to restore this kind of society. Perhaps we have. Others would argue that we really are in a doom loop, so even if we are not there yet, this is the future that almost certainly awaits us. If we are indeed going down, they say, better to go down swinging. Again, John Adams wrote over two hundred years ago that "there was never a democracy yet, that did not commit suicide."[1] It might be that even after all this time, we may end up proving him right.

Perhaps. But it is also possible that despite the obscenity of January 6, 2021, we have not sunk that low yet, that something yet remains of the common commitments that make us all Americans. I noted Joe Biden's 2020 inaugural address in the introduction. Here in the conclusion, I want to reference it one last time, for Biden spoke to this more hopeful possibility: "Through civil war, the Great Depression, world war, 9/11, through struggle, sacrifice and setbacks, our better angels have always prevailed. In each of these moments, enough of us have come together to carry all of us forward."[2]

The agreement that undergirds society is never fully complete. There are always outliers. Those who have a prior and more essential moral commitment that is not wholly commensurate with society at large. Those who dispute the terms or legitimacy of the agreement. Those who simply want to be left alone. Yet even in the midst of our nation's greatest challenges, there have been *enough* citizens who did agree, who did strive to live up to the virtues that were most important for the times in which they found themselves. There is no reason to assume that this moment of crisis is somehow unlike all those that came before. We have every reason to hope that even at this moment, there are enough Americans, members of both tribes, who may once again carry all of us and sufficiently restore the fabric of our society.

These Americans might prove willing to commit to the practice of the democratic virtues in their own lives, stepping up to the opportunities that present themselves daily. Just as importantly, there might be enough who are willing to highlight and praise the acts of others when they exhibit those same virtues. It would be especially useful if, for the sake of consistency, enough Americans were able and willing to call out virtuous acts when they are undertaken by those in the other tribe. That is assuredly not the most powerful theory of change you are ever going to hear. But it is only through little acts like these that our nation can rise to the challenge that presents itself to this generation and thereby restore the culture upon which our democracy rests.

In fact, this moment might well be better than most. In Biden's appeals to unity, to giving each other a chance, and the like, we see more opportunity to change than we have in a long while. Of course, as we saw with the Delta variant of COVID-19, things can change back drastically and quickly. Moments can come and go. As daunting as the prospects are, however, they are better than they have been in years.

Let's be clear. The alternative, whether it ends in tyranny or civil war, ought to fill us with dread. It should therefore summon us to action regardless of the prospects for success. But even if there are not enough Americans heeding this call, even if our democracy does end up committing suicide, there are still reasons to practice democratic virtues.

As I noted in chapter 8, the best long-term strategy for our democracy is for us to periodically find opportunities to practice democratic charity, always hoping that when we do, those actions will be met with a spirit of reciprocity. Democratic virtue is a manifestation of that hope. Again, sometimes hope is all we have, and for many of us, now is one of those times. Ensconced in our separate tribes, we find ourselves in the same position as those two prisoners: stuck in a never-ending game, distrustful, hostile, happy to win and just as happy when the other side loses. Whatever decision we make this round, though, the game just goes on. Just like the prisoners, we polarized Americans are stuck with each other, and the rewards of pragmatic coexistence remain whether we choose to agree to them or not. Sooner or later, we must accept the reality that we cannot *not* find a way to live together, and that means we must restore some modicum of mutual respect and concern.

That fact—and it is a fact—offers enough reason for hope. Though oriented toward the future, hope works in the here and now to sustain the possibility that a time will come when animosity has played itself out, when we recognize that good and evil reside in all of us, and when citizens are no longer so ready, even eager, to listen to lies. When that happens, democracy will become viable once again.

Democratic virtue helps sustain the possibility of democracy for that future, whether it belongs to us or to those who come after us.

Acts that affirm democracy are not merely acts of hope. They are also acts of defiance—defiance at the soul-crushing thought that the way things are now is the way they must be. Practicing democratic virtue means witnessing for a better conception of what we are all capable of and what we all deserve: self-determination and the dignity that comes with it. Practicing democratic virtue is an act against authoritarianism, against those who disdain our humanity, who are so indifferent about our hard-won rights and freedoms and about the sacrifices of so many over the years that made them possible. It is an act against the violence and tyranny that loom as alternatives when democracy fails.

There is one more reason to practice democratic virtues. For Aristotle, virtue is not only about knowing and doing the right thing; it is about living a full and happy life. Even more fundamentally, it is about becoming an excellent person. By encouraging the right habits in ourselves, we come closer to achieving our potential, becoming better selves, becoming the kind of people whom we ourselves and others can respect. Nothing changes when we talk about democratic virtues, except that along with a distinctive set of virtues comes a distinctive kind of excellence: *democratic* excellence.

Being an excellent democrat means standing up for oneself as a person with a point of view who is worthy of being heard. It means allowing others, even encouraging them, to do the same. It means striving to assess the world as best as we can, even as we recognize that we cannot escape the constrained and compromised condition of our own perspective. It means spurning those who appeal to our worst, most undemocratic impulses. It means fighting for what we believe in, but fighting well and fairly. It means respecting others enough to let them do the same. It means winning and losing with class. Whether it changes the nation or not, this distinctively democratic excellence is worthy of the effort it takes to create and sustain it.

In this moment of crisis and opportunity, we should do our part to improve democracy, constraining tribalism and restoring what has been lost. The democratic virtues offer us a guide for how to do that. But even if enough people take on that challenge and things do improve, even if we are able to step away from the brink and build back our democracy, the problem will always remain. Democracy is a chronic struggle against aspects of our humanity that we can never fully escape. Owning our part in this struggle is part of the price of admission for a society that strives to be free and decent, equal and just. If nothing else, recent events have made this fact inescapable. We therefore undertake the task before us with a more realistic sense of what we have signed up for—and a more urgent sense of what is at stake.

Notes

INTRODUCTION

1. Thomas, Ordonez, and Larramendia, "Capitol Police Officer."
2. Antidemocratic thought exists on both sides of the partisan divide, but in terms of power and influence, they are in no way equivalent. In their study of web traffic data, Thomas Main and Jessica Miller conclude that "if the penetration of illiberalism into American political culture is a matter of concern, the problem is to be found exclusively on our right flank. The Illiberal Left is minute, entirely isolated, and unengaged. The Illiberal Right is sizeable, closely connected with mainstream political tendencies, and dramatically more engaged with political discourse than any other ideological tendency." Main and Miller, "Audience," 41.
3. This quotation is referenced in Friedersdorf, "How Breitbart Destroyed."
4. See Foot, *Virtues and Vices*, 170.
5. For comparison, here is the definition that Alasdair MacIntyre offers in *After Virtue*, one of the most important books on virtue ethics in the last fifty years: "A virtue is an acquired human quality, the possession and exercise of which tends to enable us to achieve those goods which are internal to practices and the lack of which effectively prevents us from achieving any such goods" (178).
6. Rawls, *Political Liberalism*, 197n32.
7. There are a number of philosophers, from a variety of schools of thought, who would reject this statement. The late American philosopher Richard Rorty, for example, argues that talking about reality *out there* is a waste of time. Worse, the pursuit of something like an *objective* reality only serves to undermine the genuine philosophical task of enhancing human happiness (Rorty, *Pragmatism as Anti-Authoritarianism*). I obviously don't agree with such a claim. To frame it simply, I would contend that democratic politics both presumes and requires a realist metaphysics. But to take up this argument would require a different, longer, and far less accessible book.
8. In Benhabib, *Democracy and Difference*, four preeminent scholars consider the necessity and metaphysical status of the foundations undergirding democratic theory. My own view is closest to Amy Gutmann's. Gutmann concludes that "democracy can be defended by

publicly accessible reasons," but these reasons "cannot be deduced from self-evident truths" (see "Philosophy, Democracy and Justification," 346).

9. Aristotle's list of the former is different from mine. My list is closer to the "responsibilist" epistemology, which sees intellectual virtues as a product of character. See Zagzebski, *Virtues of the Mind*.
10. The list of the cardinal virtues, but not the term, comes from Plato. Let me say a word about the two cardinal virtues I leave off. As I noted, I use "consistency" to get at the virtue of justice as it applies to individuals. As for prudence, here is what Thomistic scholar Joseph Pieper said: "Prudence is cause, root, mother, measure, precept, guide, and prototype of all ethical virtues; it acts in all of them, perfecting them to their true nature; all participate in it, and by virtue of this participation they are virtues" (Pieper, *Four Cardinal Virtues*, 8). I talk about practical wisdom frequently in what follows, but because prudence is so inseparable from any ethical act, it is unnecessary to give it its own chapter.
11. For all of the quotations in this paragraph and the next, see Biden, Inaugural Address.
12. Gorman, "Hill We Climb."

CHAPTER I

1. Hobfoll, *Tribalism*, 24.
2. The brands we choose help us define ourselves, and cultivating this sense of identity is central to many ad campaigns. See Vedantam, "Our Brands, Our Selves."
3. For more on this taxonomy of groups, see Lickel et al., "Varieties of Groups."
4. Kelly et al., "Other-Race Effect."
5. See, for example, Tatum, *Why Are All the Black Kids*.
6. Frame, "Study Finds Evidence of Social Disconnect."
7. Smith et al., "Categorization."
8. Harnad, "To Cognize Is to Categorize."
9. Duarte et al., "Tribal Love."
10. Bigler, Jones, and Lobliner, "Social Categorization," 6.
11. Tajfel, "Experiments in Intergroup Discrimination," 96.
12. Another famous example of children adopting and defending arbitrary tribes is the famous Robbers' Cave experiment, led by Muzafer Sherif. I discuss this experiment in Beem, *Democratic Humility*, 49–51.
13. Yagoda, "Cognitive Biases."
14. See Kahneman, *Thinking Fast and Slow*.

15. See, for instance, Iacozza, Meyer, and Lev-Ari, "How In-Group Bias," 308.
16. Tajfel et al., "Social Categorization and Intergroup Behaviour," 172.
17. Cikara, Botvinick, and Fiske, "Us Versus Them."
18. Haslam et al., "More Human Than You."
19. Hobfoll, *Tribalism*, 175.
20. Drutman, *Breaking the Two-Party Doom Loop.*
21. See Wang, "Partisan Marriage Gap."
22. Pew Research Center, "Partisan Antipathy."
23. Miller and Conover, "Red and Blue States of Mind," 9.
24. Pierce, Rogers, and Snyder, "Losing Hurts."
25. Martherus et al., "Party Animals."
26. See Edsall, "No Hate Left Behind," and Kalmoe and Mason, "Lethal Mass Partisanship," 23.

CHAPTER 2

1. Lipset, *Political Man*, 31.
2. See Jones, "Support for Third U.S. Political Party." For January/February 2021 Gallup poll results on party identification, and those following, see https://news.gallup.com/poll/15370/party-affiliation.aspx.
3. Pew Research Center, "Partisan Antipathy."
4. See Klar and Krupnikov, *Independent Politics.*
5. Mason and Wronski, "One Tribe to Bind Them All," 274.
6. Newport, "Percentage of Christians in U.S."
7. Thompson, "Where Did All the Workers Go?"
8. In "The Truth About Taxes," Blodget writes that "during the 1950s and early 1960s, the top bracket income tax rate was over 90%." It is currently 37 percent.
9. Tienda and Sánchez, "Latin American Immigration."
10. Frey, "US Will Become 'Minority White.'"
11. Parker, Morin, and Horowitz, "Looking to the Future."
12. There is an argument that all this partisan division comes down to one's neurological makeup. Republicans and Democrats line up according to the size of their amygdala, on the one hand, and their anterior cingulate cortex, on the other. See, for example, Denworth, "Conservative and Liberal Brains." I am confident that this argument is important and revealing, and the more we learn about the brain, the more likely this perspective will be filled in. But the "might" in the title of Denworth's piece is operative. It is not a sufficient explanation.
13. Pew Research Center, "Generation Gap in American Politics."

14. Abramowitz, *Great Alignment*, 14.
15. Muro and Liu, "Another Clinton-Trump Divide."
16. Muro et al., "Biden-Voting Counties."
17. Kaplan, Spenkuch, and Sullivan, "Partisan Spatial Sorting."
18. Some scholars argue that the difference goes down, instead, to a very local, even neighborhood level. The operative difference in terms of establishing which side of the partisan divide you are on is population density. If your neighborhood reflects a low population density, that is, if you live in rural or suburban and especially exurban communities, you are likely to be a Republican. If you live closer to your neighbors and in neighborhoods that have a comparatively higher population density, then you are likely to be a Democrat. This connection between density and partisanship represents a new, dramatic, and ubiquitous change. For most of the first half of the twentieth century, the correlation between voting and density was zero. See Gimpel et al., "Urban–Rural Gulf."
19. Abramowitz writes, "African Americans and (to a lesser extent) Hispanic voters have been less attuned to cultural issues and more focused on social welfare and economic issues." See Abramowitz, *Great Alignment*, 53.
20. Interestingly, this division is also reflected within Judaism, between Reformed and Conservative Jews on the one hand and Orthodox on the other. See Hetherington and Weiler, *Prius or Pickup*, 80.
21. Cox and Jones, "Majority of Americans Oppose."
22. Wehner, "Trump's Words Are Poison."
23. Cox and Jones, "America's Changing Religious Identity." The term "nones" refers to those who have no religious affiliation.
24. Abramowitz, *Great Alignment*, 49.
25. Horowitz, Brown, and Cox, *Race in America 2019*.
26. Conroy and Bacon, "There's a Huge Gap."
27. Pew Research Center, "Examination of the 2016 Electorate."
28. Abramowitz, *Great Alignment*, 159.
29. I asked Abramowitz if the same patterns were operative in the 2020 election. In an email, he responded, "Racial resentment and hostility toward immigrants and outgroups are certainly still central, but in my view, his [Trump's] appeal has become much more ideological as he has aligned himself closely with the views of the conservative wing of the Republican Party."
30. Pape, "What an Analysis."
31. In chapter 6, I argue that if we truly want to be consistent, we need those who disagree with us because they can see our biases with much more clarity than we can ourselves.

32. For more on this split, see Talisse, *Overdoing Democracy*, 84–85.
33. Some of this data comes from my analysis of results from the McCourtney Institute's Mood of the Nation poll. But see also Pew Research Center, "In Views of U.S. Democracy." See also Fitzgerald, "What Does 'Political' Mean to You?," 472. Fitzgerald concludes that "there is nothing simple about defining the political, and . . . survey participants' minds can go to very different places when answering questions that hinge on this term."
34. Brown, "Is Geographic Polarization Self-Reinforcing?"
35. Krieg, "Donald Trump Reveals."
36. See Hetherington and Weiler, *Prius or Pickup*, 220. On January 5, 2021, the day before the insurrection at the Capitol, Will Cain, host of *Fox and Friends Weekend*, said that Trump supporters "can be forgiven for their skepticism" around the 2020 election because "it certainly feels like society is rigged right now. . . . The entire society is rigged against people who hold my values." See https://twitter.com/i/status/1346420512168275969.
37. For more on this pattern, see Wehner, "Trump's Words Are Poison."
38. L. Mason, "'I Disrespectfully Agree,'" 141.

CHAPTER 3

1. Adams to John Taylor, December 17, 1814.
2. Montesquieu, *Spirit of the Laws*, 8.16.
3. Less convincingly, Montesquieu argues that in a city-state, there is less likely to be significant differences in wealth and therefore less cause for animosity between the rich and the poor. Of course, that argument does not hold up. For any metropolitan area you want to name, extreme wealth and poverty exist cheek by jowl. Perhaps for similar reasons, Montesquieu refers to the Pennsylvania established by William Penn but does not even mention contemporary European city-states like Venice or Geneva.
4. See Storing, introduction to *The Anti-Federalist*. See also Nicgorski, "Review."
5. Madison, Federalist 10.
6. Hamilton, Federalist 9.
7. This and all following quotations from Madison, Federalist 10.
8. Bentley, *Process of Government*, cited in Achen and Bartels, *Democracy for Realists*, 307.
9. Roccas and Brewer, "Social Identity Complexity," 104.
10. Madison, Federalist 51.
11. Montesquieu, *Considerations on the Causes*, chapter 10.

12. Montesquieu, *Spirit of the Laws*, 4.5.
13. Ibid.
14. Madison, Federalist 55.
15. See Smylie, "Madison and Witherspoon."
16. Madison, "Virginia Ratifying Convention."
17. G. Mason, "Virginia Declaration of Rights," sec. 15.
18. Franklin to the Abbés Chalut and Arnoux, April 17, 1787.
19. Henry to Archibald Blair, January 8, 1799, in Witte, *No Establishment of Religion*, 274.
20. Quoted in Philp, "Thomas Paine."
21. Morris to George Gordon, June 28, 1792, in McDonald, "Political Thought of Gouverneur Morris."
22. Rush, *Thoughts Upon the Mode of Education.*
23. Jefferson, *Notes on the State of Virginia*, 53.
24. Adams, "To the Inhabitants."
25. Adams to the Massachusetts Militia, October 11, 1798.
26. Washington, "Farewell Address."
27. Hamilton, Federalist 1.
28. Hamilton to Rufus King, June 3, 1802. The editors of Hamilton's letters provide the quotation and translation of Vergil.
29. Kloppenberg, "Virtues of Liberalism," 19.

CHAPTER 4

1. My last book was called *Democratic Humility: Reinhold Niebuhr, Neuroscience, and America's Political Crisis*. It was my first effort to address the inescapable fact of bias, what it means for a democracy, and what we can do about it. The argument here is similar, but they are wholly separate works. There is nothing in what follows that presumes familiarity with that book.
2. Applebaum, "'I Alone Can Fix It.'"
3. The Hindu scripture Bhagavad Gita lists humility as the first of the twenty qualities that divine wisdom comprises. For the Buddhist, the diminishment of the ego is the key to spiritual enlightenment; humility is both a means to that end and one of its inevitable manifestations. In the Hebrew Bible, too, the faithful are called to recognize God's majesty, power, and righteous justice and to respond to it with humility. Humility—the Hebrew word *anav* is also often translated as "meekness"—is thus understood to follow naturally from genuine understanding of our place in God's creation.
4. This and the following quotations are from Hume, *Enquiry Concerning the Principles of Morals*, 9.1.

5. Bernard of Clairvaux, *Steps of Humility*, 149.
6. Ibid., 125.
7. Hume, *Enquiry Concerning Human Understanding*, 687.
8. For one example, see Davis et al., "Distinguishing Intellectual Humility."
9. One early paper tentatively defined humility as "a nondefensive willingness to see the self accurately, including strengths and limitations." See Exline and Geyer, "Perceptions of Humility."
10. Leary, "Psychology of Intellectual Humility" (original emphasis), 4. The author notes that the "interdisciplinary group . . . involved philosophers with expertise in intellectual virtues (Jason Baehr, Heather Battaly, Dan Howard-Snyder, Dennis Whitcomb) and social, personality, clinical, counseling, and organizational psychologists with expertise in egotism and humility (Don Davis, Julie Exline, Peter Hill, Joshua Hook, Rick Hoyle, Mark Leary, Bradley Owens, Wade Rowatt, Steven Sandage)" (4).
11. Deffler, Leary, and Hoyle, "Knowing What You Know." See also Porter and Schumann, "Intellectual Humility and Openness."
12. Porter, "Benefits of Admitting." See also Krumrei-Mancuso et al., "Links Between Intellectual Humility," 9.
13. Krumrei-Mancuso, "Intellectual Humility and Prosocial Values," 8.
14. Porter and Schumann, "Intellectual Humility and Openness."
15. Krause et al., "Humility."
16. For a broad overview, see, for example, the Greenleaf Center for Servant Leadership website, https://www.greenleaf.org/what-is-servant-leadership.
17. Sousa and Van Dierendonck, "Servant Leadership," 15.
18. See Cable, "How Humble Leadership Really Works," 8.
19. Ou, Waldman, and Peterson, "Do Humble CEOs Matter?" See also Collins, "Level 5 Leadership."
20. See Estephan, "Relationship Between Marital Humility," 2334. For a study of college student relationships, see Farrell et al., "Humility and Relationship Outcomes."
21. Porter and Schumann, "Intellectual Humility and Openness," 157.
22. Ibid.
23. Ibid., 141.
24. Duhigg, "Real Roots of American Rage."
25. Leary et al., "Cognitive and Interpersonal Features," 793.
26. Ibid., 809.
27. Hand, "Spirit of Liberty Speech."
28. For an excellent overview, see Kraut, "Aristotle's Ethics."

29. In "Intellectual Humility," Baehr et al. present a similar take on humility as a virtuous mean.

CHAPTER 5

1. Orwell, "Politics and the English Language."
2. Kessler, "Not Just Misleading."
3. Mayer, "What Joe Biden Hasn't Owned Up."

4. This is why I will argue in chapter 6 that consistency is another democratic virtue.
5. Elving, "What Happened with Merrick Garland."
6. Leung, "'Oh, We'd Fill It.'"
7. See the *Seinfeld* clip here: https://www.youtube.com/watch?v=vn_PSJsloLQ.
8. Roosevelt, "Fireside Chat #18."
9. See PBS, "FDR on Lying."
10. Nye, *Do Morals Matter?*, 23.
11. Stevenson, *Man Called Intrepid*, 270.
12. Niebuhr, *Love and Justice*, 67.
13. Ibid.
14. Arendt, "Truth and Politics," 296.
15. See Shaffer, "Dress That Broke the Internet."
16. Arendt, "Karl Jaspers," 86. For more on Arendt and truth, see Beem, "Burden of Truth."
17. Arendt, *Origins of Totalitarianism*, 382.
18. See National Intelligence Council, "Foreign Threats."
19. See, for example, Dudziak, *Cold War Civil Rights*.
20. Boghardt, "Operation INFEKTION," 8.
21. Pomerantsev, *This Is Not Propaganda*, 115.
22. Frankfurt, *On Bullshit*, 55.
23. Ibid., 51.
24. Ibid., 34.
25. Ibid., 56.
26. Ibid., 61.
27. Pomerantsev, "Inside Putin's Information War."
28. Paul and Matthews, *Russian "Firehose of Falsehood."*
29. Ramsay and Robertshaw, *Weaponising News*.
30. For the complete story, see Urban, *Skripal Files*.
31. Ramsey and Robertshaw, *Weaponising News*, 44.
32. See Navalny, *Putin's Palace*.
33. The report by the Organization for the Prohibition of Chemical Weapons did note that the type of Novichok was one that they had not seen before. See Meduza, "OPCW Confirms."

34. See Babich, "West Rushes to Accuse Moscow."
35. See RT, "Developers of 'Novichok.'"
36. See RT, "Czech President Admits."
37. Part of the effort to obfuscate is to accuse your accusers of what they claim you to be doing; see MacDonald, "Latest."
38. In "Democracy Demotion," Larry Diamond offers a similar description of Russian propaganda: "The Kremlin's central tactic is to destroy the very premise that there can be objective truth, not to mention universal values. If there is no objective truth, and no deeper moral value than power itself, then the biggest liar wins. And that, is Vladimir Putin." This book was written long before the Russian invasion of Ukraine, but Russian responses to charges of war crimes demonstrate the very same pattern.
39. Ioffe, "What Is Russia Today?"
40. During the COVID-19 crisis, this propaganda model made yet another comeback, this time from a new international actor. Seeking to deflect attention from its mishandling of the outbreak of a worldwide pandemic, the Chinese Communist Party has also adopted the "firehose of falsehood" strategy. In a 2020 article for *Foreign Affairs*, Laura Rosenberger writes that "Beijing has taken a more aggressive approach than usual, even experimenting with tactics drawn from Russia's more nihilistic information operations playbook. That strategy aims not so much to promote a particular idea as to sow doubt, dissension, and disarray—including among Americans—to undermine public confidence in information and prevent any common understanding of facts from taking hold." See Rosenberger, "China's Coronavirus Information Offensive."
41. See Kessler, Rizzo, and Kelly, "Trump Is Averaging."
42. Downie, *Trump Administration and the Media.*
43. Coppins, "Billion-Dollar Disinformation Campaign," 35.
44. Downie, *Trump Administration and the Media.*
45. See Chalfant, ""Trump.'"
46. Naylor, "Read Trump's Jan. 6 Speech."
47. McConnell, speech on Senate floor, January 6, 2021.

CHAPTER 6

On the epigraph: It is not clear that Groucho ever said this, and even if he did, there were many before him. See Quote Investigator: https://quoteinvestigator.com/2010/05/09/groucho-principles.

1. Emerson, *Self-Reliance.*
2. Ibid.
3. Ibid.

4. Recall the epigraph for chapter 1 from Walter Lippman: "Where all think alike, no one thinks very much."
5. Everly, "Trauma of Intimate Partner Betrayal."
6. See, e.g., Swide, "Jets Fan Group."
7. See Macur, "Why Do Fans Excuse."
8. Pettigrew, "Ultimate Attribution Error."
9. Hewstone, "'Ultimate Attribution Error'?"
10. Barden, "Order of Actions," 599.

11. Maynes, "Critical Thinking and Cognitive Bias," 187.
12. Lord, Ross, and Lepper, "Biased Assimilation and Attitude Polarization."
13. Ibid., 2102.
14. Ibid., 2107.
15. Lord, Lepper, and Preston, "Considering the Opposite," 1232.
16. Ibid.
17. Ibid.
18. See Justinian, *Institutes.*
19. This connection is one reason why I chose not to add a chapter on justice. The relevant point is covered here.
20. McGurn, "Slogans to Fit the Occasion," 170–74.
21. Rothman, *Unjust*, 31.
22. All quotations are from Winston Churchill, "Consistency in Politics." This piece also begins with Emerson's remark. When you are talking about consistency, it really is impossible to ignore.
23. See PC Mag Staff, "25 Optical Illusions."
24. Kruger and Gilovich, "'Naive Cynicism,'" 743–53.
25. Here is the exact quotation, translated into English: "Whoever wills the end also wills (in so far as reason has decisive influence on his actions) the indispensably necessary means to it that is in his control." Kant, *Groundwork of the Metaphysics of Morals*, 30.

CHAPTER 7

1. Compare this frequently cited definition from the literature: Courage is "(a) a willful, intentional act, (b) executed after mindful deliberation, (c) involving objective substantial risk to the actor, (d) primarily motivated to bring about a noble good or worthy end, (e) despite, perhaps, the presence of the emotion of fear." Rate et al., "Implicit Theories of Courage," 95.
2. It is true that bravery is frequently immediate. Courageous people will often reflect afterward that at the moment, there wasn't time to be scared, or to think; they just reacted. So perhaps it is more

accurate to say that fear is often but not always part of being courageous. Yet it is certainly true that faced with the same circumstance, not everyone would have reacted in the same way. And it is almost certainly true that at some level, more or less conscious, these courageous people did indeed have a sense of the risk they were undertaking. Fear or no, risk—and recognition of that risk—is an essential dimension of courage.

3. Aristotle, *Nicomachean Ethics*, 70–72.
4. For a very good introduction, see Taylor, "Who Were the Freedom Riders?" The American Experience *Freedom Riders* episode is also excellent.
5. Here is one definition of civil courage: "brave behavior accompanied by anger and indignation which intends to enforce societal and ethical norms without considering one's own social costs." See Greitemeyer et al., "Civil Courage," 115.
6. See National Women's Hall of Fame, "Maggie Kuhn."
7. See, for example, Johnson, "Latest Battlefield"; Gabriel, "American Suburbs."
8. Cuff, "Experience of Courage," 8.
9. See Osswald et al., "What Is Moral Courage?," 149–64; Kramer and Zinbarg, "Recalling Courage," 528–37.
10. Osswald, Frey, and Streicher, "Moral Courage," 396.
11. The notion that bees ostracize other bees was an arresting piece of information for me. Williams, "Ostracism."
12. Ibid., 433.
13. Ibid., 432, citing Baumeister, Twenge, and Nuss, "Effects of Social Exclusion," 817–27.
14. Kennedy, *Profiles in Courage*, 130.
15. Ibid., 127.
16. Ibid., 130.
17. Klein, *Why We're Polarized*, 97.
18. Many people find political disagreement particularly distasteful. See Hibbing and Theiss-Morse, *Stealth Democracy*, especially chapter 8, "The Realities of Popular Deliberation and Group Involvement."
19. Williams, "Ostracism," 428.
20. Ibid., 439.
21. Garrett, Sude, and Riva, "Toeing the Line," 167.
22. Ibid.
23. Aristotle, *Nicomachean Ethics*, 172.
24. The question of the so-called unity of the virtues is complex and ongoing. I am not inclined to go down that rabbit hole. But what I say here must make it clear that, niceties aside, I side with Aristotle.

For more on this debate, see Russell, *Practical Intelligence and the Virtues.*

CHAPTER 8

1. Lyman, "Domestication of Anger," 133–47.
2. Merriam-Webster, s.v. "grievance," https://www.merriam-webster.com/dictionary/grievance.
3. Ibid.
4. Merriam-Webster, s.v. "petition," https://www.merriam-webster.com/dictionary/petition.
5. Webster, *American Rage,* 6.
6. Lounge Group, "Nearly 80 Percent."
7. Aristotle, *Rhetoric* 2.2, 1378a.
8. Ibid.
9. Lazarus, "How Emotions Influence Performance," 234. Lazarus notes that he is working in the tradition of Aristotle and Plato.
10. Seneca, *On Anger* 1.8.
11. Aristotle, *Nicomachean Ethics,* 101.
12. For an excellent presentation of a broader reading of Aristotle's conception of anger, see Christensen, "Aristotle on Anger."
13. Aristotle, too, speaks of temperance as a virtue, but he associates it only with food, drink, and sex. This is another example of what I see as Aristotle inordinately limiting the scope of each virtue.
14. Aristotle, *Rhetoric* 2.4, 1382a, 1–14.
15. Friendship is the opposite of hate, but for Aristotle, it, too, is more a disposition than an emotion.
16. Beck, *Prisoners of Hate,* quoted in Konstan, "Anger, Hatred, and Genocide," 178.
17. Lamoureux, "Former Neo-Nazis."
18. See PRRI, *Dueling Realities.*
19. Levitsky and Ziblatt, *How Democracies Die,* 218–19.
20. Beem, *Democratic Humility,* chapter 10.
21. Allcott et al., "Welfare Effects," 629–76.
22. Here, I am expanding on an idea that I first heard in conversation with David Frum. I referenced this idea in a TEDx Talk I gave at Penn State: https://www.ted.com/talks/christopher_beem_how_you_can_fix_democracy_yes_really. My point is similar to one raised by Talisse in his book *Overdoing Democracy.*
23. Lamoureux, "Former Neo-Nazis."
24. Lincoln, "First Inaugural Address."

25. Velasquez-Manoff, "How to Make Fun of Nazis."
26. Popovic with McClennen, *Pranksters vs. Autocrats*. Popovic was awarded the Brown Democracy Medal by the McCourtney Institute for Democracy in 2020.
27. Velasquez-Manoff outlines the lesson this story offers to Americans in "How to Make Fun of Nazis."

CHAPTER 9

1. Niebuhr, *Moral Man and Immoral Society*, 127.
2. See, for example, Siegel, *Charity and Condescension*.
3. Technically, for David Davidson, thought itself can only emerge through communication and interpretation. But this is really inside baseball.
4. "This necessarily requires us to see others as much like ourselves in point of overall coherence and correctness—that we see them as more or less rational creatures mentally inhabiting a world much like our own." Davidson, "Expressing Evaluations," 35.
5. Ibid., 36.
6. Murray, *We Hold These Truths*, 32.
7. This story is well documented. See, for example, Shelden and Alexander, "Americans Worry About 2020."
8. Aquinas, *Summa Theologica* 2.2.25.4.
9. Allen, *Talking to Strangers*, 156 (emphasis added).
10. Bernard of Clairvaux, *Steps of Humility*, 147.
11. Ibid.
12. Harris, "Francis Preaches on St. Thérèse."
13. Reid, "Bernard of Clairvaux."
14. Exline and Hill, "Humility," 216.
15. Ibid., 215.
16. Dionne, "Biden Reaches Out." The following quotations are also from this article.
17. See, for example, Dombrowski, "Nonviolent Resistance and Hitler (Milosevic)."
18. See Matthew 5:38, 18:21–22.
19. Allen, *Talking to Strangers*, 155.
20. There are myriad accounts readily available. For one that ably explores the many philosophical issues associated with the story, see Kuhn, "Prisoner's Dilemma."
21. See Axelrod, *Evolution of Cooperation*.

CHAPTER 10

1. See Madison, "Notes on Ancient and Modern Confederacies."
2. Aquinas, *Summa Theologica* 2.2.4.1.
3. Ibid. 2.2.1.2.
4. Achen and Bartels, *Democracy for Realists*, 1 and passim.
5. Ibid., 299.
6. Ibid., 44.
7. Ibid., 181.
8. Ibid., 118–28.
9. Ibid., 143.
10. Ibid., 299.
11. Ibid., 214–15.
12. Ibid., 311, 313.
13. Ibid., 342.
14. Ibid., 321.
15. Madison, Federalist 55.
16. Thunberg, speech before the US. Congress reproduced in *The Independent*: https://www.independent.co.uk/voices/greta-thunberg-congress-speech-climate-change-crisis-dream-a9112151.html.
17. See Vindman's opening statement reproduced in the *New York Times*: https://www.nytimes.com/2019/11/19/us/politics/vindman-statement-testimony.html.
18. Associated Press, "'Here, Right Matters.'"
19. Cheney-Rice, "Bryan Stevenson."
20. See Ayesh, "Trump Justifies Firing Alexander Vindman."
21. Vindman, "Coming Forward."
22. Aquinas, *Summa Theologica* 2.2.17.1.
23. Niebuhr, *Irony of American History*, 63.

CONCLUSION

1. Adams to John Taylor, December 17, 1814.
2. Biden, Inaugural Address.

Bibliography

Abramowitz, Alan. *The Great Alignment: Race, Party Transformation, and the Rise of Donald Trump*. New Haven: Yale University Press, 2018.

Achen, Christopher H., and Larry M. Bartels. *Democracy for Realists: Why Elections Do Not Produce Responsive Government*. Princeton: Princeton University Press, 2018.

Adams, John. Letter to John Taylor. Quincy, MA, December 17, 1814. Founders Online. National Archives. https://founders.archives.gov/documents/Adams/99-02-02-6371.

———. Letter to the Massachusetts Militia. Quincy, MA, October 11, 1798. Founders Online. National Archives. https://founders.archives.gov/documents/Adams/99-02-02-3102.

Adams, John [under pen name Novanglus]. "To the Inhabitants of the Colony of Massachusetts-Bay." *Boston Gazette, and Country Journal*, February 6, 1775. Adams Papers: Digital Edition. Massachusetts Historical Society. http://www.masshist.org/publications/adams-papers/index.php/view/PJA02d092.

Allcott, Hunt, Luca Braghieri, Sarah Eichmeyer, and Matthew Gentzkow. "The Welfare Effects of Social Media." *American Economic Review* 110, no. 3 (2020): 629–76. https://pubs.aeaweb.org/doi/pdfplus/10.1257/aer.20190658.

Allen, Danielle. *Talking to Strangers*. Chicago: University of Chicago Press, 2004.

Appelbaum, Yoni. "I Alone Can Fix It." *The Atlantic*, July 21, 2016. https://www.theatlantic.com/politics/archive/2016/07/trump-rnc-speech-alone-fix-it/492557.

Aquinas, Thomas. *Summa Theologica*. Translated by English Dominican Province. Vol. 5. Westminster, MD: Christian Classics, 1981.

Arendt, Hannah. "Karl Jaspers: Citizen of the World?" In *Men in Dark Times*, 81–94. New York: Harvest, 1968.

———. *The Origins of Totalitarianism*. New York: Harcourt Brace Jovanovich, 1973.

———. "Truth and Politics." *The New Yorker*, February 17, 1967, 49. https://idanlandau.files.wordpress.com/2014/12/arendt-truth-and-politics.pdf.

Aristotle. *Nicomachean Ethics*. Translated by Martin Ostwald. Indianapolis: Bobbs-Merrill, 1962.

———. *Rhetoric*. Translated by W. Rhys Roberts. The Internet Classics Archive. http://classics.mit.edu/Aristotle/rhetoric.2.ii.html.

Associated Press. "'Here, Right Matters': Vindman Explains Why He Testified." *New York Times*, November 19, 2019. https://www.nytimes.com/video/us/politics/100000006834102/impeachment-inquiry-vindman-applause.html.

Axelrod, Robert. *The Evolution of Cooperation*. Rev. ed. New York: Basic Books, 2006.

Ayesh, Rashaan. "Trump Justifies Firing Alexander Vindman for Being 'Insubordinate.'" *Axios*, February 8, 2020. https://www.axios.com/trump-tweet-vindman-insubordiante-firing-a9929087-fe9a-44ef-b95b-12d07e235682.html.

Babich, Dmitry. "West Rushes to Accuse Moscow of 'Novichok-Type' Poisoning of Navalny . . . but Would Russia Really Have Reason to Get Rid of Him?" *RT*, September 2, 2020. https://www.rt.com/op-ed/499741-navalny-poisoning-western-blame-russia.

Baehr, Jason, Dennis Whitcomb, Heather Battaly, and Dan Howard-Snyder. "Intellectual Humility: Owning Our Limitations." *Philosophy and Phenomenological Research* 94, no. 3 (2017): 509–39. doi: 10.1111/phpr.12228.

Barden, Jamie, Derek D. Rucker, Richard E. Petty, and Kimberly Rios. "Order of Actions Mitigates Hypocrisy Judgments for Ingroup More Than Outgroup Members." *Group Processes and Intergroup Relations* 17, no. 5 (2014): 590–601. doi: 10.1177/1368430213510192.

Baumeister, Roy F., Jean M. Twenge, and Christopher K. Nuss. "Effects of Social Exclusion on Cognitive Processes: Anticipated Aloneness." *Journal of Personality and Social Psychology* 83, no. 4 (2002): 817–27. doi: 10.1037//0022-3514.83.4.817.

Beck, Aaron. *Prisoners of Hate: The Cognitive Basis of Anger, Hostility, and Violence*. New York: Harper Collins, 1999.

Beem, Christopher. "The Burden of Truth: Hannah Arendt, Democracy, and Donald Trump's Lies." *The Critique*, January 15, 2017. http://www.thecritique.com/articles/the-burden-of-truth/#_ftn7.

———. *Democratic Humility: Reinhold Niebuhr, Neuroscience, and America's Political Crisis*. Lanham, MD: Lexington Books, 2015.

Benhabib, Seyla, ed. *Democracy and Difference: Contesting the Boundaries of the Political*. Princeton: Princeton University Press, 1996.

Bentley, Arthur F. *The Process of Government: A Study of Social Pressures*. Edited by Peter H. Odegard. Cambridge: Harvard University Press, 1908, 1965.

Bernard, Abbot of Clairvaux. *The Steps of Humility*. Edited by George Bosworth Burch. Translated by George Bosworth Burch. Cambridge: Harvard University Press, 1940.

Biden, Joseph R. Inaugural Address. Washington, DC, January 20, 2021. The White House. Briefing Room. https://www.whitehouse.gov/briefing-room/speeches-remarks/2021/01/20/inaugural-address-by-president-joseph-r-biden-jr.

Bigler, Rebecca S., Lecianna C. Jones, and Debra B. Lobliner. "Social Categorization and the Formation of Intergroup Attitudes in Children." *Child Development* 68, no. 3 (1997): 530–43. doi: 10.2307/1131676.

Blodget, Henry. "The Truth about Taxes: Here's How High Today's Rates Really Are." *Business Insider*, July 12, 2011. https://www.businessinsider.com/history-of-tax-rates.

Boghardt, Thomas. "Operation INFEKTION: Soviet Bloc Intelligence and Its AIDS Disinformation Campaign." *Studies in Intelligence* 53, no. 4 (2009): 1–24. https://digitallibrary.tsu.ge/book/2019/september/books/Soviet-Bloc-Intelligence-and-Its-AIDS.pdf.

Brown, Jacob R. "Is Geographic Polarization Self-Reinforcing?" 2021. Unpublished manuscript.

Cable, Dan. "How Humble Leadership Really Works." *Harvard Business Review*, April 23, 2018. https://hbr.org/2018/04/how-humble-leadership-really-works.

Chalfant, Morgan. "Trump: 'The Only Way We're Going to Lose This Election Is if the Election Is Rigged.'" *The Hill*, August 17, 2020. https://thehill.com/homenews/administration/512424-trump-the-only-way-we-are-going-to-lose-this-election-is-if-the.

Cheney-Rice, Zak. "Bryan Stevenson on His 'Not Entirely Rational' Quest for Justice." *New York*, June 25, 2019. https://nymag.com/intelligencer/2019/06/bryan-stevensons-not-entirely-rational-quest-for-justice.html.

Christensen, Niels Aslak. "Aristotle on Anger, Justice and Punishment." Master's thesis, University College London, 2016. https://discovery.ucl.ac.uk/id/eprint/1557934/1/Aristotle%20on%20Anger,%20Justice%20and%20Punishment.pdf.

Churchill, Winston S. "Consistency in Politics." In *Thoughts and Adventures*, 39–50. London: Thornton Butterworth, 1932. https://matiane.wordpress.com/2019/09/07/consistency-in-politics-by-winston-churchill.

Cikara, Mina, Matthew M. Botvinick, and Susan T. Fiske. "Us Versus Them: Social Identity Shapes Neural Responses to Intergroup Competition and Harm." *Psychological Science* 22, no. 3 (2011): 306–13. doi: 10.1177/0956797610397667.

Collins, Jim. "Level 5 Leadership: The Triumph of Humility and Fierce Resolve." *Harvard Business Review*, July–August 2005. https://

hbr.org/2005/07/level-5-leadership-the-triumph-of-humility-and-fierce-resolve.
Conroy, Meredith, and Perry Bacon Jr. "There's a Huge Gap in How Republicans and Democrats See Discrimination." FiveThirtyEight, June 17, 2020. https://fivethirtyeight.com/features/theres-still-a-huge-partisan-gap-in-how-americans-see-discrimination.
Coppins, McKay. "The Billion-Dollar Disinformation Campaign to Reelect the President." *The Atlantic,* February 10, 2020. https://www.theatlantic.com/magazine/archive/2020/03/the-2020-disinformation-war/605530.
Cox, Daniel, and Robert P. Jones. *America's Changing Religious Identity.* PRRI, September 6, 2017. https://www.prri.org/research/american-religious-landscape-christian-religiously-unaffiliated/.
———. *Majority of Americans Oppose Transgender Bathroom Restrictions.* PRRI, March 10, 2017. https://www.prri.org/research/lgbt-transgender-bathroom-discrimination-religious-liberty.
Cuff, William Thomas. "The Experience of Courage and the Characteristics of Courageous People." PhD diss., University of Minnesota, 1993.
Davidson, Donald. "Expressing Evaluations." In *Problems of Rationality,* 19–38. Oxford: Clarendon Press of Oxford University Press, 2004.
Davis, Don E., Kenneth Rice, Stacey McElroy, and Cirleen DeBlaere. "Distinguishing Intellectual Humility and General Humility." *Journal of Positive Psychology* 11, no. 3 (2016): 215–24. doi: 10.1080/17439760.2015.1048818.
Deffler, S. A., M. R. Leary, and R. H. Hoyle. "Knowing What You Know: Intellectual Humility and Judgments of Recognition Memory." *Personality and Individual Differences* 96 (2016): 255–59. doi: 10.1016/j.paid.2016.03.016.
Denworth, Lydia. "Conservative and Liberal Brains Might Have Some Real Differences." *Scientific American,* October 26, 2020. https://www.scientificamerican.com/article/conservative-and-liberal-brains-might-have-some-real-differences.
Diamond, Larry. "Democracy Demotion: How the Freedom Agenda Fell Apart." *Foreign Affairs,* July–August 2019. https://fsi.stanford.edu/news/democracy-demotion-how-freedom-agenda-fell-apart.
Dionne, E. J. "Biden Reaches Out. The GOP Slaps Him in the Face." *Washington Post,* November 22, 2020. https://www.washingtonpost.com/opinions/biden-reaches-out-the-gop-slaps-him-in-the-face/2020/11/20/5111029e-2b76-11eb-92b7-6ef17b3fe3b4_story.html.

Dombrowski, Daniel. "Nonviolent Resistance and Hitler (Milosevic)." *Peace Research* 32, no. 1 (2000): 42–51. http://www.jstor.org/stable/23607684.

Downie, Leonard, Jr. *The Trump Administration and the Media*. New York: Committee to Protect Journalists, 2020. https://cpj.org/reports/2020/04/trump-media-attacks-credibility-leaks.

Drutman, Lee. *Breaking the Two-Party Doom Loop: The Case for Multiparty Democracy in America*. Oxford: Oxford University Press, 2020.

Duarte, Isabel C., Sonia Afonso, Helena Jorge, Ricardo Cayolla, Carlos Ferreira, and Miquel Castelo-Branco. "Tribal Love: The Neural Correlates of Passionate Engagement in Football Fans." *Social Cognitive and Affective Neuroscience* 12, no. 5 (2017): 718–28. doi: 10.1093/scan/nsx003.

Dudziak, Mary. *Cold War Civil Rights: Race and the Image of American Democracy*. Princeton: Princeton University Press, 2011.

Duhigg, Charles. "The Real Roots of American Rage." *The Atlantic*, January–February 2019. https://www.theatlantic.com/magazine/archive/2019/01/charles-duhigg-american-anger/576424.

Edsall, Thomas B. "No Hate Left Behind." *New York Times*, March 13, 2019. https://www.nytimes.com/2019/03/13/opinion/hate-politics.html.

Elving, Ron. "What Happened with Merrick Garland in 2016 and Why It Matters Now." *NPR*, June 29, 2018. https://www.npr.org/2018/06/29/624467256/what-happened-with-merrick-garland-in-2016-and-why-it-matters-now.

Emerson, Ralph Waldo. *Self-Reliance*. White Plains, NY: Peter Pauper Press, 1967. https://emersoncentral.com/texts/essays-first-series/self-reliance.

Estephan, A. S. "The Relationship Between Marital Humility, Marital Communication, and Marital Satisfaction." *Dissertation Abstracts International Section A: Humanities and Social Sciences* 68 (6-A) (2007), 2334. https://psycnet.apa.org/record/2007-99230-469.

Everly, George S., Jr. "The Trauma of Intimate Partner Betrayal." *Psychology Today*, June 8, 2018. https://www.psychologytoday.com/us/blog/when-disaster-strikes-inside-disaster-psychology/201806/the-trauma-intimate-partner-betrayal.

Exline, Julie J., and Anne L. Geyer. "Perceptions of Humility: A Preliminary Study." *Self and Identity* 3, no. 2 (2004): 95–114. doi: 10.1080/13576500342000077.

Exline, Julie J., and Peter C. Hill. "Humility: A Consistent and Robust Predictor of Generosity." *Journal of Positive Psychology* 7, no. 3 (2012): 208–18. doi: 10.1080/17439760.2012.671348.

Farrell, Jennifer E., Joshua N. Hook, Marciana Ramos, Don E. Davis, Daryl R. Van Tongeren, and John M. Ruiz. "Humility and Relationship Outcomes in Couples: The Mediating Role of Commitment." *Couple and Family Psychology: Research and Practice* 4, no. 1 (2015): 14–26. doi: 10.1037/cfp0000033.

Fitzgerald, Jennifer. "What Does 'Political' Mean to You?" *Political Behavior* 35, no. 3 (2013): 453–79. http://www.jstor.org/stable/43653078.

Foot, Philippa. *Virtues and Vices*. Oxford: Oxford University Press, 1978.

Frame, Carson. "Study Finds Evidence of Social Disconnect Between Veterans, Civilians." Texas Public Radio, December 20, 2017. https://www.tpr.org/post/study-finds-evidence-social-disconnect-between-veterans-civilians.

Frankfurt, Harry G. *On Bullshit*. Princeton: Princeton University Press, 2005.

Franklin, Benjamin. "Letter to the Abbés Chalut and Arnoux." Philadelphia, April 17, 1787. *The Papers of Benjamin Franklin*, March 1, 1786–April 30, 1787. https://franklinpapers.org/framedVolumes.jsp?vol=44&page=605.

Frey, William H. "The US Will Become 'Minority White' in 2045, Census Projects." *Brookings*, March 14, 2018. https://www.brookings.edu/blog/the-avenue/2018/03/14/the-us-will-become-minority-white-in-2045-census-projects.

Friedersdorf, Conor. "How Breitbart Destroyed Andrew Breitbart's Legacy." *The Atlantic*, November 14, 2017. https://www.theatlantic.com/politics/archive/2017/11/how-breitbart-destroyed-andrew-breitbarts-legacy/545807.

Gabriel, Trip. "American Suburbs Are Tilting for Biden. But Not Milwaukee's." *New York Times*, September 23, 2020. https://www.nytimes.com/2020/09/23/us/politics/wisconsin-trump-biden-suburbs.html.

Garrett, R. Kelly, Daniel Sude, and Paolo Riva. "Toeing the Party Lie: Ostracism Promotes Endorsement of Partisan Election Falsehoods." *Political Communication* 37, no. 2 (2020): 157–72. doi: 10.1080/10584609.2019.1666943.

Gimpel, James, Nathan Lovin, Bryant Moy, and Andrew Reeves. "The Urban–Rural Gulf in American Political Behavior." *Political Behavior* 42 (2020): 1343–68. doi: 10.1007/s11109-020-09601-w.

Gorman, Amanda. "The Hill We Climb." [Poem read for Joseph R. Biden's presidential inauguration, Washington, DC.] *CNN Politics*, January 20, 2021. https://www.cnn.com/2021/01/20/politics/amanda-gorman-inaugural-poem-transcript/index.html.

Greitemeyer, Tobias, Silvia Osswald, Peter Fischer, and Dieter Frey. "Civil Courage: Implicit Theories, Related Concepts, and Measurement." *Journal of Positive Psychology* 2, no. 2 (2007): 115–19. doi: 10.1080/17439760701228789.

Gutmann, Amy. "Philosophy, Democracy, and Justification." In *Democracy and Difference: Contesting the Boundaries of the Political*, edited by Seyla Benhabib, 340–47. Princeton: Princeton University Press, 1996.

Hamilton, Alexander. Federalist No. 1. 1788. Federalist Papers: Primary Documents in American History. Library of Congress. https://guides.loc.gov/federalist-papers/text-1-10#s-lg-box-wrapper-25493264.

———. Federalist No. 9. 1788. Federalist Papers: Primary Documents in American History. Library of Congress. https://guides.loc.gov/federalist-papers/text-1-10#s-lg-box-wrapper-25493272.

———. Letter to Rufus King. June 3, 1802. Founders Online. National Archives. https://founders.archives.gov/documents/Hamilton/01-26-02-0001-0011.

Hamilton, Alexander, James Madison, and John Jay. *The Federalist Papers*. Edited by Clinton Rossiter. New York: Mentor, 1961.

Hand, Learned. "'The Spirit of Liberty' Speech by Judge Learned Hand, 1944." Foundation for Individual Rights in Education. https://www.thefire.org/first-amendment-library/special-collections/the-spirit-of-liberty-speech-by-judge-learned-hand-1944.

Harnad, Stevan. "To Cognize Is to Categorize: Cognition Is Categorization." In *Handbook of Categorization in Cognitive Science*, edited by Henri Cohen and Claire Lefebvre, 21–54. Amsterdam: Elsevier, 2017.

Harris, Elise. "Francis Preaches on St. Thérèse: Charity Without Humility Is Sterile." *National Catholic Register*, October 2, 2013. https://www.ncregister.com/news/francis-preaches-on-st-therese-charity-without-humility-is-sterile.

Haslam, Nick, Paul Bain, Lauren Douge, Max Lee, and Brock Bastian. "More Human Than You: Attributing Humanness to Self and Others." *Journal of Personality and Social Psychology* 89, no. 6 (2005): 937–50. doi: 10.1037/0022-3514.89.6.937.

Hetherington, Marc, and Jonathan Weiler. *Prius or Pickup? How the Answers to Four Simple Questions Explain America's Great Divide*. Boston: Houghton Mifflin Harcourt, 2018.

Hewstone, Miles. "The 'Ultimate Attribution Error'? A Review of the Literature on Intergroup Causal Attribution." *European Journal*

of Social Psychology 20, no. 4 (1990): 311–35. doi:10.1002/ejsp.2420200404.
Hibbing, John R., and Elizabeth Theiss-Morse. *Stealth Democracy: Americans' Beliefs About How Government Should Work*. Cambridge: Cambridge University Press, 2002. doi:10.1017/CBO9780511613722.
Hobfoll, Stevan E. *Tribalism: The Evolutionary Origins of Fear Politics*. London: Palgrave Macmillan, 2018.

Horowitz, Juliana Menasce, Anna Brown, and Kiana Cox. *Race in America 2019*. Washington, DC: Pew Research Center, 2019. https://www.pewsocialtrends.org/wp-content/uploads/sites/3/2019/04/PewResearchCenter_RaceStudy_FINAL-1.pdf.
Hume, David. "An Enquiry Concerning Human Understanding." In *English Philosophers from Bacon to Mill*, edited by Edwin A. Burtt, 585–689. New York: Modern Library, 1967.
———. *An Enquiry Concerning the Principles of Morals*. 1912. Reprint of 1777 edition. Project Gutenberg. https://www.gutenberg.org/files/4320/4320-h/4320-h.htm.
Iacozza, Sara, Antje Meyer, and Shiri Lev-Ari. "How In-Group Bias Influences Source Memory for Words Learned from In-Group and Out-Group Speakers." *Frontiers in Human Neuroscience* 13 (2019): 308. doi: 10.3389/fnhum.2019.00308.
Ioffe, Julia. "What Is Russia Today?" *Columbia Journalism Review*, September–October 2010. https://archives.cjr.org/feature/what_is_russia_today.php.
Johnson, Jenna. "The Latest Battlefield in a Heated Presidential Campaign: Front Yards Bearing Biden Signs." *Washington Post*, August 29, 2020. https://www.washingtonpost.com/politics/the-latest-battlefield-in-a-heated-presidential-campaign-front-yards-bearing-biden-signs/2020/08/29/5264dc70-e962-11ea-970a-64c73a1c2392_story.html#comments-wrapper.
Jones, Jeffrey M. "Support for Third U.S. Political Party at High Point." *Gallup*, February 15, 2021. https://news.gallup.com/poll/329639/support-third-political-party-high-point.aspx.
Justinian. *The Institutes of Justinian*. Translated by Richard Laird Cole. N.d. http://thelatinlibrary.com/law/institutes.html.
Kahneman, Daniel. *Thinking Fast and Slow*. New York: Farrar, Straus and Giroux, 2011.
Kalmoe, Nathan P., and Lilliana Mason. "Lethal Mass Partisanship: Prevalence, Correlates, and Electoral Contingencies." Prepared for the NCAPSA American Politics Meeting, January 2019. https://www

.dannyhayes.org/uploads/6/9/8/5/69858539/kalmoe___mason_ncapsa_2019_-_lethal_partisanship_-_final_lmedit.pdf.
Kant, Immanuel. *Groundwork of the Metaphysics of Morals*. Edited and translated by Mary Gregor and Jens Timmermann. Cambridge: Cambridge University Press, 2012.
Kaplan, Ethan, Jörg L. Spenkuch, and Rebecca Sullivan. "Partisan Spatial Sorting in the United States: A Theoretical and Empirical Overview." Unpublished paper, 2020. http://econweb.umd.edu/~kaplan/big_sort_APSA.pdf.
Kelly, David, Paul C. Quinn, Alan M. Slater, Kang Lee, Liezhong Ge, and Olivier Pascalis. "The Other-Race Effect Develops During Infancy: Evidence of Perceptual Narrowing." *Psychological Science* 18, no. 12 (2007). doi: 10.1111/j.1467-9280.2007.02029.x.
Kennedy, John F. *Profiles in Courage*. New York: Harper Perennial, 2015.
Kessler, Glenn. "Not Just Misleading. Not Merely False. A Lie." *Washington Post*, August 22, 2018. https://www.washingtonpost.com/politics/2018/08/23/not-just-misleading-not-merely-false-lie.
Kessler, Glenn, Salvador Rizzo, and Meg Kelly. "Trump Is Averaging More Than 50 False or Misleading Claims a Day." *Washington Post*, October 22, 2020. https://www.washingtonpost.com/politics/2020/10/22/president-trump-is-averaging-more-than-50-false-or-misleading-claims-day.
Klar, Samara, and Yanna Krupnikov. *Independent Politics: How American Disdain for Parties Leads to Political Inaction*. Cambridge: Cambridge University Press, 2016.
Klein, Ezra. *Why We're Polarized*. New York: Avid Reader Press, 2020.
Kloppenberg, James T. "The Virtues of Liberalism: Christianity, Republicanism, and Ethics in Early American Political Disourse." *Journal of American History* 19, no. 1 (1987): 9–33 . http://www.jstor.org/stable/1908503.
Konstan, David. "Anger, Hatred, and Genocide in Ancient Greece." *Common Knowledge* 13, no. 1 (2007): 170–87. https://www.muse.jhu.edu/article/210770.
Kramer, Amanda, and Richard Zinbarg. "Recalling Courage: An Initial Test of a Brief Writing Intervention to Activate a 'Courageous Mindset' and Courageous Behavior." *Journal of Positive Psychology* 14, no. 4 (2019): 528–37. doi: 10.1080/17439760.2018.1484943.
Krause, Neal, Kenneth I. Pargament, Peter C. Hill, and Gail Ironson. "Humility, Stressful Life Events, and Psychological Well-Being: Findings from the Landmark Spirituality and Health Survey." *Journal of Positive Psychology* 11, no. 5 (2016): 499–510. doi: 10.1080/17439760.2015.1127991.

Kraut, Richard. "Aristotle's Ethics." Stanford Encyclopedia of Philosophy Archive, Summer 2018 Edition. https://plato.stanford.edu/archives/sum2018/entries/aristotle-ethics.

Krieg, Gregory. "Donald Trump Reveals When He Thinks America Was Great." *CNN Politics*, March 28, 2016. https://www.cnn.com/2016/03/26/politics/donald-trump-when-america-was-great/index.html.

Kruger, Justin, and Thomas Gilovich. "'Naive Cynicism' in Everyday Theories of Responsibility Assessment: On Biased Assumptions of Bias." *Journal of Personality and Social Psychology* 76, no. 5 (1999): 743–53. doi: 10.1037%2F0022-3514.76.5.743.

Krumrei-Mancuso, Elizabeth. "Intellectual Humility and Prosocial Values: Direct and Mediated Effects." *Journal of Positive Psychology* 12, no. 1 (2017): 13–28. doi: 10.1080/17439760.2016.1167938.

Krumrei-Mancuso, Elizabeth J., Megan C. Haggard, Jordan P. LaBouff, and Wade C. Rowatt. "Links Between Intellectual Humility and Acquiring Knowledge." *Positive Psychology* 15, no. 2 (2020): 155–70. doi: 10.1080/17439760.2019.1579359.

Kuhn, Steven. "Prisoner's Dilemma." Stanford Encyclopedia of Philosophy Archive, Winter 2019 Edition. https://plato.stanford.edu/archives/win2019/entries/prisoner-dilemma.

Lamoureux, Mack. "Former Neo-Nazis Tell Us How They Finally Left the Movement." *Vice*, June 21, 2018. https://www.vice.com/en/article/59qeqa/former-neo-nazis-told-us-how-they-finally-left-the-movement.

Lazarus, Richard S. "How Emotions Influence Performance in Competitive Sports." *The Sport Psychologist* 14, no. 3 (2000): 229–52. doi: 10.1123/tsp.14.3.229.

Leary, Mark. "The Psychology of Intellectual Humility." Department of Psychology and Neuroscience, Duke University. The John Templeton Foundation, 2018.

Leary, Mark, Kate J. Diebels, Erin Davisson, Katrina P. Jongman-Sereno, Jennifer C. Isherwood, Kaitlin T. Raimi, Samatha A. Deffler, and Rick H. Hoyle. "Cognitive and Interpersonal Features of Intellectual Humility." *Personality and Social Psychology Bulletin* 43, no. 6 (2017): 793–813. doi: 10.1177/0146167217697695.

Leung, Hillary. "'Oh, We'd Fill It.' Mitch McConnell Says He'd Fill a Supreme Court Vacancy in 2020." *Time*, May 29, 2019. https://time.com/5597395/mitch-mcconnell-supreme-court-2020.

Levitsky, Steven, and Daniel Ziblatt. *How Democracies Die*. New York: Crown Books, 2018.

Lickel, Brian, David L. Hamilton, Grazyna Wieczorkowska, Amy Lewis, Steven J. Sherman, and A. Neville Uhles. 2000. "Varieties of Groups and the Perception of Group Entitativity." *Journal of Personality and Social Psychology* 78 (2000): 223–46.

Lincoln, Abraham. "First Inaugural Address of Abraham Lincoln." Washington, DC, March 4, 1861. The Avalon Project: Documents in Law, History and Diplomacy. Yale Law School. doi: https://avalon.law.yale.edu/19th_century/lincoln1.asp.

———. "Lincoln's Second Inaugural Address." Washington, DC, March 4, 1865. National Park Service. doi: https:// www.nps.gov/linc/learn/historyculture/lincoln-second-inaugural.htm.

Lipset, Seymour Martin. *Political Man*. London: Heinemann, 1960.

Lord, Charles G., Mark R. Lepper, and Elizabeth Preston. "Considering the Opposite: A Corrective Strategy for Social Judgment." *Journal of Personality and Social Psychology* 47, no. 6 (1984): 1231–43. doi: 10.1037/0022-3514.47.6.1231.

Lord, Charles G., Lee Ross, and Mark R. Lepper. "Biased Assimilation and Attitude Polarization: The Effects of Prior Theories on Subsequently Considered Evidence." *Journal of Personality and Social Psychology* 37, no. 11 (1979): 2098–109. doi: 10.1037/0022-3514.37.11.2098.

Lounge Group. "Nearly 80 Percent of American Voters are Angry, Fearful or Sad According to New Poll." *Cision PR Newswire*, October 22, 2020. https://www.prnewswire.com/news-releases/nearly-80-percent-of-american-voters-are-angry-fearful-or-sad-according-to-new-poll-301158329.html.

Lyman, Peter. "The Domestication of Anger: The Use and Abuse of Anger in Politics." *European Journal of Social Theory* 7, no. 2 (2004): 133–47. doi: 10.1177/1368431004041748.

MacDonald, Bryan. "Latest Navalny Novichok Water Bottle Poisoning Claim Stretches All Credibility, but Western Media Swallows It Without Question." *RT*, September 18, 2020. https://www.rt.com/russia/501041-navalny-novichok-media-credibility.

MacIntyre, Alasdair. *After Virtue*. Notre Dame: University of Notre Dame Press, 1984.

Macur, Juliet. "Why Do Fans Excuse the Patriots' Cheating Past?" *New York Times*, February 5, 2017. https://www.nytimes.com/2017/02/05/sports/football/new-england-patriots-super-bowl-cheating.html.

Madison, James. Federalist No. 10. 1788. Federalist Papers: Primary Documents in American History. Library of Congress. https://guides.loc.gov/federalist-papers/text-51-60#s-lg-box-wrapper-25493427.

———. Federalist No. 51. 1788. Federalist Papers: Primary Documents in American History. Library of Congress. https://guides.loc.gov/federalist-papers/text-51-60#s-lg-box-wrapper-25493427.

———. Federalist No. 55. 1788. Federalist Papers: Primary Documents in American History. Library of Congress. https://guides.loc.gov/federalist-papers/text-51-60#s-lg-box-wrapper-25493431.

———. "Notes on Ancient and Modern Confederacies." 1786. Founders Online. National Archives. https://founders.archives.gov/documents/Madison/01-09-02-0001.

———. "Speech Before the Virginia Ratifying Convention." 1788. Founders Online. National Archives. https://founders.archives.gov/documents/Madison/01-11-02-0101.

Main, Thomas J., and Jessica Miller. "The Audience for Illiberalism Today." In *The Rise of Illiberalism*, by Thomas J. Main, 22–79. Washington, DC: Brookings Institution Press, 2021.

Martherus, J. L., A. G. Martinez, P. K. Piff, et al. "Party Animals? Extreme Partisan Polarization and Dehumanization." *Political Behavior* 43 (2021): 517–40. doi: 10.1007/s11109-019-09559-4.

Mason, George. "The Virginia Declaration of Rights." Richmond, VA, June 12, 1776. America's Founding Documents. National Archives. https://www.archives.gov/founding-docs/virginia-declaration-of-rights.

Mason, Lilliana. "'I Disrespectfully Agree': The Differential Effects of Partisan Sorting on Social and Issue Polarization." *American Journal of Political Science* 59, no. 1 (2015): 128–45. http://www.jstor.org/stable/24363600.

Mason, Lilliana, and Julie Wronski. "One Tribe to Bind Them All: How Our Social Group Attachments Strengthen Partisanship." *Political Psychology* 39 (2018): 257–77. doi: 10.1111/pops.12485.

Mayer, Jane. "What Joe Biden Hasn't Owned Up to with Anita Hill." *The New Yorker*, April 27, 2019. https://www.newyorker.com/news/news-desk/what-joe-biden-hasnt-owned-up-to-about-anita-hill.

Maynes, Jeffrey. "Critical Thinking and Cognitive Bias." *Informal Logic* 35, no. 2 (2015): 183–203. doi: 10.22329/il.v35i2.4187.

McConnell, Mitch. "Mitch McConnell Senate Speech Transcript January 6: Rejects Effort to Overturn Presidential Election Results." Washington, DC, January 6, 2021. Rev Transcript Library. https://www.rev.com/blog/transcripts/mitch-mcconnell-senate-speech-on-election-confirmation-transcript-january-6.

McDonald, Forrest. "The Political Thought of Gouverneur Morris." *The Imaginative Conservative*, May 18, 2013. https://theimaginativeconservative.org/2013/05/political-thought-gouverneur-morris.html.

McGurn, Barrett. “Slogans to Fit the Occasion.” In *United States Supreme Court Yearbook*, edited by William F. Swindler, 170–74. Washington, DC: Supreme Court Historical Society, 1982.
Meduza. “OPCW Confirms That Navalny Was Poisoned with a Toxin Resembling Novichok Not Included Under Its Existing Bans.” *Meduza*, October 6, 2020. https://meduza.io/en/news/2020/10/06/opcw-confirms-that-navalny-was-poisoned-with-a-toxin-resembling-novichok-not-included-under-its-existing-bans.
Miller, Patrick R., and Pamela Johnston Conover. “Red and Blue States of Mind: Partisan Hostility and Voting in the United States.” *Political Research Quarterly* 68, no. 2 (2015): 225–39. doi: 10.1177/1065912915577208.
Montesquieu, Baron de, Charles Louis de Secondat. *Considerations on the Causes of the Grandeur and Declension of the Roman Empire*. Vol. 3 of *The Complete Works*. London: T. Evans, 1777. https://oll.libertyfund.org/title/montesquieu-complete-works-vol-3.
———. *The Spirit of the Laws*. Vol. 1 of *The Complete Works*. London: T. Evans, 1777. https://oll.libertyfund.org/title/montesquieu-complete-works-vol-1-the-spirit-of-laws.
Muro, Mark, Eli Byerly-Duke, Yang You, and Robert Maxim. “Biden-Voting Counties Equal 70% of America’s Economy. What Does This Mean for the Nation’s Political-Economic Divide?” *Brookings: The Avenue*, December 8, 2020. https://www.brookings.edu/blog/the-avenue/2020/11/09/biden-voting-counties-equal-70-of-americas-economy-what-does-this-mean-for-the-nations-political-economic-divide.
Muro, Mark, and Sifan Liu. “Another Clinton-Trump Divide: High-Output America vs Low-Output America.” *Brookings Report*, November 29, 2016. https://www.brookings.edu/blog/the-avenue/2016/11/29/another-clinton-trump-divide-high-output-america-vs-low-output-america.
Murray, John Courtney. *We Hold These Truths: Catholic Reflections on the American Proposition*. New York: Sheed and Ward, 1960.
National Intelligence Council. “Foreign Threats to the 2020 US Federal Elections.” Intelligence Community Assessment, Washington, DC, March 10, 2021. https://int.nyt.com/data/documenttools/2021-intelligence-community-election-interference-assessment/abd0346ebdd93e1e/full.pdf.
National Women’s Hall of Fame. “Maggie Kuhn.” 1995. https://www.womenofthehall.org/inductee/maggie-kuhn.
Navalny, Alexei. *Putin’s Palace: History of World’s Largest Bribe*. January 19, 2021. https://www.youtube.com/watch?v=ipAnwilMncI.

Naylor, Brian. "Read Trump's Jan. 6 Speech, a Key Part of Impeachment Trial." NPR, February 10, 2021. doi: https://www.npr.org/2021/02/10/966396848/read-trumps-jan-6-speech-a-key-part-of-impeachment-trial.

Newport, Frank. "Percentage of Christians in U.S. Drifting Down, but Still High." *Gallup Reports*, December 24, 2015. https://news.gallup.com/poll/187955/percentage-christians-drifting-down-high.aspx.

New York Times. "Read Alexander Vindman's Prepared Opening Statement from the Impeachment Hearing." *New York Times*, November 19, 2019 (updated June 18, 2020). https://www.nytimes.com/2019/11/19/us/politics/vindman-statement-testimony.html.

Nicgorski, Walter. "Review: The Anti-Federalists: Collected and Interpreted." *Review of Politics* 46, no. 1 (1984): 113–25.

Niebuhr, Reinhold. *The Irony of Amerian History*. New York: Scribners, 1952.

———. *Love and Justice: Selections from the Shorter Writings of Reinhold Niebuhr*. Edited by D. B. Robertson. Louisville, KY: Westminster John Knox Press, 1992.

———. *Moral Man and Immoral Society*. New York: Scribners, 1932.

Nye, Joseph. *Do Morals Matter? Presidents and Foreign Policy from FDR to Trump*. Oxford: Oxford University Press, 2020.

Orwell, George. "Politics and the English Languge." *Horizon*, May 1946, 252–65. http://www.public-library.uk/ebooks/72/30.pdf.

Osswald, Silvia, Dieter Frey, and Bernhard Streicher. "Moral Courage." In *Justice and Conflicts: Theoretical and Empirical Contributions*, edited by Elisabeth Kals and Jürgen Maes, 391–406. Heidelberg: Springer, 2012.

Osswald, Silvia, Tobias Greitemeyer, Peter Fischer, and Dieter Frey. "What Is Moral Courage? Definition, Explication and Classification of a Complex Construct." In *The Psychology of Courage: Modern Research on an Ancient Virtue*, edited by Cynthia L. S. Pury and Shane J. Lopez. Washington, DC: American Psychology Association, 2010.

Ou, Amy Y., David A. Waldman, and Suzanne J. Peterson. "Do Humble CEOs Matter? An Examination of CEO Humility and Firm Outcomes." *Journal of Management* 44, no. 3 (2015): 1147–73. doi: 10.1177/0149206315604187.

Pape, Robert A. "What an Analysis of 377 Americans Arrested or Charged in the Capitol Insurrection Tells Us." *Washington Post*, April 6, 2021. https://www.washingtonpost.com/opinions/2021/04/06/capitol-insurrection-arrests-cpost-analysis/.

Parker, Kim, Rich Morin, and Juliana Menasce Horowitz. "Looking to the Future, Public Sees an America in Decline on Many Fronts." *Pew Center Reports*, March 21, 2019. https://www.pewresearch.org/social-trends/2019/03/21/public-sees-an-america-in-decline-on-many-fronts.

Paul, Christopher, and Miriam Matthews. *The Russian "Firehose of Falsehood" Propaganda Model: Why It Might Work and Options to Counter It.* Santa Monica, CA: RAND Corporation, 2016. https://www.rand.org/pubs/perspectives/PE198.html.

PBS. "FDR on Lying: Creating a Reason to Go to War." *American Experience*, October 31, 2011. https://www.pbs.org/video/american-experience-fdr-on-lying-creating-a-reason-to-go-to-war.

PBS Learning Media. *Freedom Riders: American Experience.* Produced by Firelight Media. 2010. https://pbslearningmedia.org/collection/frriders.

PC Mag Staff. "25 Optical Illusions That Prove Your Brain Sucks." *PC Mag*, March 10, 2020. https://www.pcmag.com/news/21-optical-illusions-that-prove-your-brain-sucks.

Pettigrew, T. F. "The Ultimate Attribution Error: Extending Allport's Cognitive Analysis of Prejudice." *Personality and Social Psychology Bulletin* 5, no. 4 (1979): 461–76. doi: 10.1177/014616727900500407.

Pew Research Center. "An Examination of the 2016 Electorate, Based on Validated Voters." August 9, 2018. https://www.pewresearch.org/politics/2018/08/09/an-examination-of-the-2016-electorate-based-on-validated-voters.

———. "The Generation Gap in American Politics." March 1, 2018. https://www.pewresearch.org/politics/2018/03/01/1-generations-party-identification-midterm-voting-preferences-views-of-trump/.

———. "In Views of U.S. Democracy, Widening Partisan Divides Over Freedom to Peacefully Protest." September 2, 2020. https://www.pewresearch.org/politics/2020/09/02/in-views-of-u-s-democracy-widening-partisan-divides-over-freedom-to-peacefully-protest.

———. *Partisan Antipathy: More Intense, More Personal.* October 10, 2019. https://www.pewresearch.org/politics/2019/10/10/partisan-antipathy-more-intense-more-personal/.

———. "Political Independents: Who They Are, What They Think." March 14, 2019. https://www.pewresearch.org/politics/2019/03/14/political-independents-who-they-are-what-they-think.

Philp, Mark. "Thomas Paine." Stanford Encyclopedia of Philosophy Archive, Winter 2019 Edition. https://plato.stanford.edu/archives/win2019/entries/paine.

Pieper, Joseph. *The Four Cardinal Virtues: Prudence, Justice, Fortitude, Temperance.* New York: Harcourt, Brace & World, 1965.

Pierce, Lamar, Todd Rogers, and Jason A. Snyder. "Losing Hurts: The Happiness Impact of Partisan Electoral Loss." *Journal of Experimental Political Science* 3, no. 1 (2016): 44–59. Published online October 12, 2015. https://scholar.harvard.edu/files/todd_rogers/files/losing.pdf.

Pomerantsev, Peter. "Inside Putin's Information War." *Politico,* January 4, 2015. https://www.politico.com/magazine/story/2015/01/putin-russia-tv-113960/.

———. *This Is Not Propaganda: Adventures in the War Against Reality.* New York: PublicAffairs, 2019.

Popovic, Srdja, with Sophia A. McClennen. *Pranksters vs. Autocrats: Why Dilemma Actions Advance Nonviolent Activism.* Ithaca: Cornell University Press, 2020.

Porter, Tenelle. "The Benefits of Admitting When You Don't Know." *Behavioral Scientist,* April 30, 2018. https://behavioralscientist.org/the-benefits-of-admitting-when-you-dont-know.

Porter, Tenelle, and Karina Schumann. "Intellectual Humility and Openness to the Opposing View." *Self and Identity* 17, no. 2 (2018): 139–62. doi: 10.1080/15298868.2017.1361861.

Public Religion Research Institute (PRRI). *Dueling Realities: Amid Multiple Crises, Trump and Biden Supporters See Different Priorities.* October 19, 2020. https://www.prri.org/research/amid-multiple-crises-trump-and-biden-supporters-see-different-realities-and-futures-for-the-nation.

Ramsay, Gordon, and Sam Robertshaw. *Weaponising News: RT, Sputnik and Targeted Disinformation.* London: Policy Institute, King's College London, 2019. https://www.kcl.ac.uk/policy-institute/assets/weaponising-news.pdf.

Rate, Christopher R., Jennifer A. Clarke, Douglas R. Lindsay, and Robert J. Sternberg. "Implicit Theories of Courage." *Journal of Positive Psychology* 2, no. 2 (2007): 80–98. doi: 10.1080/17439760701228755.

Rawls, John. *Political Liberalism.* New York: Columbia University Press, 1993.

Reid, W. Stanford. "Bernard of Clairvaux in the Thought of John Calvin." *Westminster Theological Journal* 41, no. 1 (1978): 127–45.

Roccas, Sonia, and Marilynn B. Brewer. "Social Identity Complexity." *Personality and Social Psychology Review* 6, no. 2 (2002): 88–106. doi: 10.1207/S15327957PSPR0602_01.

Roosevelt, Franklin D. "Fireside Chat #18: On the Greer Incident." September 11, 1941. Miller Center, University of Virginia. https://millercenter.org/the-presidency/presidential-speeches/september-11-1941-fireside-chat-18-greer-incident.
Rorty, Richard. *Pragmatism as Anti-Authoritarianism*. Edited by Eduardo Mendieta. Cambridge: Harvard University Press, 2021.
Rosenberger, Laura. "China's Coronavirus Information Offensive." *Foreign Affairs*, April 22, 2020. https://www.foreignaffairs.com/articles/china/2020-04-22/chinas-coronavirus-information-offensive.
Rothman, Noah. *Unjust: Social Justice and the Unmaking of America*. New York: Gateway Editions, 2019.
RT. "Czech President Admits His Country Produced Novichok—but British Mainstream Media Remain Silent." *RT*, May 4, 2018. https://www.rt.com/uk/425826-czech-zeman-skripal-novichok.
———. "Developers of 'Novichok' Say Navalny's Symptoms Aren't Consistent with Poisoning by Their Deadly Creation, Reject German Claims." *RT*, September 2, 2020. https://www.rt.com/russia/499732-novichok-developers-navalny-symptoms.
Rush, Benjamin. *Thoughts Upon the Mode of Education Proper in a Republic*. Philadelphia, PA, 1786. ExplorePAhistory. https://explorepahistory.com/odocument.php?docId=1-4-218.
Russell, Daniel C. *Practical Intelligence and the Virtues*. Oxford: Oxford University Press, 2009.
Seneca, Lucius Annaeaus. *On Anger*. In *Moral Essays*, vol. 1. Translated by John W. Basore. London: Heinemann, 1928. Electronic text © SophiaOmni, 2005. http://www.sophia-project.org/uploads/1/3/9/5/13955288/seneca_anger.pdf.
Shaffer, Leslie. "The Dress That Broke the Internet." *CNBC*, February 27, 2015. https://www.cnbc.com/2015/02/27/the-dress-that-broke-the-internet.html.
Shelden, Rachel, and Erik B. Alexander. "Americans Worry About 2020 Being Another 2000, but the Real Worry Is Another 1876." *Washington Post*, October 20, 2020. https://www.washingtonpost.com/outlook/2020/10/20/americans-worry-about-2020-being-another-2000-real-worry-is-another-1876.
Siegel, Daniel. *Charity and Condescension: Victorian Literature and the Dilemmas of Philanthropy*. Athens: Ohio University Press, 2012.
Smith, J. David, Alexandria C. Zakrzewski, Jennifer M. Johnson, Jeanette C. Valleau, and Barbara A. Church. 2016. "Categorization: The View from Animal Cognition." *Behavioral Sciences* 6, no. 2 (2016): 12. doi: 10.3390/bs6020012.

Smylie, James H. "Madison and Witherspoon: Theological Roots of American Political Thought." *American Presbyterians* 73, no. 3 (1995): 155–64. http://www.jstor.org/stable/23333418.

Sousa, Milton, and Dirk Van Dierendonck. "Servant Leadership and the Effect of the Interaction Between Humility, Action, and Hierarchical Power on Follower Engagement." *Journal of Business Ethics* 141 (2017): 13–25. doi: 10.1007/s10551-015-2725-y.

Stevenson, William. *A Man Called Intrepid*. Guildford, CT: The Lyons Press, 1976.

Storing, Herbert, ed. *The Anti-Federalist*. Chicago: University of Chicago Press, 1985.

Swide, Joseph. "Jets Fan Group Talks About Why They Trolled the Patriots with a Banner." *Vice*, July 30, 2015. https://www.vice.com/en/article/jp7vdp/jets-fan-group-talks-about-why-they-trolled-the-patriots-with-a-banner.

Tajfel, Henri. "Experiments in Intergroup Discrimination." *Scientific American* 223, no. 5 (1970): 96–102.

Tajfel, Henri, M. G. Billig, R. P. Bundy, and Claude Flament. "Social Categorization and Intergroup Behaviour." *European Journal of Social Psychology* 1, no. 2 (1971): 149–78. doi: 10.1002/ejsp.2420010202.

Talisse, Robert. *Overdoing Democracy: Why We Must Put Politics in Its Place*. Oxford: Oxford University Press, 2019.

Tatum, Beverly Daniel. *Why Are All the Black Kids Sitting Together in the Cafeteria: And Other Conversations About Race*. New York: Basic Books, 2017.

Taylor, Derrick Bryson. "Who Were the Freedom Riders?" *New York Times*, July 18, 2020. https://www.nytimes.com/2020/07/18/us/politics/freedom-riders-john-lewis-work.html.

Thomas, Pierre, Victor Ordonez, and Eliana Larramendia. "Capitol Police Officer Recounts Jan. 6 Attack: Exclusive." *ABC News*, February 22, 2021. https://abcnews.go.com/Politics/capitol-police-officer-recounts-jan-attack-exclusive/story?id=76036587.

Thompson, Derek. "Where Did All the Workers Go? 60 Years of Economic Change in 1 Graph." *The Atlantic*, January 26, 2012. https://www.theatlantic.com/business/archive/2012/01/where-did-all-the-workers-go-60-years-of-economic-change-in-1-graph/252018.

Thunberg, Greta. Speech before the US Congress. *The Independent*, September, 20, 2019. https://www.independent.co.uk/voices/greta-thunberg-congress-speech-climate-change-crisis-dream-a9112151.html.

Tienda, Marta, and Susana Sánchez. "Latin American Immigration to the United States." *Daedalus* 142, no. 3 (2013): 48–64. doi: 10.1162/DAED_a_00218.

Urban, Mark. *The Skripal Files: The Life and Near Death of a Russian Spy.* London: Pan Macmillan, 2018.

Vedantam, Shankar. "Our Brands, Our Selves." Interview with Americus Reed. *Hidden Brain.* Podcast. 2019. https://hiddenbrain.org/stories.

Velasquez-Manoff, Moises. "How to Make Fun of Nazis." *New York Times,* August 17, 2017. https://www.nytimes.com/2017/08/17/opinion/how-to-make-fun-of-nazis.html.

Vindman, Alexander. "Coming Forward Ended My Career. I Still Believe Doing What's Right Matters." *Washington Post,* August 1, 2020. https://www.washingtonpost.com/opinions/2020/08/01/alexander-vindman-retiring-oped.

Wang, Wendy. "The Partisan Marriage Gap Is Bigger Than Ever." *The Hill,* October 27, 2020. https://thehill.com/opinion/white-house/522987-the-partisan-marriage-gap-is-bigger-than-ever.

Washington, George. "Washington's Farewell Address 1796." The Avalon Project: Documents in Law, History and Diplomacy. Yale Law School. https://avalon.law.yale.edu/18th_century/washing.asp.

Webster, Steven W. *American Rage: How Anger Shapes Our Politics.* Cambridge: Cambridge University Press, 2020.

Wehner, Peter. "Trump's Words Are Poison." *The Atlantic,* August 6, 2019. https://www.theatlantic.com/ideas/archive/2019/08/what-trump-has-done/595585.

Williams, Kipling D. "Ostracism." *Annual Review of Psychology* 58 (2007): 425–52. https://www.hendrix.edu/uploadedFiles/Academics/Faculty_Resources/2016_FFC/Williams%20(2007).pdf.

Witte, John. *No Establishment of Religion: America's Original Contribution to Religious Liberty.* Oxford: Oxford University Press, 2012.

Yagoda, Ben. "The Cognitive Biases Tricking Your Brain: Science Suggests We're Hardwired to Delude Ourselves. Can We Do Anything about It?" *The Atlantic,* September 2018. https://www.theatlantic.com/magazine/archive/2018/09/cognitive-bias/565775.

Zagzebski, Linda. *Virtues of the Mind: An Inquiry into the Nature of Virtue and the Ethical Foundations of Knowledge.* Cambridge: Cambridge University Press, 1996.

Index

Abramowitz, Alan, 9, 41, 45–46, 186n19, 186n29
Achen, Christopher, 12, 165–70
Adams, John, 52, 61, 63, 179
Aeneid (Vergil), 62
African Americans. *See* Black people
After Virtue (MacIntyre), 183n5
agape (love), 148
AIDS, 88
Alcoholics Anonymous, 69
Allcott, Hunt, 138
Allen, Danielle, 153–54, 158
American Bible Society, 63
American Rage (Webster), 129
amygdala, 185n12
anchoring bias, 24
anger
  Aristotle on, 131–34
  articulation of, 127–29
  hatred, 11, 134–37, 140–41
  limits on expression, 129
  See also temperance
anterior cingulate cortex, 185n12
antidemocratic thought, 6, 95, 170, 175, 177, 183n2
Anti-Federalists, 53, 55, 58
Aquinas, Thomas, 11–12, 145, 153–54, 164
Arendt, Hannah, 10, 84–87
argument, as necessary for democracy, 2–7, 85–86, 125, 150, 163, 165
Aristotle
  on anger, 131–34
  committing to democratic virtues, 12
  on courage, 114
  on a good life, 181
  on hate, 134–35
  on temperance, 194n13
  on unity of the virtues, 125, 193n24
  on virtue as between two vices, the golden mean, 78–79, 177
Athens, as example of small republic, 53
Axelrod, Robert, 160–61

Barden, Jamie, 101
Barrett, Amy Coney, 81
Bartels, Larry, 12, 165–70
Beck, Aaron T., 135
Beem, Christopher
  and Aristotle's views, 193n24
  in conversation with Frum, 194n22
  on current democracy, 169–70
  Democratic Humility, 188n1
  on humility, 69
Benhabib, Seyla, 183n8
Bentley, Arthur, 55
Berlin, Isaiah, 7
Bernard of Clairvaux (saint), 9–10, 69–72, 154–55
Bhagavad Gita, 188n3
biases
  about, 23–25
  critical thinking to counteract, 119–20
  and democracy, 188n1
  in-group bias, 22, 25–27, 49, 82, 101
  as laziness, 99
  metacognitive strategies against, 102
  reduced by consistency, 97
  ultimate attribution errors, 101–2
Bible, 188n3
Biden, Joseph
  "Biden Reaches Out. The GOP Slaps Him in the Face" (Dionne), 157
  on democratic charity, 11, 151–52, 155
  demographics in counties won, 42
  inaugural address, 12–13, 179–80
  mention, 155
Bigler, Rebecca, 22
bigotry, 19, 27, 30
Bill of Rights, 62
Black people
  Congressional Black caucus, 136–37

end of Jim Crow era, 39
and Jim Crow era, 152
and police violence, 30
and political affiliation, 44–45
racism, 25–26, 29–30, 37, 39, 46
and Russian propaganda, 87–88
segregation laws, 114
social welfare issues, 186n19
Boston Marathon bombing (2013), 31
brand identification, 18, 47–48, 184n2
Breitbart, Andrew, 4–5
Brewer, Marilynn, 57
Brooks, David, 122
Brown, Jacob, 48
Buddhism, 188n3
bullshit *versus* lies, 89

Cain, Will, 187n36
Calvin, John, 155
capitalism, 4, 87
Capitol Hill, January 6, 2021, riot. *See* riot, January 6, 2021
cardinal virtues, 11, 111, 184n10
See also democratic acting
Carlson, Tucker, 140
cars/trucks, political party preference for, 47
Carthage, as example of small republic, 53
Catholicism, 155
Center for the Study of Democratic Institutions, Vanderbilt University, 31–32
charity, 147–62
about, 11
Aquinas on, 153–54
Bernard on, 154–55
compared to democratic charity, 159
Davidson on, 149–50
humility as foundation for, 154–56
Lincoln on, 151–52, 156
and philanthropy, 147–49
term usage, 147–48
as theological virtue, 11, 145
See also democratic charity
Charlottesville march, 128, 141, 142
Chicago Bears, NFL, 21
Chick-fil-A, 47
Chinese Communist Party, 191n40
Chipotle, 47
Christianity, 148, 158
Churchill, Winston, 10, 106
Cikara, Mina, 26
civil rights, 39, 44, 62, 88, 129, 173
Civil War, 141
Clinton, Hillary Rodham, 41, 42, 45
conflict. *See* argument
Congressional Black Caucus, 136–37
Conover, Pamela Johnston, 31
Considerations on the Causes of the Greatness of the Romans and Their Decline (Montesquieu), 58
consider the opposite (metacognitive strategy), 102–4
consistency, 97–109
about, 9–10
as aid to manage bias, 97, 107–9
as basis for reasonable argumentation, 164
consider the opposite (metacognitive strategy), 102–4
Emerson on, 97–100
and hypocrisy, 101–2
and justice, 104–5, 184n10
in politics, 105–7
and the ultimate attribution error, 100–102
See also inconsistency
"Consistency in Politics" (Churchill), 106
Constitution of the US
Anti-Federalists on, 55
and checks and balances, 57
designed to discourage rash action, 59
First Amendment, 85, 145
and gun owners, 30
Madison's drafting of, 164
Montesquieu's arguments, 53–54
Publius argument, 56
Coppins, McKay, 93
Costanza, George (Seinfeld), 82

courage, 113–27
and anger, 117–19
in battle, 113–14
as cardinal virtue, 10, 111
characteristics of brave people, 117
definitions, 115, 192n1, 193n5
and democratic thinking, 119, 125–26, 143
everyday courage, 115–17, 127
needed to counter tribal animosity, 11
ostracism and reaction to, 120–25
and risk, 113–17, 119–22, 125–27
speaking up to friends and neighbors, 119–20
COVID-19, 94, 116, 191n40
Cracker Barrel, 47
critical thinking, 119–20
Cuff, William, 117
culture, as upstream from politics, 4–5

Daniels, Stormy, 80
Davidson, David, 149, 195n3
debate. *See* argument
defend and aggress, 28, 30–31, 119, 142, 157
Deffler, Samantha, 72
dehumanization, 27, 31–32, 49–50, 135–36
democracy
about, 2–7, 65
antidemocratic thought, 6, 95, 170, 175, 177, 183n2
argument, as necessary for, 2–7, 85–86, 125, 150, 163, 165
dependent on tribalism, 35
folk theory compared to reality, 165–70
foundational assumptions, 7–8, 163
foundations of, 183n8
as midpoint between civil war and tyranny, 2, 5
versus representative republic, 56
requirement of compromise, 136
requirement of democratic faith, 175
Trump's assault on, 177–78
See also biases; democratic virtues; lies
"Democracy" (Hughes), 3
Democracy and Difference (Benhabib), 183n8
"Democracy Demotion" (Diamond), 191n38
Democracy for Realists (Achen and Bartels), 165, 170
democratic acting
about, 9–10, 111
follows democratic thinking, 111, 125–26, 143
See also courage; temperance
democratic belief, 9, 131–32, 145
See also charity; faith
democratic charity
about, 153–54
Biden on, 151–52
and democratic humility, 156
Lincoln on, 11, 147, 151–52, 155
random acts of, 159–62
response to, 156–59
term usage, 148–49
See also charity
Democratic Humility: Reinhold Niebuhr, Neuroscience, and America's Political Crisis (Beem), 188n1
Democratic Party
beliefs about Republican Party, 136
characteristics of members, 20, 185n12
demographics of, 42, 47, 186n18
members' partisanship, 31–32
self-awareness of members, 70
democratic republics, 52–64
American conception of civic virtue, 59–62
classic conception of virtue, 58
Montesquieu and the small republic, 53–54
Publius and the large republic, 54–57
types of virtue, 63–64
democratic thinking
about, 9–10, 65, 79
and courage, 119, 125, 143

necessary for democratic action, 111, 125–26
See also consistency; honesty; humility
democratic virtues
about, 5–9, 180–81
as acts of defiance, 181
commitment to, 12–13, 63, 143, 179
democratic action preceded by democratic thinking, 111, 125–26
and reciprocity, 158, 178
and respect, 158
undermined by tribalism, 170
See also democratic acting; democratic belief; democratic thinking
demonization, 135
Diamond, Larry, 191n38
Dionne, E. J., 157
disagreement. *See* argument
distrust
and in-group bias, 108
and partisanship, 31, 50, 136
and racial resentment, 45
and racism, 25, 30–31
versus temperance, 147
of those outside the group, 5–6, 9, 23, 26
See also trust
doom loop, 31, 125, 130–31, 134, 159, 179
Douthat, Ross, 49
dress, debate on color, 85, 107
Drutman, Lee, 31
Duarte, Isabel, 21
Dunkin' Donuts, 47
Dunn, Harry, 1–2

economy (US), 38, 41–42
Edsall, Thomas, 31–32
education, 3, 58, 72
Emerson, Ralph Waldo, 10, 97–99
Enquiry Concerning the Principles of Morals (Hume), 68, 71
epistemology, 84
equality, 3–4, 7, 163, 165
Equal Justice Initiative, 172
Exline, Julie, 156

Facebook, 87, 138
faith, 163–76
about, 11–12
definition, 164–65
Thomas Aquinas on, 12, 164
Faith and Freedom Coalition, 43–44
favoritism, 22–23, 25–28, 32, 50
Federalist Papers, 54, 62, 168, 170
firehose of falsehood, 77, 89, 90–95, 191n40
Fitzgerald, Jennifer, 187n33
Floyd, George, 40, 44–45
Foot, Philippa, 4–5
Foreign Affairs, 191n40
Founders, 9, 52–54, 58–61, 63–64
Fox Television, 47, 187n36
Francis, (pope), 155
Frankfurt, Harry, 89
Franklin, Benjamin, 61
Freedom Riders, 12, 114–15, 117, 127, 170–71
Frey, Dieter, 118
Frum, David, 194n22
Fulbright, William, 163

game theory, 12, 159–61
Gandhi, Mahatma, 158, 173
Garland, Merrick, 81, 95
Garrett, Kelly, 123
gender issues, 30, 37, 39–40, 72
generosity, 156
Geneva, Switzerland, 187n3
Gilovich, Thomas, 108
Ginsburg, Ruth Bader, 81
the golden mean, 78, 177
Gorman, Amanda, 13
Gray Panthers, 116
Green Bay Packers, NFL, 21
Greer (US destroyer), 82–83
GRU, Russian intelligence agency, 90
Gutmann, Amy, 183n8

halo effect, 24
Hamilton, Alexander, 54, 62

Hand, Learned, 67, 77, 116
happiness, 3, 11, 60, 63, 68, 145, 183n7
Harnad, Stevan, 20
hatred, 11, 134–37, 140–41
    See also anger
Hebrew Bible, 188n3
Henry, Patrick, 61
Hess, Rudolf, 141–43
Hidden Figures (film), 46
Hill, Anita, 81
Hill, Peter, 156
hindsight bias, 24
Hispanic voters, 186n19
Hitler, Adolf, 141
Hobfoll, Stevan, 28–29
homophily, 19
honesty, 9–10, 164
    See also lies
hope, 175–76
How Democracies Die (Levitsky and Ziblatt), 137
Hughes, Evan, 105
Hughes, Langston, 3
Hume, David, 9–10, 63, 68–73, 98
humility, 67–79
    about, 9–10
    Bernard on, as self-awareness, 69–72, 154–55
    definitions, 71–72, 189n9
    as a golden mean, 76–79
    Hume on, claims as vice, 68–73
    intellectual humility, 71–72
    in many world religions, 188n3
    usefulness of, 72–76
Hutcheson, Francis, 63
hypocrisy, 101–2

illiberalism, 183n2
immigration, 29, 38–39, 186n29
Immigration and Nationality Act (1965), 38
inconsistency and authenticity, 98–99
independent voter (neither Democrat or Republican), 36
in-group bias, 22, 25–27, 49, 82, 101
Institutes of Justinian, 104
intellectual virtues, 9
    See also democratic thinking

January 6, 2021, riot. *See* riot, January 6, 2021
Jay, John, 54, 63
Jefferson, Thomas, 61, 63
Jesus, 132
Johnson, Andrew, 121–22
journalism, 93
Judaism, 186n20
justice, 10, 104, 111, 118, 165, 172

Kaepernick, Colin, 48
Kahneman, Daniel, 25
Kalmoe, Nathan, 31–32
Kandinsky, Wassily, 22, 26
Kant, Immanuel, 108
Kennedy, John F., 121
Kennedy, Robert, 177
Kierkegaard, Søren, 164–65
King, Rufus, 62
Klar, Samara, 37
Klee, Paul, 22, 26
Klein, Ezra, 122
Kloppenberg, James, 63–64
Kruger, Justin, 108
Krupnikov, Yanna, 37
Kuhn, Maggie, 116

Lambeau Field, Green Bay Packers, 21
laughtivism, 142
Lavelle, Peter, 92
Lazarus, Richard, 131
Lepper, Mark, 102–3
Levitsky, Steven, 137
Lewis, C. S., 113
LGBTQ issues, 30, 39–40, 72
lies, 80–96
    Arendt on, 84–87
    versus bullshit, 89
    democracy threatened by, 86
    versus false beliefs, 95–96
    firehose of falsehood, 77, 89, 90–95, 191n40
    lying for good reasons, 82–84

versus obfuscation, 191n37
Soviet propaganda, 87–89
Lincoln, Abraham, 11, 141, 147, 151, 155
Lippmann, Walter, 17
Lord, Charles, 102–3
Lowell, James Russell, 34
Lyman, Peter, 127

MacIntyre, Alasdair, 183n5
Madison, James, 9, 54–60, 126, 164, 168, 169–70
MAGA, 1–2, 49
See also riot, January 6, 2021
Main, Thomas, 183n2
March on Washington for Jobs and Freedom (1963), 171
Marx, Groucho, 97
Mason, George, 61
Mason, Lilliana, 8, 31–32, 37, 50
Matthews, Miriam, 89
McConnell, Mitch, 10, 81, 95
metacognitive strategies, 102–4, 107–8
Me Too Movement, 30, 40
Mexican immigration, 39
Miller, Jessica, 183n2
Miller, Patrick R., 31
Milwaukee Bucks, NBA, 48
modesty, 71
Montesquieu, Baron de, Charles Louis de Secondat, 53–59, 62, 63, 187n3
Morris, Gouverneur, 61, 63
MSNBC Television, 47
Murdoch, Rupert, 92
Muro, Mark, 41
Murray, John Courtney, 150

naive realism, 107
NASCAR, 47
Nash, Diane, 114
National Intelligence Council, 87
National Rifle Association, 30
Native Americans, 39–40
Navalny, Alexei, 91
NBA (National Basketball Association), 47–48
neo-Nazis, 135, 140, 141–43
nerve agent (Novichok), 90–92, 190n33
New Jersey, US, 167
Newtown, Connecticut, school shooting, 31
Niebuhr, Reinhold, 52, 83, 148, 176
1960s, 39–40, 41
Nixon, Richard, 40, 44
Novichok (Russian nerve agent), 90–92, 190n33
Nye, Joseph, 83

Obama, Barack, 81
On Bullshit (Frankfurt), 89
Organization for the Prohibition of Chemical Weapons, 190n33
Orwell, George, 80
Osswald, Silvia, 118
ostracism, 120–26, 132, 135, 193n11

Paine, Thomas, 61
Pape, Robert, 45, 56
Parchman State, Mississippi State Penitentiary, 114
Parks, Rosa, 173
partisanship
and anger, 129–31, 136, 157
and consistency, 107
and courage, 11
and distrust, 31–32, 50, 136
function as a marker, 47
and honesty, 95–96
and in-group bias, 101–4
and media infotainment, 138
non-partisan organizations, 139–40
and ostracism, 122–25
and Russian influence, 87
and tribal alignment, 31–32, 35–37, 46–50, 82, 118–19, 139
and ultimate attribution error, 101
and white Christians, 43
See also tribal alignment; us and them
paternalism, 148, 159
patriotism, 161
Paul, Christopher, 89
Pearl Harbor, US, 82–83

penance, 68
Penn, William, 187n3
people of color. *See* Black people
philanthropy. *See* charity
Pieper, Joseph, 184n10
Plato, 104, 184n10
politics
committing to democratic virtues, 12
as downstream from culture, 4–5
friendship in, 158
lies told, 10, 82–84
and ostracism, 123, 193n18
science of, 56–57, 59
See also democracy; Democratic Party; democratic virtues; partisanship; Republican Party
"Politics and the English Language" (Orwell), 80
Pomerantsev, Peter, 88, 89
Pope Francis, 155
Popovic, Srdja, 142
population densities, 186n18
Porter, Tenelle, 73, 74–75
Preston, Elizabeth, 103
pride, 70, 78
prisoner's dilemma, 159–60, 180
Prisoners of Hate (Beck), 135
Prius, Toyota, 47
The Process of Government (Bentley), 55
Profiles in Courage (Kennedy), 121
protests, 12, 30, 40, 171
prudence, 10, 111, 132, 161, 184n10
Public Religion Research Institute, 136
Publius, 54–60, 62, 63
Puritan New England, 63
Putin, Vladimir, 91, 191n38

racial resentment, 45–46, 186n29
racism, 19, 25–26, 29–30, 37, 39, 44–46, 114
See also Black people; white people
Ramsay, Gordon, 90
Rand Corporation, 89
Rawls, John, 7
reality/realism, 7, 107, 163, 165, 170, 183n7
Reed, Ralph, 43–44
religion
American Bible Society, 63
Bible, 188n3
Catholicism, 155
Christianity, 148, 158
evangelical support for Trump, 43
evangelism, 29–30
humility as religious virtue, 68–70
Jesus, 132
Judaism, 186n20
theological virtues, 11, 145
and ultimate attribution error, 101
and white, male, Christian establishment, 42–44
Republican Party
beliefs about Democratic Party, 136
characteristics of members, 43, 44, 185n12, 186n18
demographics of, 47
members' partisanship, 31–32
and Trump, 157, 186n29
respect, 3
revenge, 141–43
Rhetoric (Aristotle), 134
riot, January 6, 2021
characteristics of individuals, 45–46
Dunn on, 1–2
rise of anger prior to, 130–31, 136
and Trump's lies, 94–96
unmoderated tribalism, 6, 177
risk
and courage, 113–17, 119–22, 125–27
and freedom, 59
physical, 76
in prisoner's dilemma, 160
taken by Thunberg, 173
taken by Vindman, 172
Robbers' Cave experiment, 184n12
Robertshaw, Sam, 90
Roccas, Sonia, 57
Roman Republic, 58
Roosevelt, Franklin D., 10, 82–83
Rorty, Richard, 183n7
Rosenberger, Laura, 191n40
Ross, Edmond, 121–22

Ross, Lee, 102–3
Rothman, Noah, 105–6
Rush, Benjamin, 61, 63
Russia
GRU, intelligence agency, 90
interference in US elections, 87
media outlet RT, 10
Russia Today (RT), 87, 90–91
Sputnik (Russian media), 87, 90–91
and use of falsehoods, 77
See also USSR

Salt March (Gandhi), 173
same-sex marriage, 72
Sandy Hook Elementary school shooting, 31
satyagraha (passive nonviolent political resistance), 158
Scalia, Antonin, 81
schadenfeude, 26, 50
Schumann, Karina, 73–74
Scottish Enlightenment, 64
segregation laws, 37, 114, 173
self-knowledge, 70, 154–55
self-reliance, 97–100
Self-Reliance (Emerson), 97
Seneca, Lucius Annaeaus, 132
shark attacks, New Jersey (1916), 167
Sherif, Muzafer, 184n12
Skripal, Sergei and Yulia, 90–91
Smith, Adam, 63
Snyder, Timothy, 80
Sparta, as example of small republic, 53
sports fandom, 18, 21–23, 26, 48, 100–101
Sputnik (Russian media), 87, 90–91
Stahl, Lesley, 93
Starbucks, 47
Stevenson, Bryan, 12, 172–73
Stoics, 132
Streicher, Bernhard, 118
Subaru, 47
Supreme Court, US, 104

Tajfel, Henri, 8, 22–23
Talking to Strangers (Allen), 153–54
temperance, 127–43
about, 11, 111, 164
as between anger and apathy, 134, 137
Aristotle on anger, 131–34
building the habit, 137–40
as cardinal virtue, 10
democratic action easier after democratic thinking, 111, 143
hatred, 11, 134–37, 140–41
tend and befriend, reaction to ostracism, 123–25
theological virtues, 11, 145
thinking
critical thinking, 119–20
fast and slow, 25
"Type 1" and "Type 2" thinking, 24–25
See also democratic thinking
Thomas, Clarence, 81
Thomas Aquinas, 11–12, 145, 153–54, 164
Thompson, Dorothy, 127
Thunberg, Greta, 12, 171, 173
Trader Joe's, 47
transgender people, 40
tribal alignment, 34–51
and brand identification, 47–48
on economy, race, and religion, 40–46
and partisan animosity, 118
postwar establishment, 37–40
prevention by multiple tribes, 57
Trump's politics, 48–49
viciousness of, 49–50
See also partisanship; us and them
tribalism, 17–33
and bias, 23–25
as commitment to our group identity, 7
democracy dependent on, 35
and democratic propositions, 165
doom loop, 31–33, 125, 130–31, 134, 159, 179
and favoritism, 22–23
in-group bias, 22, 25–27, 49, 82, 101
as instinctual, a natural tendency, 17–22, 55, 119

tribalism (*continued*)
as laziness, 99
term usage, 5–6
tribal threats, real or perceived, 28–31
tribe success and brain activity, 21, 23
viciousness of, 27–28
Tribalism: The Evolutionary Origins of Fear Politics (Hobfoll), 28–29
tribes
inherited and chosen, 18–19, 47
little, 47–48, 139–40
viciousness of, 49–50
the Troubles (Northern Ireland), 34
Trump, Donald
assault on democracy, 177–78
evangelical support for, 43
exploitation of tribal politics, 48–49
lies, 80, 92–95
payments to Stormy Daniels, 80
racial resentment of voters, 45
and Republican Party, 157, 186n29
Russian interference in election, 87
trust
Arendt on, 86
and democratic charity, 150, 154, 156
Emerson on, 98
Founders on, 59–62, 170
and the government, 129
members in the group, 17–18
in the Prisoner's Dilemma, 160, 180
See also distrust
The Twelve Steps of Humility (Bernard of Clairvaux), 69
2020 election, 130, 186n29, 187n36
"Type 1" and "Type 2" thinking (Kahneman), 24–25

ultimate attribution error, 101–2
United States
Founders, 9, 52–54, 58–61, 63–64
post-war economy, 38
Supreme Court, 104
threats Americans feel, 29–31
2020 election, 130, 186n29, 187n36
See also Constitution of the US
Unjust (Rothman), 105–6
urban/rural divide, 29–30, 42
us and them
in American politics, 9, 35–37
and dehumanization, 27
difficulties for democratic propositions, 165
emotion *versus* reason, 168
inevitability of, 169
instinctive categorization, 21
interactions between, 50
and perception of bias, 108
Republicans and non-whites, 45
Tajfel's experiment, 23
during the Troubles, 34–35
and the ultimate attribution error, 101–2
See also partisanship; tribal alignment
USSR, 87–89
Utilitarians, 68

vices, 17, 71
consistency as, 98
as easy choice, 10
and hate, 137
human inclination, 27–28, 49
humility as, 69, 73
and virtues, 9, 78–79, 89, 113, 170
vulnerability to, 6
See also tribal alignment; tribalism
viciousness of tribes, 27–28, 49–50
Vietnam War protests, 40
Vindman, Alexander, 12, 171–74
violence
consequence of bias, 27
descent from tribalism, 31
at January 6, 2021, riot, 1–2
justification by political party members, 32
Kaepernick protest against, 48
viciousness of tribes, 27–28, 49–50
virtues
and Christianity, 63–64
classic conception of, 58
and classic (Roman) republicanism, 64

Founders on, 59–62
general relevance to democracy, 7–8
justice, 10, 104, 118, 165
monkish, 9, 68–69
necessary for democratic society, 60–61
prudence, 10, 111, 132, 161, 184n10
as social agreement, 178
term usage, 6, 183n5
as between two vices (Aristotle), 78
types of, 63–64
See also democratic virtues
voting, method of, 167–68

Walmart, 47
Washington, George, 61
Webster, Steven, 129
wedding cake for gay marriage (Masterpiece Cakeshop v. Colorado Civil Rights Commission), 150
white people
belief in diversity, 40–41
Charlottesville march, 128, 141, 142
declining populations of, 44, 46
feeling threatened, 29
male, Christian (WMC) cultural establishment, 37–39, 41, 42–43, 49
as minority, 39
racial resentment, 45–46, 186n29
racism, 25–26, 29–30, 37, 39, 46
in Republican Party, 44–45
segregation laws, 114
white nationalism, 106
white supremacy, 135–36
Why We're Polarized (Klein), 122
Williams, Kipling, 121, 123
Wilson, Bill, 69
Wilson, James, 63
Wilson, Woodrow, 167
Witherspoon, John, 60
World War II, 37–38
Wronski, Julie, 37
Wunsiedel, Germany, 141–43

Yagoda, Ben, 24

Zelenskyy, Volodymyr, 172
Ziblatt, Daniel, 137